At Home
in the World

At Home
in the World

A STUDY IN

PSYCHOANALYSIS,

RELIGION, AND ART

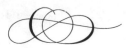

Donald Capps

 CASCADE *Books* • Eugene, Oregon

AT HOME IN THE WORLD
A Study in Psychoanalysis, Religion, and Art

Cascade Books
An Imprint of Wipf and Stock Publishers
199 W. 8th Ave., Suite 3
Eugene, OR 97401

www.wipfandstock.com

ISBN 13: 978-1-61097-969-6

Cataloging-in-Publication data:

Capps, Donald.

At home in the world : a study in psychoanalysis, religion, and art / Donald Capps.

xxvi + 188 p. ; illus. ; 23 cm.—Includes bibliographical references, illustrations, and index.

ISBN: 978-1-61097-969-6

1. Melancholy. 2. Mothers and sons. 3. Freud, Sigmund, 1856–1939. 4. Erikson, Eric H. (Erik Homburger), 1902–1994. 5. Gifford, Sanford Robinson, 1823–1880. 6. Inness, George, 1825–1894. 7. Leonardo da Vinci, 1452–1519. 8. Rockwell, Norman, 1894–1978. 9. Vermeer, Johannes, 1632–1675. 10. Whistler, James McNeill, 1834–1903. 11. Moses, Grandma, 1860–1961. I. Title.

BL625.65 C37 2013

Contents

Illustrations

PAINTINGS

Leonardo da Vinci's *Mona Lisa*, The Louvre (Paris). Photo credit: Réunion des Musées Nationaux / Art Resource, New York.

Leonardo da Vinci's "Saint Anne with Virgin and Child," The Louvre (Paris). Photo credit: Réunion des Musées Nationaux / Art Resource, New York.

James McNeill Whistler's *Arrangement in Gray and Black No. 1* or *The Artist's Mother*, Musée d'Orsay (Paris, France). Photo credit: Réunion des Musées Nationaux / Art Resource, New York.

Ken Brown's *Whistler's Brother Ernie from Duluth*. Used by permission of Ken Brown.

Norman Rockwell's *Shuffleton's Barbershop*, Norman Rockwell Family Agency. Works by Norman Rockwell printed by permission of the Norman Rockwell Family Agency. Book Rights Copyright © 2012 The Norman Rockwell Family Entities. Photo credit: Courtesy of the Berkshire Museum, Pittsfield, Massachusetts USA

Johannes (Jan) Vermeer's *Soldier and Young Girl Smiling*, The Frick Collection (New York). Copyright the Frick Collection. Photo credit: The Frick Collection.

Johannes (Jan) Vermeer's *Christ in the House of Martha and Mary*, The Scottish National Gallery. Photo credit: The National Galleries of Scotland.

Sanford R. Gifford's *Kauterskill Clove*, The Metropolitan Museum of Art collection. Photo credit: Art Resource, New York.

George Inness's *Sunrise*, The Metropolitan Museum of Art collection. Photo credit: Art Resource, New York.

Norman Rockwell's *Saying Grace*, Norman Rockwell Family Agency. Work by Norman Rockwell printed by permission of the Norman Rockwell Family Agency. Book Rights Copyright © 2012 The Norman Rockwell Family Entities. Photo credit: The Norman Rockwell Museum Collections.

Norman Rockwell's *Christmas Homecoming*, Norman Rockwell Family Agency. Works by Norman Rockwell printed by permission of the Norman Rockwell Family Agency. Book Rights Copyright © 2012 The Norman Rockwell Family Entities. Photo credit: The Norman Rockwell Museum Collections.

Grandma Moses's *Little Boy Blue*, Grandma Moses Properties Co. (New York). Credit line: Grandma Moses: *Little Boy Blue.* Copyright © 1969 (renewed 1997) Grandma Moses Properties Co., New York. Photo credit: Grandma Moses Properties Co.

POEM:

Billy Collins's "Rip Van Winkle" from *Questions about Angels*. Copyright © 1991. Reprinted by permission of the University of Pittsburgh Press.

SONG LYRICS:

Ray Evans and Jay Livingston, "Mona Lisa." Reprinted by permission of The Ray & Wyn Ritchie Evans Foundation.

Acknowledgments

I WANT TO THANK the editorial team at Wipf and Stock Publishers for their support along the way, including K. C. Hanson, editor-in-chief; Jim Tedrick, managing editor; Christian Amondson, assistant managing editor; Jeremy Funk, copyeditor; and Kristen Brack, typesetter. I would also like to express appreciation to James Stock, marketing director, and Raydeen Cuffe, marketing coordinator.

I would also like to thank Ken Brown, Denise Faife of Musée d' Orsay, Liz Kurtelik at Art Resource, Leanne Hayden at Berkshire Museum, John Rockwell of Norman Rockwell Family Entities, Philip Hunt and Shona Corner at the National Gallery of Scotland, Thomas Mesquita at Norman Rockwell Museum, Isabel Silva at Frick Collection, Hannah Bary and Jane Kallir at Grandma Moses Properties Company for their assistance in securing permission and photographic images for the art works I have used in this book; and Margie K. Bachman of University of Pittsburg Press and Angela Hanka of The Ray & Wyn Ritche Evans Foundation for their assistance in securing permissions for the poem and song lyrics I have also included here.

I am especially grateful to Robert Dykstra, Lewis Rambo, Allan Hugh Cole Jr., Nathan Carlin, and Carl Meier for their friendship over the years, and to my wife, Karen, for her friendship and love. While writing this book, I was especially conscious of the fact that she has been my beacon of hope ever since we met in the summer of 1963. Readers familiar with John Bunyan's *The Pilgrim's Progress* will understand what I mean when I say that she has been the very personification of faith and hope throughout my life's journey.

January 1, 2013

Introduction

SOMETIMES A NEW BOOK reflects the author's interest in an entirely new subject. Other times, a new book reflects the author's continuing interest in a subject in which the author has been interested for many years. This book fits into the latter category. Because it focuses on men and their experience of melancholy, it takes up a subject that I have written about in two previous books: *Men, Religion, and Melancholia* and *Men and Their Religion.*[1] Where it breaks new ground, however, is in the fact that it focuses on works of art.

This book is also related to a more recent book, *Striking Out: The Religious Journey of Teenage Boys,*[2] which focuses on teenage boys' plans to leave home and make their way in the world. In this new book I focus on men's desire to be at home in the world. It is based on the claim that these two psychosocial processes—leaving the security of home to take one's place in the world and the desire to be at home in the world—have roots in early childhood, and especially in the experience of emotional separation from one's mother that begins around the age of two to three years of age. The reasons for this emotional separation are the natural maturation of the child and the fact that his mother is helping him identify with his father and his father's world. The earlier books mentioned above focus on the fact that the effect of this emotional separation is the development of a propensity for melancholy, which is reflected in sadness, sober musing, and pensiveness.[3]

In the late 1940s John Bowlby emphasized the necessity of a warm, intimate, and continuous relationship between an infant and young child and his mother (or mother substitute), and suggested that those who do not experience such a relationship may experience significant and irreversible

1. Capps, *Men, Religion, and Melancholia*; Capps, *Men and Their Religion.*
2. Capps, *Striking Out.*
3. Agnes, *Webster's New World*, 896.

mental health consequences.[4] At about the same time, Erik H. Erikson, a child analyst, pointed out that year-old infants are already beginning to pull away from their mothers. He attributed this to physical developments such as acquiring teeth and the growing child's greater use of his arms and legs.[5]

While their views might seem to conflict with one another, the fact is that the two processes are occurring at about the same time. In fact, the warm, intimate and continuous relationship between the mother and her young boy may make it easier for the pulling away to occur. A bit later in the child's development, mothers begin to encourage their boys to become more independent of them so that they may develop a stronger identification with their fathers and their father's world.

But even though they are motivated to pull away from their mothers and their mothers are motivated to help them do so, boys sense that something has been lost in their achievement of this independence. What often happens is that the boy feels guilty for pulling away from his mother and also misinterprets his mother's efforts to help him separate from her as a sign that she is unhappy with him and doesn't love him as much as she used to love him. He may begin to feel that he has to do something to win back her unconditional love for him by being a good, even a perfect little boy. He may also begin to search through other relationships and in other social contexts for what he senses he has lost.

I will be suggesting throughout this book that this sense of having lost something precious remains with us throughout our lives, but that what we do about this sense of having lost something precious shapes our religious sensibility. By *sensibility* I mean what the dictionary says its means, namely, a capacity for or having an appreciation or understanding of.[6] Thus, it does not mean our religious beliefs and practices but our receptiveness to a religious way of thinking about our lives. Although an infant is already endowed with a nascent religious sensibility, I believe that it begins to take form in the second and third years of a child's life, and that, especially for boys, the emotional separation that they experience in relation to their mothers plays a very significant role in the very form that it takes. To make this point more concrete, I will be making particular use of Sigmund Freud's essay "Mourning and Melancholia" and the view of the "composite

4. Bowlby, *Maternal Care and Mental Health*.
5. Erikson, *Childhood and Society*, 67–76.
6. Agnes, ed., *Webster's New World*, 1306.

Self" proposed by Erik H. Erikson.[7] Drawing on these writings of Freud and Erikson, a central thesis of this book is that the development of a *melancholy self* is a lasting consequence of the emotional separation that a boy experiences in early childhood from his mother, and that this *melancholy self* play a critical role in the development of the boy's religious sensibility.

I believe that the word *melancholy* captures the sense of loss that a boy feels as a result of the emotional separation that occurs in his relationship with his mother in the second or third year of his life. Support for this view is provided by Freud's "Mourning and Melancholia." But before discussing his essay, I need to say a few words about Erikson's view of the composite Self.

In *Youth: Identity and Crisis* Erikson suggests that we possess a "composite Self," which is made up of various selves. Which of these selves is expressed at any given time usually depends on the situation. For example, there is the relaxed self among friends, the guarded self in the company of higher-ups, the imperial self in the company of lower-downs, the anxious self in the dentist's chair, or the expansive self while walking on the beach or listening to inspiring music. He suggests that it takes "a healthy personality for the 'I' to be able to speak out of all these conditions in such a way that it can testify to a reasonably coherent Self."[8]

The *melancholy self* may be viewed as one among the various selves that make up one's composite Self. Because it is so closely associated with the boy's relationship with his mother, it is more enduring than some of the more occasional selves that Erikson describes here, but this does not necessarily mean that it is always among the more predominant selves. In fact, if it becomes one of these predominant selves for a particular individual, we may view him as one of the relatively small percentage of men who are clinically depressed.[9] The development of the *melancholy self* may also be viewed as the necessary price a boy pays for the simultaneous development

---

7. Freud, "Mourning and Melancholia"; Erikson, *Identity: Youth and Crisis,* 216–18.

8. Erikson, *Identity: Youth and Crisis,* 217.

9. In *Men and Their Depression* Cochran and Rabinowitz cite a major study (n=19, 282; w=10,971; m=8311 sponsored in part by the National Institute of Mental Health that found that approximately 5 percent of the men had experienced an Affective disorder (i.e., Major depressive episode, Manic episode, Major depression, Bipolar I, Bipolar II, and Dysthymia). Although this was half the rate of women with an Affective disorder, the authors caution that the large numbers of men in the alcohol abuse/dependence category (24 percent as compared with 4 percent of the women) may suggest that men who are "depressed" are manifesting these symptoms in these other undocumented syndromes (13–14).

of a *resourceful self.*[10] But if the *melancholy self* is not among a person's more predominant selves, this also means that he may not be consciously aware of its presence and of its role in his life, especially how it expresses itself in feelings of having lost something that was very precious to him, in the sense that he does not quite fit into the home environment, and in the desire to be at home in the world. This unconsciousness of its presence may also be true of a man who is clinically depressed, because there can be various other reasons for his depression in addition to or separate from the *melancholy self*.

Thus, a major purpose of this book is to raise our consciousness of the existence of the *melancholy self* so that we can be more cognizant of the role that it plays in our lives, especially as it expresses itself in the desire to be at home in the world. There are various ways that this purpose might be addressed, but the one that I have chosen here is to focus on works of art and on the lives of the artists who painted them and on some of the representative ways in which male viewers have responded to these paintings. My contention is that the paintings are a reflection of the artist's *melancholy self* and that this is also true of the viewers' responses. This does not mean that the artists' work as a whole is a reflection of their *melancholy selves*, but it does mean that this particular painting was under the guidance, as it were, of the painter's *melancholy self*, and that this was largely because the subject of this particular painting evoked feelings and perceptions that were associated with the emotional separation from his mother in the second or third year of his life. If this particular artist returned to this subject time and again, which is the case with some of the artists presented here, it is also likely that his attraction to this form of self-expression was itself related to difficulties and struggles associated with the *melancholy self* and that his decision to become a painter was an expression of his *resourceful self*, for one of the characteristics of the *resourceful self* is the ability to use one's imagination in a constructive way.

This brings us to Freud's essay "Mourning and Melancholia."[11] In this essay he compares his melancholic patients with persons who have lost a loved one as a result of death. He suggests that they are similar in a certain sense because melancholic patients come across to him as persons who have also lost a loved one. But there is a noticeable difference as well. For with those who are mourning, the object of their love has actually died, but

10. See Capps, "Erikson's Schedule of Human Strengths and the Childhood Origins of the Resourceful Self."

11. Freud, "Mourning and Melancholia."

with melancholic patients, the person has not actually died but has become lost as an object of love.

He suggests that melancholic patients are rather like the bride who has been stood up on her wedding day by the man she intended to marry. Here the lost loved object is easy to identify. In other cases of melancholic patients, one gets the feeling from how they talk and act that they have experienced a loss, but it is unclear as to what has in fact been lost. Sometimes the patient knows the identity of the person he has lost but is not at all clear as to what he has lost.

Another difference between mourning and melancholia is that in mourning the world itself becomes poor and empty, but in melancholia it is the ego of the sufferer that becomes poor and empty. Freud tells about patients who are suffering from melancholia who represent their ego as worthless and morally despicable. They reproach themselves, commiserate with family members who have to put up with them, and imagine that they have always been this way. Freud suggests that some of these self-accusations ring true, for the melancholic patient often has a keener eye for the truth about oneself than do persons who are not melancholic. But much of this self-accusation is a gross exaggeration, and it is not difficult to see that there is no correspondence between the degree of self-abasement and its real justification, especially when this person is compared with other persons who have a much higher opinion of themselves.

Freud says that he hasn't found it useful to try to talk a melancholic patient out of this low opinion of himself because he will merely respond by adding more self-accusations. Freud also notes that the analyst needs to keep in mind that the patient is correctly describing his psychological situation regardless of whether it is congruent with the real truth. This, after all, is how he feels about himself. Instead, Freud advises the analyst to consider the likelihood that an unconscious process is going on here, that these self-reproaches are actually reproaches against a loved object which have been redirected toward the patients' own ego. He uses the analogy of the woman who pities her husband for being bound up with such a poor creature as herself, suggesting that she may actually be accusing her husband of being a poor creature in some way or other. These self-reproaches are therefore masks that disguise the fact that someone else is the object of accusation or blame. Freud notes that this interpretation of what is going on here is supported by the fact that melancholic patients are not ashamed to hide their heads. In fact, they do not adopt the attitude of humility and submissiveness toward others that one would expect of someone as despicable as the person they portray themselves to be. On the contrary, they tend to give others a great deal of trouble, perpetually taking offence and behaving as if they had been treated with great injustice.

With these observations in hand, Freud suggests that it is not all that difficult to figure out what has happened to make the melancholic the way he is today. First, there was an object-choice (i.e., the patient loved a certain person). Then, due to a real injury or disappointment with the loved person, the object-relationship was undermined. The result was not the normal one of withdrawing one's love from this person and transferring it to another person, but a different process took place. Love, instead of transferred to another person, was withdrawn into the ego, and an *identification* of the ego with the abandoned object was established. Thus, the shadow of the object fell upon the ego, so that the ego could from then on be criticized as though it was in fact the forsaken object. Meanwhile, because the person who was loved did not die (as in the case of mourning), there is the possibility that this person is "still in the neighborhood."[12]

If this person is still living and one continues to have contact with this person, there is a sense that for the melancholic patient this person is not one person but two persons. There is the person he knew before the loss took place, and there is the person he knows after the loss has taken place. Thus, the lost loved object that has been withdrawn into the ego is not the same as the "object" who manifests herself in the melancholic patient's daily life. Nor do the reproaches and accusations against this object displaced onto his own ego have any necessary connection with how the melancholic relates to this person today. To be sure, the relationship may be flawed in various ways, but the patient's complaint is not against this person but against the object that was loved and has since been lost.

Because Freud is talking about adult patients who are suffering from an illness known as melancholia, it may seem somewhat far-fetched to suggest that something comparable to this occurs between the two- or three-year-old boy and his mother. But if we keep in mind that we are not talking here about the child suffering from an emotional illness but of the emergence of one of several selves that make up the composite Self (and not necessarily a predominant one at that), plus if we bear in mind the fact that Freud is concerned here with the loss of a loved object who (unlike one who has died and so is mourned) is still "in the neighborhood," then it makes a

12. Ibid., 173.

great deal of sense to apply his reconstruction of the process of the emergence of melancholia to what happens between a boy and his mother in the normal course of development. There may be situational circumstances that make this process more traumatic for a particular boy. Also, a very positive relationship between a mother and her son may help to moderate the felt sense of loss. But the important point here is that the boy has sustained a loss and this loss tends to manifest itself in self- reproach. Also, as the word "reproach" implies, the criticism is *moral* in nature. Thus, the idea that the *melancholy self* emerges in early childhood is consistent with Freud's view that this is the time when a child's superego begins to form.

Because he is a physician dealing with an emotional illness, Freud was naturally concerned with the question whether melancholia is curable. As I do not assume that the development of a *melancholy self* is an illness—it is the consequence of a normal process of development—much of his discussion of this question does not concern us here. But his view that there are two possible curative scenarios is relevant because these two scenarios identify ways one may come to terms with the loss that he has experienced in early childhood and even make constructive use of it. One scenario relates to the fact that in most cases of melancholia there are often manic states as well. Freud suggests that such manic states are comparable to winning a lottery. In one single victory the winner is able to throw off a heavy burden of poverty or indebtedness that he or she has endured for a long time. In a similar way, the manic state is one in which the ego surmounts the loss of the loved object in one single blow. Instead of a seemingly interminable process of struggling with ambivalent feelings of love and hate toward the lost loved object, in one decisive act one withdraws one's feelings of love toward the object and abandons it as no longer of value. Thus, the manic state enables one to break the loved object's hold upon the ego by deeming it unworthy of loyalty or longing.

The other scenario is one in which the process is more comparable to mourning. Here, one gradually accepts the reality of the fact that the object is dead and withdraws the feelings of love that are felt toward it in order to make it possible for the ego itself to live again. While it may seem rather odd to say that the mother the infant boy experienced is no longer living and needs, therefore, to be relinquished, this is in a real sense true. The consoling factor—one that also often provides consolation in mourning—is that the mother continues to exist, albeit in a different form, and *this* mother may be no less worthy of love and affection. I suggest that it is precisely boy's emerging *resourceful self* that avails itself of this very possibility and in doing so takes initiatives that compensate for the loss of the original loved object. This process, in turn, may inspire alternative ways of experiencing love that are patterned after the relationship with the mother but involve new "objects" discovered in the world beyond the maternal sphere itself.

This is where the boy's religious sensibility comes in. As I noted earlier, we have reason to believe that a nascent religious sensibility is present in and through the infant's relationship with his mother. But the religious sensibility that remains with us throughout our lives begins with a loss that evokes a desire to reverse the loss and to find ways to overcome it. This personal experience may, in fact, be the basis for a biblical view of how religion itself began. As Genesis 3 suggests, man became religious as a result of the fall. That is, he began to engage in behaviors designed to regain God's favor or recapture some sense of being in God's good graces.[13]

I suggest that the boy's religious sensibility takes two different forms initially, and that a third form is added somewhat later. The first is a *sense of honor*, which is based on his assumption that if he is a good boy, he may regain his mother's favor and get back into her good graces.[14] The second is a *sense of hope*, which is based on the view that he may be able to find what he has lost in the world beyond the maternal environment; thus, unlike the hope based on the infant's relationship with his mother, this is a hope that looks beyond the maternal relationship for intimacy and love. The third is a *sense of humor* that makes light of the other two senses, suggesting that they are not what they are cracked up to be. Thus, it satirizes the *sense of honor*, suggesting that moral rectitude does not always secure the desired

13. In *Young Man Luther* Erik H. Erikson discusses the relationship between the Genesis story, the role that the infant's maturing organs play in the emotional separation that occurs between the infant and his mother in the second year of life, and melancholia (120–22).

14. I have chosen the word *honor* because one of the dictionary definitions of the word is "a keen sense of right and wrong" and one of the meanings of the word "honorable" is "having or showing a sense of right and wrong; characterized by honesty and integrity; upright" (Agnes, *Webster's New World,* 685). The tendency to venerate the word *honor* is reflected in the fact that we use the terms *honor student* and *honor role* for exemplary academic achievement, *honor system* to convey the idea that individuals can be trusted to obey the rules without direct supervision or oversight, and *honorable mention* to convey the idea that even if one has not achieved the highest level in a competition, one's achievement is nonetheless worthy of recognition. Also, the phrase "on my honor" is not only an affirmation of one's trustworthiness but also a declaration that one will stake one's name and reputation on this claim. See also Baden-Powell's emphasis on the sacred nature of honor in *Scouting for Boys,* 222–23.

outcome, and also pokes fun at the *sense of hope,* by remarking on the absurdity of the efforts expended in the search of someone or something to compensate for the loss. By poking fun at the other two senses, the *sense of humor* saves them from outright ridicule or cynical rejection. By relativizing them it helps to preserve them.

An essay by Freud titled "The 'Uncanny'" offers another perspective on the loss that the boy experiences and also enables us to make some connections between this loss and the works of art that we will be considering in this study.[15] As the English word *uncanny* is a translation of the German word *unheimlich,* Freud notes that "the uncanny" is something that was once "homelike" (*heimlich*) but has since turned into its opposite, the "unhomelike" *(unheimlich).* One thinks here of our sense of uneasiness when we enter a house that has been vacant for years. Even if we are not superstitious, we may find ourselves thinking that it is haunted by the spirits of the family members who used to live in it.

Freud also endorses the view of the German philosopher Friedrich Schelling that the *uncanny* is the sense that something familiar has become unfamiliar. He notes, for example, that male patients sometimes observe that there is something uncanny about the female genital organs. He suggests that behind this feeling is the patient's experience of his mother's genitals or her body, with which he was originally so familiar (having lived inside her body for the first nine months of his existence), but which became unfamiliar in the course of time, often as a result of the weaning process. Freud cites the humorous saying that "Love is home-sickness," and adds that whenever a man dreams of a place or a country and says to himself that "this place is familiar to me; I have been here before," we may interpret the place as that of his mother's genitals or her body. His point is that this familiar place has become defamiliarized, and the defamiliarization of the mother's body (the place where he was originally at home) together with its attendant anxieties are implicated in all subsequent experiences of the uncanny.

Freud's allusion to male patients implies that the sense of the uncanny in this case is greater for the male than for the female child because his physical difference from his mother is precisely what the *heimlich/unheimlich* ambivalence is about. As a result, men are more likely than women to experience "home-sickness" and to express the melancholy view that "you cannot go home again." Indeed, they frequently experience themselves as strangers or intruders in that most familiar of places: the family home.

15. Freud, "The 'Uncanny,'" 152–53.

Freud does not make an explicit connection between the uncanny and melancholia in this essay, but his analysis of the uncanny suggests that they are in fact related: If melancholia focuses on emotions relating to the loss itself, then the uncanny draws attention to the fact that what was once "homelike" is no longer experienced as such. One is on the outside looking in or condemned, as it were, to make one's way in the external world. Thus, the question with which I will be concerned throughout this book is how art works assist in our efforts to recover creatively from the loss of the loved one we experienced in early childhood. There are two ways in which it does so. One is to help us to recover through the imaginative process that which we have lost. The other is to help us experience the world that is external to the maternal environment as a place in which we can be at home.

We saw earlier that Freud envisioned two possible curative scenarios for his male patients' melancholia. One is the employment of a manic state in which one withdraws through a single decisive act one's feelings of love toward the object, and summarily abandons it as no longer of value. The other is more comparable to mourning in which one gradually accepts the reality of the fact that the lost object no longer exists and withdraws the feelings of love that are felt towards it. This acceptance and withdrawal are then followed by the consoling realization that the mother continues to exist albeit in a different form, one that is no less worthy of love and affection.

Although there may be occasions when a painting may be so overwhelmingly powerful that a cure is realized in a single blow, I believe that the more common experience is that repeated exposure to several paintings is likely to have a more enduring effect. In other words, the second scenario is the more likely one. The psychoanalytic term for this scenario is *displacement*, a psychological mechanism by which emotions associated with one object are directed toward another object, one less likely to evoke overwhelming anxieties of dread, fear, and helplessness.[16]

The works of art that will be the focus of our study here have associations with the lost loved object, but at the same time they invite the displacement of the strong emotional feelings associated with this object by means of a representation that has less intensity of feeling. And because this is so, the work of art enables the artist and the viewer to work through their ambivalent feelings toward the lost object without resorting to the psychological violence that Freud describes in the first curative scenario he identifies in "Mourning and Melancholia." These works of art represent a

16. Freud, *The Interpretation of Dreams*, 209–10.

variety of such displacements, each of which serves the purpose of working through the ambivalent feelings, but doing so in quite different ways.

Among the various genres of pictorial art, the ones that are most germane to this project are portraiture, interiors, still life, and landscapes. Portraits play a central role because they enable us to focus on the development of the *melancholy self* and to trace it to the relationship between the mother and son in early childhood. As Richard Brilliant points out in his book on portraiture, the core of this genre "involves the representation of the structuring of human relationships going back to the earliest stages of life, when the interacting self comes into existence," and that the "dynamic nature of portraits" and the "occasionality" that anchors their imagery in life may be traced to "the primary experience of the infant in arms."[17] As the baby gazes up at her, her vitally important image becomes so firmly imprinted in the baby's mind that before long she can be recognized almost instantaneously and without conscious thought. A little later a name ("Mama") will be attached to her familiar face and body and soon thereafter a more conscious acknowledgment of her role as "nurturer" or provider will emerge. An understanding of her character as loving and warmly protective will also begin to form unless, of course, her behavior towards her little one is neither loving nor protective. Eventually the infant will acquire a sense of its own independent existence, of a being in its own right, capable of responding to the other, and of having its own given name.[18]

Especially noteworthy here is Brilliant's observation that the "dynamic nature of portraits" depends on the primary experience of the infant being held in the mother's arms and gazing up at her face. As time goes on, reading the mother's face becomes an interpretive task, one that is rarely straightforwardly clear. As he points out, "Visual communication between mother and child is effected face-to-face, and when those faces are smiling, everybody is happy, or appears to be." Thus, the human face is not only the most important key to identification based on appearance, but is also the primary field of expressive action, "replete with a variety of 'looks' whose meaning is subject to interpretation, if not always correctly, as any poker player knows."[19] As we will see, there is a profound connection between the development of a *melancholy self* and the male viewer's uncertainty as to what is being communicated in and through this "primary field of expressive action."

17. Brilliant, *Portraiture*, 9.
18. Ibid., 9.
19. Ibid., 10

Portraiture, then, enables us to explore the experiential roots and emotional sources of our *melancholy self,* and the chapters that focus on Leonardo da Vinci's *Mona Lisa* and James Whistler's *Mother* are essentially concerned with these experiential and emotional factors. I view these two portraits as the defining paintings of the religious sensibilities—the *sense of honor,* the *sense of hope,* and the *sense of humor*—that emerge in and through the development of the *melancholy self.* The responses and reactions of male viewers to these two paintings reflect the very different emotions that the maternal figure evokes in them. I suggest that Leonardo's *Mona Lisa* is the iconic center of the religious sensibilities associated with the *melancholy self,* but that her very elevation to iconic status also invites an iconoclastic backlash, which has been expressed in both aggressive and nonaggressive ways (e.g., humor). I also suggest that Whistler's *Mother* is the devotional center of the religious sensibilities associated with the *melancholy self,* but that her status as object of devotion also renders her vulnerable to irreverent reactions expressed mostly in humorous terms. I note that the painter himself initiated this irreverence.

The chapter on Norman Rockwell's *Shuffleton's Barbershop* shifts the focus from portraits of the maternal figure to the desire to recover a sense of being at home. If men are exiles in the world—no longer at home in their original maternal environment—they are condemned, as it were, to find for themselves a place to be at home in the world in some other actual or imaginary environment. Some men have recovered a sense of being at home in the homes they have cocreated with spouses or significant others. Others have recovered a sense of being at home in other physical settings, especially ones in which men congregate together. The local tavern or bar is one such place. The barbershop is another. But what gives *Shuffleton's Barbershop* a distinctly melancholy tone and force is the fact that the painter—and viewer—are on the outside looking in.

The chapters on Sanford R. Gifford's *Kauterskill Clove* and George Inness's *Sunrise* take a different approach in that they suggest that the world to which men have been exiled is—or at least can be experienced as—a maternal environment. In effect, they express the view that what one has lost in the domestic world may be recovered in the exterior world, if not in the very same form, at least in a form that is reminiscent of the feelings and aspirations associated with it. Thus, the paintings discussed in these chapters are expressions of the *sense of hope,* and they suggest to their viewers that their hope is not in vain.

The chapters on Grandma Moses's *Little Boy Blue* and Washington Irving's *Rip Van Winkle* build on this suggestion that their hope is not in vain because the painting and the story portray a boy and a man who are truly at home in the world. That Anna Mary Robertson Moses was known as Grandma Moses means that she does not seem to evoke the range of ambivalent feelings associated with the mother. Furthermore, unlike Whistler's mother, Anna, Grandma Moses was not the subject of a painting. She was a painter, and this means that she could *represent* the world as she chose to represent it. I focus on her *Little Boy Blue* because it portrays the reassuring mother who continues to make her presence felt to men who carry within themselves the self-image of the little boy who sleeps peacefully on the hay while the men toil and try to control the world around them. I also introduce Eugene Field's poem "Little Boy Blue" to explore his suggestion that the boy has experienced a rude awakening that challenges but also supports and reinforces his sense of being watched over by a maternal presence that is not his mother—who is, in a sense, more than a mother. I view this painting and accompanying poem as representing a self-reconciliation, that is, the *melancholy self's* reception into the company of the selves that comprise the composite Self, thereby overcoming its own sense of being an exile or dysfunctional aspect of an otherwise well-integrated Self.

The chapter on Irving's *Rip Van Winkle* focuses on a poem by Billy Collins that was inspired by visual portrayals of Rip Van Winkle.[20] His poem presents us with a picture of a man who is thoroughly at home in the world because he has chosen to imitate the non-anxious presence of Mother Nature herself.

In *The Individual and His Religion* Gordon W. Allport concludes that a man's religion "is his ultimate attempt to enlarge and to complete his personality by finding the supreme context in which he rightly belongs."[21] I suggest that the art of painting is one of the ways that men may make this ultimate attempt and that those of us who are not painters may nevertheless participate in this attempt by opening ourselves to their work. Writers who have made the art of painting an object of study can be of help in this regard, and as these introductory remarks should also make clear, this

20. In his *Museum of Words* James A. W. Heffernan focuses on *ekphrasis,* i.e., the verbal representation of visual art. He traces the literary use of *ekphrasis* to the lengthy description of the shield that Hephaestus made for Achilles in the eighteenth book of Homer's *Iliad* (9). Gail Levin's *The Poetry of Solitude*, a collection of poems inspired by paintings by Edward Hopper, is illustrative of poets' use of *ekphrasis.*

21. Allport, *The Individual and His Religion*, 142.

study is especially indebted to Sigmund Freud who worked through issues relating to his own *melancholy self* by studying the life and art of Leonardo da Vinci.[22] In his monograph on Leonardo da Vinci, he placed in juxtaposition two of Leonardo's paintings. One is Leonardo's painting of the young Italian gentlewoman now known as Mona Lisa. The other is his painting of St. Anne, Jesus's grandmother, her daughter, Mary, and the boy Jesus. If we look closely at the boy's face as he looks at his mother's face, we can see that he will not be spared the melancholy feelings that will instigate his own ultimate attempt to find the supreme context in which he rightly belongs. Yet, through this attempt, he will also experience the self-reconciliation for which the *melancholy self* residing in us all yearns and longs.[23]

22. Freud, *Leonardo da Vinci and a Memory of His Childhood*.

23. Although this book focuses on men, Julia Kristeva explores the relevance of melancholia to women in *Black Sun*. See also Jennifer Radden's "Love and Loss in Freud's *Mourning and Melancholia*: A Rereading"; and Radden, *The Nature of Melancholy: From Aristotle to Kristeva*.

PART I

The Melancholy Self

chapter one

Da Vinci's *Mona Lisa*: Maternal Icon

UNTIL 2003, THE FIVE hundredth anniversary of the *Mona Lisa* by Leonardo da Vinci, this small painting (roughly 30 x 21 inches) occupied a room at the Louvre in Paris with twenty-three other Venetian paintings (by Titian, Verones, and Tintoretto). Just outside the room, on the walls of the Grande Galerie—said to be the longest corridor in Europe—are paintings by Raphael, Correggio, Fra Angelico, Caravaggio, and five other paintings by Da Vinci.

In *Becoming Mona Lisa*, Donald Sassoon observes that these works of art can all be contemplated at leisure by any of the five and a half million people who visit the Louvre every year, even during the peak summer months. But this is not true of the *Mona Lisa*. The constantly shifting crowd in the room (fifty or more persons during the summer), all trying to catch a glimpse of the portrait, makes a contemplative viewing of it virtually impossible, and the reflection from the camera flashes continually bouncing off the glass makes an examination of it even more difficult.

Sassoon suggests that the unprepared visitor might assume that the object of such commotion is not a painting at all but some celebrity, a renowned personality from the world of the cinema, television, fashion or music, or a member of a major royal family. The museum rule that no more than thirty people are allowed in front of a single painting is disregarded. Also, otherwise-well-behaved tourists, who are somewhat in awe of the museum, ignore the prohibition of flash photography, and the guards have pretty much given up trying to stop them. The *Mona Lisa* now has its own room.[1]

Leonardo da Vinci's *Mona Lisa*, The Louvre, Paris. Photo credit: Réunion des Musées Nationaux / Art Resource, New York.

Sassoon asks, why is the *Mona Lisa* the best-known painting in the entire world? And how is it that a painting with impeccable cultural credentials has also become the most popular? Lest anyone doubt that it *is* the most popular, he cites a survey conducted in Italy for his book. He found that 86 percent of respondents said that it is the best known, followed by

1. Sassoon, *Becoming Mona Lisa*, 2–3.

4

Van Gogh's *Sunflowers* (at less than 4 percent) and Botticelli's *Spring* and Munch's *Scream* (2 percent each). A survey conducted on a February day in 2000 also revealed that "Where is the *Mona Lisa*?" was by far the most frequently asked question at information desks at the Louvre (76 queries). It was followed by "Where am I?" (53 queries), and "Where is the *Venus de Milo*?" (1 query).[2]

THE LOST OBJECT AND THE SYMBOLIC FIGURE

Sassoon's *Becoming Mona Lisa* is concerned to answer the questions: How did the *Mona Lisa* become the best-known painting worldwide, and how did it ascend to the status of a global icon? My concern here is a much narrower one. It picks up on Sassoon's observation that few of the visitors who jostle before the painting know why it is the most famous work of art in the world, but that many think it has something to do with the mystery of the *Mona Lisa*'s smile. This mystery originated in the nineteenth century. Previously, the almost imperceptible smile attracted little notice, and was not regarded as enigmatic or mysterious.[3]

Why did interest in the *Mona Lisa*'s smile emerge in the nineteenth century? I believe that it was part of a newfound interest in *Mona Lisa* herself, and that a central feature of this interest was her special appeal to the *melancholy self*, which, as the introduction notes, is one of the enduring selves that make up a man's composite Self. Also, because it appealed to the *melancholy self*, it evoked the full range of religious sensibilities identified the introduction: the *sense of honor*, the *sense of hope*, and the *sense of humor*. This means that the painting performed a therapeutic function, and did so by means of the art of displacement. As we also saw in the introduction, Freud envisions the therapy occurring in one of two ways—either by means of a manic act in which one defeats the internalized lost object with a single blow, or through a gradual process of withdrawing one's love for the lost object. Since displacement of feelings felt toward the original loved object onto another object may be therapeutic, it is not surprising that *Mona Lisa* has invited both scenarios—the most common, of course, being the gradual withdrawal of feelings toward the lost loved object in a process akin to mourning.

2. Ibid., 8–9.
3. Ibid., 11.

Although Sassoon is concerned to show how *Mona Lisa* has become a global icon, the interest the painting evoked in the nineteenth century was centered in Europe. The official religious context, then, was Western Christianity. Thus, in theory, the most likely symbolic figure for any redirection of melancholy feelings toward the lost love object would be the Virgin Mary, the mother of Jesus. The problem here is that for some the Virgin Mary was highly idealized, and for others, especially those of Protestant leanings, was not taken all that seriously. Thus, for some, she may possibly serve as an appropriate means of displacing feelings of loss and the sense that something is missing due to the emotional separation from the mother, but not for the displacement of feelings of criticism and reproach; and, for others, she is rather inconceivable as a symbolic replacement for the lost love object.

To be sure, as Michael P. Carroll shows in *Madonnas That Maim*, there is a "dark side" in certain apparitions of the Virgin Mary reported in the annals of Italian Catholicism.[4] For example in a document dated 1530 there is the story of a humble peasant named Benedetto Pareto. The Virgin Mary appeared to him when he was cutting hay for his flocks on Mount Figogna, and she told him she wanted him to erect a chapel in her honor on top of the mountain. When he replied that he was just a poor peasant, she told him not to worry, that with her help he would find everything easy. But when he told his wife about the apparition, she didn't believe him and ridiculed him for telling such a story, so he put aside any thoughts of carrying out the Virgin Mary's request. The next day he was punished by being hurled to the ground from a tree he had climbed to get some figs for his breakfast and was badly mangled in the process. Although Mary subsequently healed him and he carried out his promise, these are the very psychodynamics of the tension that occurs in the boy who develops a will of his own that conflicts with that of his mother.[4] Even the fact that Benedetto climbed a tree to get some figs for breakfast reflects the development of muscular strengths that are typical of a boy of this age.[5]

Carroll also relates the story told by a German Jesuit in 1652 about a soldier who urinated against a wall that had a painted image of the Madonna. He was struck blind and suffered strong pain "in the parts that offended the Madonna." He repented and was healed, but his behavior was

4. Carroll, *Madonnas That Maim*, 67–87.

5. Ibid., 68. In his essay "Human Strength and the Cycle of Generations," in *Insight and Responsibility*, Erik H. Erikson assigns the development of the *will* to the second stage of the life cycle (the stage of *autonomy vs. shame and doubt*) which is about one to three years of age, 118–20.

reflective of the little boy who has a mischievous penchant for urinating on walls or other targets. The fact that he is struck blind suggests an association of visual loss and sexual misbehavior relating to the genitals (e.g., masturbation).[6]

These and other stories of persons being maimed or killed through the agency of the Virgin Mary are certainly not all sweetness and light. On the other hand, they are far removed from the mainstream Marian piety that prevailed in the nineteenth century. Carroll notes that the Marian apparitions of the nineteenth century fall into two broad categories: those in which the apparition is gentle and those in which the tone is apocalyptic. While the apocalyptic apparitions may appear similar to the earlier apparitions described above, they do not, in fact, represent the Virgin Mary as punitive or vengeful. As Carroll points out, a Madonna who causes the body of Benedetto Pareto to be mangled can hardly be compared to the gentle lady who appeared at Lourdes, and even though there may be a surface similarity with the appearances at LaSalette and Fatima, this similarity breaks down on closer inspection, for the Virgin Mary who appeared at LaSalette and Fatima threatened punishment because there was too much sin in the world, and her concern was to get people to abandon their sinful ways. Unlike the Virgin Mary who inflicted injury on Benedetto Pareto, these apparitions were simply working hard to promote the moral and religious codes endorsed by the Universal Church,[7] and do not, therefore, invoke the psychodynamics of the emergence of the *melancholy self*.

Thus, even for nineteenth-century men whose belief in or devotion to the Virgin Mary was strong, she would not seem to be an effective means for the therapeutic displacement of feelings felt toward the lost loved object. But perhaps more importantly, there were a great number of men, especially in countries like England and France, and particularly among the educated classes, for whom the Virgin Mary would not have been a useful resource for such displacement even if she had afforded the therapeutic working out of the full range of ambivalent feelings felt toward the lost loved object. This would be especially true of the men who had more or less abandoned the churches in favor of museums, men whose contemplative and reverential dispositions were directed toward paintings on the wall instead of the altars and candles that adorned the walls of chapels.

6. Carroll, *Madonnas That Maim*, 73.

7. Ibid., 70–71.

It is unnecessary, though, to claim that *Mona Lisa* became the Virgin Mary's rival as the Madonna of a secularized form of Christianity. It is sufficient to suggest that in the nineteenth century men began to invest her with feelings that were originally aroused in their early childhood experience of losing the lost object, and that she enabled them to work through their ambivalence toward the maternal object. For this reason, she is adaptable to all three of the religious sensibilities identified in the introduction: men have made her the object of their commitment to moral goodness and high-minded duty (their *sense of honor*), of their quest for love and a sense of being at home in the world (their *sense of hope*), and the target of humor, light banter, and affectionate ridicule (their *sense of humor*). While the emotion of sadness—longing, sense of being bereft—has predominated, she has also been the object of reproach as exhibited in various helpless and gratuitous attacks inflicted on the woman in the painting. That these attacks involve men's religious sensibilities is reflected in the prevalent judgment that the expressions of satire and rage against *Mona Lisa* are a "sacrilege."

PSYCHOANALYTIC REFLECTIONS ON LEONARDO'S EARLY CHILDHOOD

Freud wrote a monograph on Leonardo da Vinci published in 1910.[8] In the Norton paperback that I have in my possession, two of Leonardo's paintings appear before the title page. One is his *St. Anne with Virgin and Child*. The other is his *Mona Lisa*. In the former, the Madonna gazes on her child and reaches out to him, and he gazes back while reaching out to the lamb (which many believe symbolizes his future suffering and death). In the latter, Mona Lisa is alone, and is looking forward, though her gaze is oriented toward her left. The viewer perceives, perhaps, that she is gazing at him, though the fact that her gaze is off-center may also suggest that she is gazing beyond her viewer, as though interested, perhaps even preoccupied, by something that does not concern him.

Freud's monograph is often referred to as the first psychoanalytic psychobiography as it focuses on the relationship between Leonardo's life and his art. Freud notes that we know very little about Leonardo's childhood and youth, but we do know that he was born in 1452 in the little town of Vinci between Florence and Empoli; that he was an illegitimate child, which in those days was certainly not considered a grave social stigma; that

8. Freud, *Leonardo da Vinci and a Memory of His Childhood*.

his father was Ser Piero da Vinci, a notary and descended from a family of notaries and farmers who took their name from the locality of Vinci; and that his mother was a certain Caterina, probably a peasant girl, who later married another native of Vinci.[9]

Leonardo da Vinci's *Saint Anne with Virgin and Child*, The Louvre (Paris). Photo credit: Réunion des Musées Nationaux / Art Resource, New York.

9. Ibid., 31.

The year that Leonardo was born his father married Donna Albiera, a sixteen-year-old girl of higher social standing than Caterina. Since taxation records of the year 1457 mention Leonardo among the members of the Vinci family household as the illegitimate son of Ser Piero, Freud surmises that the boy was taken into his paternal home sometime after his birth and before the age of five. However, Freud doubts that this would have happened immediately after his birth. Furthermore, he guesses it might not have happened at all were it not for the fact that his father's wife was childless. Freud points out that it is unusual at the start of a marriage to put an illegitimate offspring into the care of the young bride who still expects to be blessed with children of her own, so several "years of disappointment must surely have elapsed before it was decided to adopt the illegitimate child— who had probably grown up an attractive young boy—as a compensation for the absence of the legitimate children that had been hoped for."[10]

Freud goes on to suggest that Leonardo spent the critical years of his life not by the side of his father and stepmother but with his poor, forsaken mother, so he had time to feel the absence of his father. At least three years, and perhaps five, elapsed before he could exchange the solitary person of his mother for a parental couple, and by then his personality was already formed, for "in the first three or five years of life certain impressions become fixed and ways of reacting to the outside world are established which can never be deprived of their importance by later experience." That he spent the first years of his life alone with his mother would have had a "decisive influence on the formation of his inner life."[11]

Leonardo's *St. Anne with Virgin and Child* especially interests Freud because it presents two mothers—the Virgin Mary and her mother St. Anne—and represents them as being very close in age. St Anne is "portrayed as being perhaps a little more mature and serious than the Virgin Mary" but she is still "a young woman of unfaded beauty." In Freud's view, Leonardo recapitulated his own early childhood in this painting because he had two mothers: "first, his true mother Caterina, from whom he was torn away when he was between three and five, and then a young and tender stepmother, his father's wife, Donna Albiera." Furthermore, the maternal figure that is further away from the boy—the grandmother—corresponds to his biological mother, Caterina, both in its appearance and in its special relation to the boy. Moreover, he "seems to have used the blissful smile of St.

10. Ibid., 41.
11. Ibid., 41–42.

Anne to disavow and to cloak the envy which the unfortunate woman felt when she was forced to give up her son to her better-born rival, as she had once given up his father as well."[12]

In his psychoanalytic and art historical study of Leonardo, Bradley I. Collins points out that Freud's view that St. Anne corresponds to Leonardo's birth mother while the Virgin Mary relates to his stepmother is supported by the fact that Caterina was twenty-five years old and Donna Albiera was only sixteen years old the year that Leonardo was born. He also notes that Leonardo omitted Joseph from nearly all of his Holy Family paintings, an omission that may be related to his exclusion from his father's will, presumably on the grounds that among Ser Piero's ten sons, only Leonardo was illegitimate. The others were progeny from his father's second marriage following the death of Donna Albiera. His father's death and his contestation of his father's will occurred in the middle of the period in which Leonardo was engaged in his paintings of the Holy Family.[13]

I believe that Leonardo's exclusion from his father's will might also be reflected in his fresco *The Last Supper*, which focuses on Jesus's shattering announcement of betrayal instead of the more traditional Eucharistic theme. Like Jesus, Leonardo had been betrayed, and Jesus's announcement of betrayal occurs in the company of a group of men, his disciples, who would represent Leonardo's stepbrothers. The fact that Leonardo does not depict Judas Iscariot slinking guiltily to the door, his moneybag in hand (which would have been appropriate in a painting focusing on the announcement of the betrayal) leaves open the possibility that Leonardo means to suggest that the betrayer is not among those to whom Jesus makes the announcement, but is the father himself. This, after all, is implied in the statement attributed to Jesus on the cross, "Father, why have you abandoned me?"

In any event, Collins concludes that Leonardo's painting of *St. Anne with Virgin and Child* enabled Leonardo both to re-create his past and to transform it: On the one hand, "he could return to a world dominated by multiple maternal figures and marked by unusual and unexpected births." On the other hand, "he could take the actual, humiliating reality of his childhood—an illegitimate birth by a peasant mother—and transfigure it." Thus, by identifying with the Christ Child, "he could become the divine, not the shameful, product of an unusual pregnancy, and by identifying Caterina with the Virgin, he could undo her degradation." Also, "the theme of

12. Ibid., 63–64.

13. Collins, *Leonardo, Psychoanalysis, and Art*, 150–51.

an untainted pregnancy leading to a miraculous birth" in the case of Anne's and Mary's pregnancies "would only have strengthened the subject's unconscious appeal for Leonardo."[14] Thus, the humiliating reality that Leonardo experienced is transfigured both for himself and for his biological mother.

Collins also discusses Kurt R. Eissler's psychoanalytic study of Leonardo, a study that has particular bearing on the theme of the *melancholy self*. In his view, Eissler's reputation "as a fierce guardian of the Freudian flame" has created the mistaken impression that his study of Leonardo consists almost entirely of a staunch defense of Freud's ideas. Although it is true that Eissler rebuts Freud's critics "with great zeal and at considerable length," there is one point on which he departs from Freud. This is his emphasis on the trauma resulting from Leonardo's separation from his birth mother and its role in shaping his character. As Collins points out, "Freud, rather surprisingly, neglected the psychological consequences of the artist's loss of his mother."[15]

As we have seen, Freud emphasized the fact that Leonardo was essentially deprived of a father in his earliest years, and suggested that this experience of father absence could never be offset by later experiences of his father's presence. For Freud, father absence was an indelible feature of "the formation of his inner life."[16] However, for Eissler, the more critical factor in Leonardo's early years was the loss of his mother when he went to live with his father and stepmother. Eissler believes that Leonardo would have experienced this event as one of "abandonment" by his mother because he would have been too young to fully appreciate the fact that she had little if any power or influence in the decision. He also surmises that the separation occurred at an earlier and more vulnerable age than Freud supposed, and that the childhood memory that Freud discusses in his book—of a bird of prey striking his lips with its tail as he lay in his cradle—suggests "that Leonardo harbored intensely ambivalent feelings toward his mother."[17]

Eissler also claims that Leonardo's separation from his mother, which would have been devastating enough the first time, may have been repeated during his childhood. If his father and stepmother occasionally left Leonardo with Caterina, he would have reexperienced the trauma of loss each time he was reclaimed. Furthermore, he may also have been aware of

14. Ibid., 167.
15. Ibid., 111–12; see Eissler, *Leonardo da Vinci*.
16. Freud, *Leonardo da Vinci and a Memory of His Childhood*, 42.
17. Collins, *Leonardo, Psychoanalysis, and Art*, 112.

the births to Caterina of his half sisters Piera and Maria and, if so, these events may have added yet another dimension to his sense of traumatic rejection: "All infants find the unexpected and undesired appearance of a sibling upsetting, but Leonardo, if he had suffered repeated separations from Caterina, would have found displacement by his half sisters especially agonizing."[18] Eissler acknowledges that there is no documentary evidence to establish that Leonardo shuttled back and forth between the two families, but it is not improbable that his father and stepmother would have eased their childrearing duties from time to time by handing him over to his natural mother, nor is it far fetched to assume that the births of Piera (when he was two) and Maria (when he was five) had a traumatic effect on him. There is, in fact, possible artistic evidence that Leonardo felt traumatically displaced by his siblings in the shifting positions of the Christ Child and St. John in three successive paintings (*The Virgin of the Rocks*, the London cartoon, and *Saint Anne with Virgin and Child*). Collins writes: "As Eissler notes, these rearrangements of the Christ Child and St. John—one moving progressively closer to a maternal figure, the other to oblivion—seem to express the fears and hopes of a child displaced by siblings." Identifying with St. John, Leonardo memorializes Caterina's rejection of him in favor of Piera and Maria, but "by identifying with Christ, he triumphs over them and becomes his mother's favorite."[19]

Thus, in light of Eissler's suggestion that Leonardo was shuttled back and forth between the two families, it would appear that his identification with St. John was reflective of the young boy's view of his actual situation and that his identification with Christ was based on the play of the imagination.[20] Eissler and Collins also cite several allegorical entries in Leonardo's notebooks that enable one to detect an implicit criticism of his birth mother for abandoning him to the harsh treatment of his stepmother. On the other hand, as their interpretations of his paintings of maternal figures indicate,

18. Ibid., 112.

19. Ibid., 113.

20. In *The Play of the Imagination*, Paul W. Pruyser identifies three worldviews: the *autistic world* (the private world of which the dream is most exemplary), the *realistic world* (the public world whose features are open to inspection and verification), and the *illusionistic world* (the world of the imagination). The first engages in untutored fantasy, the second employs sense perceptions, and the third involves tutored fantasy. Also, the first involves utter whimsicality, the second involves reality testing, and the third involves orderly imagination. For additional characteristics, see the chart on page 65. The chapter "Illusion Processing in the Visual Arts" is especially relevant to the focus of this book (73–98).

he was able, through his art, to displace his ambivalent feelings—of nostalgia and longing on the one hand, and anger or rage on the other—toward the lost love object, and this brings us back to *Mona Lisa* and to Freud's commentary on the painting itself.

FREUD AND MONA LISA'S UNCANNY SMILE

Freud's commentary on the painting begins with the observation that "the smile of Mona Lisa del Giocondo had awakened in [Leonardo] as a grown man the memory of the mother of his earliest childhood."[21] This, of course, was Caterina. Noting that this smile reappears on the faces of both women in *St. Anne with Virgin and Child*, he adds this important qualification: "But although the smile that plays on the lips of the two women is unmistakably the same as that in the picture of Mona Lisa, it has lost is uncanny and mysterious character; what it expresses is inward feeling and quiet blissfulness."[22] This very qualification—that "it has lost its uncanny and mysterious character"—raises a serious question as to whether it is the same smile. At the very least, it prompts us to look at other features of the two paintings to try to discover why the very same smile could have such a different emotional expression.

Freud's use of the word "uncanny" with reference to Mona Lisa's smile recalls our brief discussion in the introduction of his essay "The 'Uncanny.'" In this essay he describes the uncanny "as that class of the terrifying which leads back to something long known to us, once very familiar," and states that the purpose of his essay is to identify the circumstances under which "the familiar can become uncanny and frightening."[23] He devotes several pages to an etymological review of the German words *heimlich* and *unheimlich*, the latter of which is translated "uncanny" in the English version of the essay. He concludes that when the various meanings of *heimlich* ("homelike") are reviewed, we discover that the word *heimlich* tends to shade into its opposite, *unheimlich*. One meaning of *heimlich* is "belonging to the house, not strange, familiar, tame, intimate, comfortable, etc.," but another meaning is "concealed, kept from sight, so that others do not get to know about it, withheld from others, i.e., secret." It is the second meaning that shades into *unheimlich*, for *unheimlich* has connotations of "uneasy,"

21. Freud, *Leonardo da Vinci and a Memory of His Childhood*, 64.
22. Ibid.
23. Freud, "The 'Uncanny,'" 125–29.

"eerie," "ghostly," and "motionless" (as in the case of a stone image) and has been described by the German philosopher Friedrich Schelling as "the name for everything that ought to have remained hidden and secret and has become visible."[24]

To support Schelling's observation, Freud turns to Jakob and Wilhelm Grimm's *Deutsches Wörterbuch*. It indicates that officials who give important advice which has to be kept secret in matters of state are called *heimlich* councilors. Also, knowledge that is mystical or allegorical is said to have "a *heimlich* meaning." On the other hand, *heimlich* means "withdrawn from knowledge, unconscious" and also has the meaning of "that which is obscure, inaccessible to knowledge." To illustrate the latter, the Grimm Brothers cite a drama by Friedrich Schiller in which the Duke of Friedland remarks, "Do you not see? They do not trust me; they fear the *heimlich* face of the Duke of Friedland."[25] In light of Freud's observation that Mona Lisa's smile has "an uncanny and mysterious character," it is notable that it is the Duke's *heimlich* face that creates fear in others. It is the same familiar face, but it has become *heimlich* to them because their trust in him has changed to fear of him.

Thus, in his monograph on Leonardo, Freud notes that Leonardo "was successful in reproducing on Mona Lisa's face the double meaning which this smile contained, the promise of unbounded tenderness and at the same time sinister menace (to quote Pater's phrase)."[26] Freud is referring here to an essay by the English essayist and critic Walter Pater, who had written an essay on Leonardo in 1869 when he was thirty years old. It became one of the chapters in his enormously influential book *The Renaissance: Studies in Art and Poetry*.[27] Freud adds that in reproducing on Mona Lisa's face the double meaning that this smile contained, Leonardo "remained true to the content of his earliest memory. For his mother's tenderness was fateful for him; it determined his destiny and the privations that were in store for him."[28]

The early memory to which Freud has reference was Leonardo's recollection, reported in a notebook entry, of a bird of prey striking him on the lips with its tail when he was lying in his cradle. Freud is uncertain as to whether this was an actual memory or a fantasy that Leonardo formulated at a later date and transposed to his childhood. Freud's assumption

24. Ibid.
25. Ibid., 131.
26. Freud, *Leonardo da Vinci and a Memory of His Childhood*.
27. Pater, *The Renaissance*.
28. Freud, *Leonardo da Vinci and a Memory of His Childhood*, 65.

that the bird was a vulture has been challenged by later writers, who claim that it was more likely a kite, a smaller bird that preys on insects, reptiles and small mammals. As Collins points out, this translation error weakens several of Freud's claims, especially his association of this memory—or fantasy—with the Egyptian legend that females vultures are not impregnated by male vultures but by the wind, which led Freud to claim that Leonardo, knowing this legend, had a narcissistic fantasy of himself as the Christ Child and of Caterina as the Virgin. The error, however, does not affect his claim that the bird symbolized Leonardo's mother. As Collins points out, "The memory refers to earliest infancy, and the most important figure for the child in that period is the mother." Furthermore, the bird "sticks its tail in Leonardo's mouth in a manner similar to the way in which a mother offers her nipple to her child."[29]

In a footnote added in 1919, nine years after the original publication of the monograph, Freud cites a review of it by Havelock Ellis, a noted British psychologist, who contended that Leonardo's account could very well have been a real childhood memory, but that the bird in question need not have been a vulture. Freud conceded that the story may not have been a fantasy that Leonardo created later and that the bird may not have been a vulture. But he did not endorse Ellis's view that the story was based on a direct memory of Leonardo's. Rather, he thinks it is possible that Caterina observed the bird's visit to her child—"an event which may easily have had the significance of an omen in her eyes"—and that she repeatedly told him about it afterwards. As a result, Leonardo retained a memory of his mother's story, and later mistakenly took it for a memory of his own. In any case, Freud doubts that this damages his interpretation of the memory, for the important thing is that Leonardo must have had "some secret reason for bringing into prominence a real event of no importance and for elaborating it in the sort of way [he] did in his story of the bird."[30] In other words, we might say that the story is itself an illustration of the uncanny and, if so, it is especially noteworthy that Leonardo's mother is so deeply implicated in it—both as the possible source of the memory and as the one symbolized by the bird of prey.

Not surprisingly, then, Freud goes on to suggest that her expressions of love toward her son were more "violent" than normally occurs between a mother and her infant son. This was because she had to "compensate

29. Collins, *Leonardo, Psychoanalysis, and Art*, 50.
30. Freud, *Leonardo da Vinci and a Memory of His Childhood*, 32–33.

herself for having no husband, but also to compensate her child for having no father to fondle him." On the other hand, there was also something quite typical about how this mother related to this son, for, as Freud continues, "A mother's love for the infant she suckles and cares for is something of a completely satisfying love-relation, which not only fulfills every mental wish but also every physical need."[31]

Thus, the difference between the smiles that play on the lips of St. Anne and Mary as Mary reaches out to her infant son and the enigmatic smile that plays on the lips of Mona Lisa is a reflection of this altered relationship between mother and child. Since Caterina was still in "the near neighborhood," we can well imagine that when Leonardo, the growing child, caught glimpses of his mother, perhaps from a distance, her smile was not one of "inward feeling and quiet blissfulness" (as are the smiles of St. Anne and Mary), but one that manifested the "uncanny and mysterious character" reproduced in the portrait of *Mona Lisa*. Glimpses of Caterina are simultaneously *heimlich* and *unheimlich*, familiar but strange, and the ambivalent feelings toward the lost love object associated with melancholia are the inevitable consequence of this estrangement.

PATER AND MONA LISA'S MELANCHOLIC APPEAL

As indicated above, Freud gives Walter Pater credit for having perceived that Mona Lisa's smile has a "double meaning"—"the promise of unbounded tenderness and at the same time sinister menace."[32] Pater's "Notes on Leonardo da Vinci" appeared in the November 1869 issue of *Fortnightly Review*. He was thirty years old at the time. The essay was reprinted unchanged as chapter 5 of his book *Studies in the History of the Renaissance*, originally published in 1873, and republished in 1877 as *The Renaissance: Studies in Art and Poetry*.[33] Freud notes that "the need for a deeper reason behind the attraction of [Mona Lisa's] smile, which so moved the artist that he was never again free from it, has been felt by more than one of his biographers," and he specifically cites Pater, who sees in the painting of Mona Lisa a presence "'expressive of what in the ways of a thousand years men had come to desire,'" and who "writes very sensitively of 'the unfathomable smile, always with a touch of something sinister in it, which plays

31. Ibid., 65.
32. Ibid., 65.
33. Pater, *The Renaissance*, 77–101.

over all Leonardo's work.'" Freud suggests that Pater's reflections on Mona Lisa's smile lead us to another clue to the attraction of Mona Lisa's smile for Leonardo when Pater declares: "Besides, the picture is a portrait. From childhood we see this image defining itself on the fabric of his dreams; and but for express historical testimony, we might fancy that this was but his ideal lady, embodied and beheld at last."[34]

Freud does not comment on Pater's reference to "express historical testimony," but the clear implication here is that Leonardo was sexually attracted to men, not to women. This, of course, makes the association of the Mona Lisa smile to his mother all the more likely, for there was no other "ideal lady" in Leonardo's life. Thus, as Freud sees it, what Pater seems to be suggesting is that "Leonardo was fascinated by Mona Lisa's smile for the reason that it awoke something in him which had for long lain dormant in his mind—probably an old memory." If so, "This memory was of sufficient importance for him never to get free of it when it had once been aroused; he was continually forced to give it new expression." If this is Pater's meaning, Freud concurs with him, noting that "Pater's confident assertion that we can see, from childhood, a face like Mona Lisa's defining itself on the fabric of [Leonardo's] dreams, seems convincing and deserves to be taken literally."[35]

The significance of Pater's essay in bringing *Mona Lisa* to the attention of men who had their own unresolved issues relating to their early loss of the loved object can hardly be exaggerated. As Donald Sassoon points out, Leonardo's *Mona Lisa* was beginning to be the subject of a literary cult in the mid-nineteenth century, and Walter Pater and Theophile Gautier (the most respected art critic in Paris in the mid-nineteenth century) were especially responsible for drawing attention to its emotional power. According to Sassoon, Gautier was "the chief maker of the *Mona Lisa* as a mysterious woman with a strange smile."[36] But Pater's influence proved the greater, as his eloquent passages on the *Mona Lisa* were themselves of such poetical power that many men committed these words to memory. It was not unusual for a man to recite Pater as he gazed at the painting itself. If, as Sassoon points out, *Mona Lisa* began her career as an icon in the mid-nineteenth century, Pater's words about the painting may be viewed as her liturgical accompaniment. Or, more psychologically, they were therapeutic in the sense that they helped these men pursue, through displacement, one

34. Freud, *Leonardo da Vinci and a Memory of His Childhood*, 60.
35. Ibid., 60–61.
36. Sassoon, *Becoming Mona Lisa*, 82, 91.

or both of the therapeutic scenarios that Freud identifies in his essay on mourning and melancholia.

As James A. W. Heffernan notes in his introduction to *The Museum of Words*, *ekphrasis*—the literary representation of art—"evokes the power of the silent image even as it subjects that power to the rival authority of language." He suggests that "the contest it stages is often powerfully gendered: the expression of a duel between male and female gazes, the voice of male speech striving to control a female image that is both alluring and threatening, of male narrative striving to overcome the fixating impact of beauty poised in space."[37]

Pater's commentary on the *Mona Lisa* in his essay on Leonardo da Vinci may be viewed as an instance of *ekphrasis*, and, as such, as a reflection of his and other men's efforts to "work through" their ambivalent feelings toward the lost loved object. It consists of only two paragraphs. The first paragraph begins with his assertion that this painting is, "in the truest sense, Leonardo's masterpiece, the revealing instance of his mode of thought and work." Continuing, he claims: "In suggestiveness, only the *Melancholia* of [Albrecht] Dürer is comparable to it and no crude symbolism disturbs the effect of its subdued and graceful mystery."[38] It is noteworthy that Pater compares the *Mona Lisa* to a painting on the theme of melancholia, as this suggests that he is aware that the *Mona Lisa's* evocation of the range of feelings associated with the *melancholy self* is central to its emotional impact.

Next, he comments on her face and hands: "We all know the face and hands of the figure, set in its marble chair, in that circle of fantastic rocks, as in some faint light under the sea. Perhaps of all ancient pictures, time had chilled it least." Then, he focuses on the famous smile:

> As often happens with works in which invention seems to reach its limit, there is an element in it given to, not invented by, the master. In that inestimable folio of drawings, once in the possession of [Giorgio] Vasari, were certain designs by [Andrea del] Verrocchio, faces of such impressive beauty that Leonardo in his boyhood copied them many times. It is hard not to connect with these designs of the elder, by-past master, as with its germinal principle, the unfathomable smile, always with a touch of something sinister in it, which plays over all Leonardo's work.[39]

37. Heffernan, *Museum of Words*, 1.

38. Pater, *The Renaissance*, 97.

39. Ibid., 97. Sassoon points out that Pater's main direct source—after Vasari—for the essay was Charles Clément's 1861 book on three great Renaissance painters

Following his attribution of the unfathomable *Mona Lisa* smile to
the influence of Leonardo's mentor, Pater observes that the painting is
a portrait but not, for its painter, an ordinary one. Rather, it has special
significance for Leonardo himself, for "from childhood we see this image
defining itself on the fabric of his dreams." That the image may be traced to
childhood prompts Pater to raise this further question: What was the relationship of the living Florentine woman in the painting to "this creature of
his thought"? And by what "strange affinities has the dream and the person
grown up thus apart, and yet so closely together?" He concludes, "Present
from the first incorporeally in Leonardo's brain, dimly traced in the designs
of Verrocchio, she is found present at last in *Il Giocondo's* house."[40]

Little wonder, then, that Freud, influenced by Pater's reference to the
"strange affinities" between the dream and the person, would conclude that
Lisa Giocondo—the woman who sat for this portrait—awakened in Leonardo long forgotten feelings toward his mother, Caterina, in whose arms
he first experienced love and from whose presence he had subsequently
become estranged. As Pater suggests, this was, for Leonardo, far more than
an ordinary portrait. And, as Sherwin B. Nuland points out, it was hardly
coincidental that Lisa Giocondo, the wife of Francesco del Giocondo, the

(Michelangelo, Leonardo, and Raphael), in particular his remarks on *Mona Lisa*: "Lovers,
poets, dreamers, go and die at her feet! Neither your desperation nor your death will
erase from her mocking mouth the enchanting smile, the implacable smile that promises
rapture and denies happiness." Sassoon adds, "This is the theme of the scornful woman.
Women are dangerous tricksters. They promise and deny. It is also the Medusa theme—
the hub of Pater's interpretation of the *Mona Lisa*. She glares at the hapless man, and
before he is aware of it he is hers, petrified." He adds that Pater unquestioningly accepted
the traditional view that Leonardo was also the creator of the Uffizi Medusa (which was
actually painted by a seventeenth-century Flemish painter), assumed by Percy Shelley
in his 1819 poem "On the Medusa of Leonardo da Vinci in the Florentine Gallery." See
Sassoon, *Becoming Mona Lisa*, 139–40. It is also noteworthy that in his short piece on
"Medusa's Head" (published posthumously) Freud, while indicating that he does not often attempt to interpret individual mythological themes, says that such an interpretation
suggests itself quite easily in the case of the horrifying decapitated head of Medusa. He
equates decapitation with castration and suggests that the terror of Medusa "is thus a terror of castration that is linked to the sight of something." He adds, "Numerous analyses
have made us familiar with the occasion for this: it occurs when a boy, who has hitherto
been unwilling to believe the threat of castration, catches sight of the female genitals,
probably those of an adult, surrounded by hair, and essentially those of his mother"
(Freud, "Medusa's Head," 264). Thus, in addition to the homesickness that he associated
with the female genitals in "The 'Uncanny,'" Freud adds here the terror of castration due
to having seen the female genitals with one's own eyes.

40. Pater, *The Renaissance*, 97–98.

Florentine silk merchant who commissioned the painting, "was twenty-four years old in 1503, which was probably the midpoint of the four years during which Leonardo is thought to have worked intermittently on her portrait."[41] Thus, since Caterina was twenty-five years old when he was born, the woman he was painting intermittently over a four year period would have been his mother's age during his infancy and early childhood.

It may also be of some significance that the work was painted intermittently, for, as Kurt Eissler suggests, Leonardo's encounters with his mother during his early childhood were also intermittent, as he was shuttled back and forth between the two families. Moreover, Nuland cites the view of Kenneth Keele, a clinical physician and author of several books and numerous articles on Leonardo, that the woman in the painting is pregnant and about to become a mother. He notes the "location of the hands and the draping of clothes," which suggests "that an enlarged abdomen is being subtly obscured by both artist and subject." He adds that this physical evidence supports the more subjective claim that "hers is the smile of inner satisfaction that the miracle of life is being created in her body."[42]

But if her smile reveals "an inner satisfaction that the miracle of life is being created within her body," it also, according to Pater, reveals much more than this, for there is also "a touch of something sinister in it," and perhaps its sinister feature has much to do with the fact that the painter is reliving his childhood experience of being replaced in his mother's affections by a second and then a third child, both of whom will live out their childhoods in the physical presence of their mother. Her clenched fist may also suggest that Leonardo was re-experiencing some of the ambivalent feelings toward the mother of his earlier childhood.

41. Nuland, *Leonardo da Vinci*, 79.

42. Ibid., 81. Keele's clinically informed observations have been supported more recently by infrared photographs of the painting. In September 2006 Bruno Mottin, a curator in the research department of the Center of Research and Restoration of the Museums of France, noted that Lisa was originally painted wearing a large transparent overdress made from gauze. Under normal light, some of the gauze is visible on the right hand side of the painting, but it appears to be part of the background. He notes that such transparent robes were worn by expecting or nursing mothers in sixteenth-century Italy. The photographs also show that some of her hair was rolled into a small bun and tucked under a tiny bonnet with an attached veil, the latter being another indication of her pregnant condition, and that at one point one of her hands was painted in a clenched rather than a relaxed position (Seeten, "New Look at 'Mona Lisa' Yields Some New Secrets"). The clenched fist, later painted over, may suggest that Leonardo was reexperiencing some of the ambivalent emotions toward the mother of his early infancy during the process of painting a young woman who was evidently pregnant.

Pater also bases his view that this is more than an ordinary portrait for Leonardo himself on the legend promoted by Giorgio Vasari in his *Lives of the Most Eminent Painters, Sculptors and Architects* (published in 1550) that "by artificial means, the presence of mimes and flute-players, that subtle expression was protracted on the face." The legend that Leonardo hired mimes and flute-players, even if merely apocryphal, suggests an association with the painter's mother, for is it not often the case that a young boy, in the developmental stage that concerns us here, will go to rather extraordinary efforts—some of which are artificially produced—to coerce his mother to smile at or for him? Adding to the sense that the portrait was extraordinary are the conflicting claims as to how the painting came to be. Pater asks, "Again, was it in four years and by renewed labor never really completed, or in four months and as by a stroke of magic, that the image was projected?"[43] Or are these apparently conflicting claims reconcilable if we view the act of painting itself as affording the release of long repressed feelings toward the mother of the painter? The theory that Leonardo was unable to finish the painting attests to its emotional significance—that he and his mother had some unfinished business—but so does the theory that the image of the face came to him as if by magic in a much abbreviated time for, after all, he has seen this face before.

The second paragraph of Pater's commentary on the *Mona Lisa* is essentially a lyrical panegyric on the painting, focusing on the woman herself. It begins with reference to the numinous presence of the woman in the painting: "The presence that rose thus so strangely beside the waters, is expressive of what in the ways of a thousand years men had come to desire. Hers is the head upon which all 'the ends of the world are come,' and the eyelids are a little weary. It is a beauty wrought out from within upon the flesh, the deposit, little cell by cell, of strange thoughts and fantastic reveries and exquisite passions."[44]

Continuing, Pater imagines what might occur should she be placed in company with other women of acclaimed beauty: "Set it for a moment beside one of those white Greek goddesses or beautiful women of antiquity, and how would they be troubled by this beauty, into which the soul with all its maladies has passed! All the thoughts and experience of the world have etched and moulded there, in that which they have of power to refine

43. Pater, *The Renaissance*, 98.

44. Ibid., 98. The quotation—"the ends of the world are come"—is from 1 Corinthians 10:11: "Now all of these things happened unto them for ensamples; and they are written for our admonition, upon whom the ends of the world are come" (KJV).

and make expressive the outward form, the animalism of Greece, the lust of Rome, the mysticism of the middle age with its spiritual ambition and imaginative lives, the return of the Pagan world, the sins of the Borgias."[45]

In effect, she is the archetypal woman; and she is more fully archetypal than the Virgin Mary, who is representative only of "the mysticism of the middle age with its spiritual ambition and imaginative loves." She is this and more. As the archetypal woman,

> she is older than the rocks among which she sits; like the vampire, she has been dead many times, and learned the secrets of the grave; and has been a diver in deep seas, and keeps their fallen day about her; and trafficked for strange webs with Eastern merchants: and, as Leda, was the mother of Helen of Troy, and, as Saint Anne, the mother of Mary; and all this has been to her but as the sound of lyres and flutes, and lives only in the delicacy with which it has moulded the changing lineaments, and tinged the eyelids and the and the hands. The fancy of a perpetual life, sweeping together ten thousand experiences, is an old one; and modern philosophy has conceived the idea of humanity as wrought upon by, and summing up in itself, all modes of thought and life. Certainly Lady Lisa might stand as the embodiment of the old fancy, the symbol of the modern idea.[46]

It is as if she has herself has been the viewer—not the viewed—of all that has gone on before her and all that will go on in the future. And, drawing on the legend of the mimes and flute players performing before her eyes, Pater suggests that so much of the history she has witnessed has been but the sound of lyres and flutes.

To underscore what he called the "revolutionary importance" of the concluding sentences of the second paragraph, W. B. Yeats, in 1936, reprinted the first sentence as free verse:

> She is older than the rocks among which she sits;
>> Like the vampire,
> She has been dead many times,
>> And learned the secrets of the grave;
>> And has been a diver in the deep seas,
>> And kept their fallen day about her;
>> And trafficked for strange webs with eastern merchants;
>> And, as Leda,

45. Ibid., 98–99.
46. Ibid., 99.

> Was the mother of Helen of Troy,
>   And, as Saint Anne,
>   The mother of Mary;
> And all this has been to her as the sound of lyres and flutes,
>   And lives
>   Only in the delicacy
>   With which it has moulded the changing lineaments,
>   And tinged the eyelids and hands.[47]

Yeats's line arrangement highlights what Sassoon calls "the rhythmic, almost biblical, Paterian use of 'and,' as in '*And* learned the secrets of the grave; *and* has been a diver in the deep seas; *and* keeps their fallen day about her."[48] The very suggestion that Pater's use of "and" is "*almost* biblical" supports the idea that this passage functioned as a liturgical accompaniment to the iconic representation of the mother figure, a representation that enabled men to displace feelings of ambivalence toward their own mothers and to invest it with the religious sensibilities that accompany the emergence of the *melancholy self.*

Sassoon also notes that "there is no mention of a smile in Pater's passage." To be sure, in the page that precedes it, Pater had mentioned an "unfathomable smile, always with a touch of something sinister in it," but he had added "that such smiles were common to Verrocchio, Leonardo's teacher."[49] In the passage itself, the most specific reference that Pater makes to a feature of the subject's face is that "the eyelids are a little weary," and towards the end of the passage, he directs the viewer to "the eyelids and the hands." This raises the interesting question whether the "un-canniness" that many experience when viewing the painting is attributable to her mysterious smile, or is it due, instead, to her mysterious eyes, to the way in which she looks at her observer? For Pater, her eyes betray her world-weariness. Perhaps, then, it is the weariness in her eyes that has such a devastating effect on the *melancholy self.* As Pater indicates, Giorgio Vasari claimed that Leonardo employed mimes and other performers to entertain the sitter while he painted her. Thus, Vasari claims that she smiled because she was at least faintly amused. But, if so, only her smile betrays amusement. Her eyes are rather dull, even more impervious to the efforts of the male performers to give her delight and provoke her pleasure. Could it be, then, that melancholy feelings

47. Sassoon, *Becoming Mona Lisa*, 133–34. This is the sentence that men would commit to memory and recite, in whole or in part, when observing the painting itself.

48. Ibid., 134.

49. Ibid.

originate in the boy's perception that he has failed to make his mother's eyes dance with joy, that he has been unable to dispel her world-weariness, and that his inability to make her smile is a secondary failure?

In any event, in a poem titled "The Sphinx," written shortly after the publication of Pater's essay, Oscar Wilde makes several veiled allusions to Pater's famous passage.[50] Its opening lines emphasize her inexpressive gaze, not her enigmatic smile: "In a dim corner of my room for longer than my fancy thinks, / A beautiful and silent Sphinx has watched me through the shifting gloom." To be sure, Wilde also alludes to her smile, noting how "subtle-secret" it is, but her "curved archaic smile" is itself a consequence of the fact that she has "watched" her lover's passion "come and go." Thus, as Sassoon points out, "The Sphinx of the poem encompasses the Mona Lisa and all the threatening females which haunt men's lives."[51] Therefore the warning: "Get hence! I weary of your sullen ways, / I weary of your steadfast gaze, your somnolent magnificence."

Thus, where Pater saw that her eyelids were "a little weary," Wilde expresses his own weariness. This weariness is attributable to her emotional distance, as reflected in the way that she observes him from a dim corner of his room. Similarly, Pierre Marcy, author of an 1867 guidebook to the Louvre, noted her "melancholic look," and then quoted this sentence from George Sand's essay on the *Mona Lisa*: "What is disquieting about this image is the soul shining through, appearing to contemplate yours, with lofty serenity reading into your eyes while you vainly try to read into hers."[52] The hands, to which Pater also alludes, add to this sense of her emotional inaccessibility, for these are not hands that reach out, as in the case of Leonardo's *St. Anne with Virgin and Child* in which the Madonna reaches out to her son. Instead, they rest on her lap, the right arm over the left arm as if to insure that neither hand will impulsively reach out to the boy—or man—who longs to feel her touch.

Thus, the parts of her body to which Pater refers in the second paragraph of his reflections on the subject of the painting—her eyes, her hands—express her emotional inaccessibility, and she therefore represents the lost loved object, her "lostness" made the more painfully frustrating by the fact that she "is to be found among those in his near neighborhood."[53]

50. Ibid., 150–51.
51. Ibid., 151.
52. Ibid., 128.
53. Freud, "Mourning and Melancholia," 173.

Although she is the archetypal woman, she *is*, after all, a local woman ("a living Florentine").[54]

Sassoon's explanation for why Pater's famous passage came to have such influence also lends support to the idea that it addressed the ambivalent feelings toward the lost loved object that are central to the emergence and persistence of the *melancholy self*. In his view, "The success of Pater's text was due to the beauty of the prose and to the literary and visual associations it conjured."[55] It was also timely:

> Women had become the hub of artistic fixation. It was as if "the feminine" was a distant and mysterious land, just sighted by apprehensive explorers who, afraid to conquer it, let alone understand it, contented themselves with describing it from afar, magnifying its danger, exaggerating its mystery, *embellishing their own predicament*. This ideal woman had—as yet—no fixed visage, but multifarious expressions and poses. Pater's great achievement was to devise resonant words with which to capture this strange *Zeitgeist* and link them to a specific painting representing an unknown woman, already mythologized, painted against a landscape equally mysterious and unknown.[56]

The key phrase in this account of "the feminine" is the one that I have emphasized: This is the *predicament* that lies at the heart of the development of the *melancholy self*: the fact that a boy's mother is both "lost" and "to be found among those in his near neighborhood." The dictionary defines *predicament* as "a condition or situation, one that is difficult, unpleasant, embarrassing, or, sometimes, comical," and indicates that it implies "a complicated, perplexing situation from which it is difficult to disentangle oneself."[57] If Freud recognized that his melancholic patients engaged in exaggeration—greater self-reproach than was warranted—Sassoon notes the tendency of these "apprehensive explorers" to *embellish* their own predica-

54. Moreover, she may not have been an especially healthy woman. Theunis Bates reports on the research by Vito Franco, Professor of Pathological Anatomy at the University of Palermo, on the health conditions of subjects painted in famous works of art. According to Franco, the subject of Leonardo's painting had very high levels of cholesterol. He made his diagnosis after spotting signs of xanthelasma (a buildup of yellowish fatty acids under the skin) under her left eye, as well as subcutaneous lipomas (benign tumors composed of fatty acids) on her hands (Bates, "Did High Cholesterol Dim Mona Lisa's Smile?").

55. Sassoon, *Becoming Mona Lisa*, 135.

56. Ibid., 137–38 (italics added).

57. Agnes, *Webster's New World*, 1132.

ment, i.e., to "decorate or improve by adding detail; ornament; adorn."[58] By linking the new *Zeitgeist*—the new disposition to explore, however tentatively, the source and the contours of the *melancholy self*—to a centuries-old painting, Pater provided these men with a visual image of their predicament. View, observe, gaze upon, and study the *Mona Lisa*, and you will discover the true locus of your predicament.

Thus, Pater and the other "aesthetes" of his time were the "apprehensive explorers" of the origins of the *melancholy self*, origins that were half revealed and half concealed. *Mona Lisa* may therefore be said to be the visual representation of that *heimlich* place that has since become *unheimlich*. As Pater emphasizes, "No crude symbolism disturbs the effect of its subdued and graceful mystery. We all know the face and hands of the figure, set in its marble chair, in that circle of fantastic rocks, as in some faint light under sea."[59] The very absence of "crude symbolism," together with the strange foreignness of the landscape behind the figure, account for much of the painting's *heimlich/unheimlich* ambiguity. As Freud recognized, the smile expresses this ambiguity, but the painting itself reflects the viewer's predicament, the predicament of knowing that the one with whom one shared a deep and profound intimacy has subsequently become strangely foreign, a foreignness all the more distressing because she remains somewhere in the "near neighborhood."[60]

Pater concludes his essay on Leonardo with the observation that after much busy antiquarianism, two questions concerning Leonardo's death remain. One is the question whether Francois I, King of France, was present at his bedside.[61] According to Sassoon, this is most unlikely.[62] The other is "the question of the exact form of his religion."[63] To Pater, neither is of much importance in the estimate of Leonardo's genius, but the second *is* important in light of my proposal that the *Mona Lisa* is the iconic center of the religious sensibilities associated with the *melancholy self*.

Pater's own conclusion as to the "form" of Leonardo's real religious proclivities supports this proposal. He writes, "The direction in [Leonardo's] will concerning the thirty masses and the great candles for the church

---

58. Ibid., 463.

59. Pater, *The Renaissance*, 97.

60. Freud, "Mourning and Melancholia," 173.

61. Pater, *The Renaissance*, 101.

62. Sassoon, *Becoming Mona Lisa*, 80.

63. Pater, *The Renaissance*, 101.

of Saint Florentin are things of course, their real purpose being immediate and practical; and on no theory of religion could these hurried offices be of much consequence. We forget them in speculating how one who has been always so desirous of beauty, but desired it always in such precise and definite forms, as hands or flowers or hair, looked forward into the vague land, and experienced the last curiosity."[64]

In suggesting that questions about Leonardo's identification with traditional Christian practices are beside the point, that these questions dissolve when we consider how "desirous" Leonardo was of beauty, but always "in such precise and definite forms, as hands or flowers or hair," Pater presents Leonardo as a man whose personal religion was centered on his longing for the lost mother. Of the three religious sensibilities associated with the *melancholy self*—the *sense of honor*, the *sense of hope*, and the *sense of humor*—he represents Leonardo's as the second—that of searching for glimpses of the lost object in the world around him. This was not, however, a search that terminated with death, for, in Pater's view, Leonardo "looked forward now into the vague land, and experienced the last curiosity." If the question of whether Francois I was at his bedside when he died centers on the paternal figure, the question of Leonardo's personal faith centers on the maternal figure, his quest in life and in death for the "lost object" of his early childhood.

As for Pater himself, he continued to work through his own experience of maternal loss in his writings, perhaps the most self-revealing of which was his brief story "The Child in the House" published 1878, nine years after his Leonardo essay was published.[65] Anthony Vidler discusses this story in his chapter on homesickness in *The Architectural Uncanny*. It concerns a man, Florian, who dreams of the house in which he spent his childhood. For him, whose "sense of home was singularly intense," this childhood home was initially so secure, so much the locus and symbol of his own sense of security, "that even the fog and smoke that occasionally drifted in from the nearby town had an ominous air." But as the dream continued, later perceptions of the house's impermanence intervened, and "the dream rapidly became a history of the growth of fear, a tracing of the sources of what, to the child, were uncanny sensations, and remained, with the adult, the permanent springs of unease."[66]

64. Ibid., 101.
65. Pater, "The Child in the House."
66. Vidler, *The Architectural Uncanny*, 58.

Vidler captures the melancholy associations implicit in the dream when he comments: "Henceforth the soul would have no rest but in nostalgia, in that malady provoked by all apparently secure enclosures, homesickness," adding: "The childhood home was transformed into no more than a locus for dreams, for what Pater called 'that clinging back towards it' that lasts for a long time and eventually spoils all anticipated pleasure."[67] Here, Vidler chooses Pater's "The Child in the House" to illustrate Freud's view of the uncanny, especially his suggestion that neurotic male patients associate homesickness with their original home, their mother's womb.

67. Ibid., 58.

chapter two

Da Vinci's *Mona Lisa*:
The Iconoclastic Backlash

THE PRECEDING CHAPTER FOCUSED on the fact that beginning in the nineteenth century men have found in Leonardo's *Mona Lisa* a way to displace the ambivalent feelings evoked by their loss of the loved object in early childhood, a loss that was central to their development of a *melancholy self*. In effect, she has become the focus—the iconic center—of the religious sensibilities that give expression to these ambivalent feelings. Because these feelings reflect considerable ambivalence toward the lost love object, men have viewed *Mona Lisa* as both attractive and threatening. In this chapter, I will focus on the fact that she became the target of iconoclastic actions, the types of actions the central icon of an established religion often evokes. However, we will also see how *Mona Lisa* has survived these attacks and has become more humanized, partly as a result of the attacks inflicted upon her but also because she is, after all, a painting.

I will begin with Freud's reflections on how Leonardo began to displace his emotional investment in his paintings, *Mona Lisa* among them, into a scientific curiosity about the real world around him. Such displacement is not normally considered an iconoclastic act. But, in this case, it was an initial stage in the process because it represented an emotional detachment from the icon itself.

THE DISPLACEMENT OF EMOTIONAL INVESTMENT INTO SCIENTIFIC CURIOSITY

In the concluding paragraph of his essay on Leonardo, Pater refers to death as "the last curiosity," thus implying that there were many instances of curiosity before this. This implication invites further consideration of Freud's monograph on Leonardo because Freud was especially interested in Leonardo's displacement of his emotional investment in the subjects of his paintings into a scientific *curiosity* about the natural world. In effect, this was a secondary displacement, for the first displacement was one in which the emotional investment in a painting's subject, as in the case of *Mona Lisa*, was a displacement of emotions evoked by another person in his life, in this case, his biological mother.

Two points that Donald Sassoon makes in his discussion of the "discovery" of the *Mona Lisa* in the mid-nineteenth century are relevant to the relationship between this secondary displacement and the religious sensibilities of the *melancholy self.* The first occurs in his consideration of the fact that those who were attracted to the painting were overwhelmingly male. Very few women had much to say about the painting, and what they *did* say was not very favorable. For example, in his 1867 popular guide to the Louvre, Pierre Marcy cited an essay on *Mona Lisa* by George Sand (the masculine pseudonym of Amandine Dupin) but was highly selective in what he included in his citation and what he left out. He quoted this sentence from the essay: "What is disquieting about this image is the soul shining through, appearing to contemplate yours, with lofty serenity reading into your eyes while you vainly try to read into hers." This citation, Sassoon notes, reinforced the dominant view of the woman in the painting. On the other hand, Marcy omitted the fact that "Sand began, daringly, to say what many have since thought—Lisa is not a beautiful woman: she has no eyebrows, her cheeks are too full, her hair too thin, her forehead too broad, her eyes do not sparkle, she is plump." She also said that "there is an undertone of cold malice in her smile, a riddle in her expression difficult to forget." So, she concluded, "The real secret lies not in the painting but in the painter: how he achieved an idealized portrait; how he instilled his powers of expression into it. What we see in the painting is the genius of the painter, the soul of a master, the hopes of a superior man."[1] Sassoon notes that this attempt to discuss the work in terms of its creator was unsuccessful, and

1. Sassoon, *Becoming Mona Lisa,* 128–29.

Sand's conclusions—"Whoever looked at her for an instant cannot forget her"—were frequently quoted, but the rest of her essay has been forgotten.[2]

Clearly, male viewers were entranced by Mona Lisa herself and much less interested in how Leonardo "instilled his powers of expression into" the painting. There was little commentary—certainly none in Pater's two paragraphs—on Leonardo's techniques, such as his invention of the *sfumato* technique, which consisted in building up layers of paint from dark to light and allowing the previous one show through, thus achieving, through a play of shadows and light, the optical illusion of a relief. This technique, applied to great effect in the *Mona Lisa*, is evident in the blurring of the corners of her eyes and mouth (the main identification points of a facial expression), thus adding to the uncertainty surrounding the expression of her face.[3]

But these early discoverers of the *Mona Lisa*—these "apprehensive explorers"—were less interested in how Leonardo achieved these effects and far more drawn to the image itself—*she* was the object of their devoted gaze. It was *she* who held them in *her* thrall. Fictional stories written at the time depicted a man standing in rapture before the painting, quoting Pater from memory, while his female companion clutched at his coat sleeve, urging him to consider that there were many other paintings in the museum that were worthy of their attention. In effect, these stories recognized his companion's dilemma, as his ability to invest himself in *her* depended upon his ability to wrench himself away from the woman depicted in the painting. Thus, a real woman took upon herself the difficult task of pulling him away from the woman on the wall who evoked reveries of the lost loved object, whose own image he had internalized and carried in his heart throughout the intervening years. She was a formidable opponent.

Sassoon's second point occurs in his discussion of the fact that the mid-nineteenth-century cult of *Mona Lisa* began in France through the writings of art critic Theopile Gautier and in England through the essay by Walter Pater. It did not gain favor in Italy despite the fact that Leonardo was Italian. Sassoon notes that the painting was almost entirely ignored in Italy until Gebriele D'Annunzio published a poem about "La Gioconda" in 1889, and even then, the poem did not become widely known until he republished it in abbreviated form immediately after the painting was stolen from the Louvre on August 21, 1911. To Italians, Leonardo's *The Last Supper* was regarded as the greater work, and, except for D'Annunzio, who was

2. Ibid., 129.

3. Ibid., 37–38.

"essentially an imitator and an importer" of a "renaissance derived from [John] Ruskin and Pater," Italians "sought to demystify their *Gioconda* as just a Florentine gentlewoman painted wonderfully well by a great painter."[4]

This view of the painting by Italian art historians continued through the nineteenth and well into the twentieth century. Sassoon does not attempt to explain why this was the case. No doubt, the reasons were multiple. But one important reason for this relative coolness toward the *Mona Lisa* was the fact that she was, in a sense, an iconic alternative to the Virgin Mary, the Mother of Jesus. In Protestant England and post-Revolutionary France, the Virgin Mary had already been dethroned, which made it easier for *Mona Lisa* to become an iconic maternal figure in these two countries. Thus, it is significant that, as Sassoon points out, "the most popular interpretation of Leonardo in Italy was neither Gautier's nor Pater's but a positivist reading that emphasized Leonardo the scientist and the philosopher."[5] Recognition of the emotional appeal of *Mona Lisa* might have threatened the traditional Christian mythology with the Virgin Mary at its center.

On the other hand, the tendency of Italians to emphasize Leonardo the scientist over Leonardo the artist has direct bearing on Freud's own view that Leonardo took recourse to a similar emotional disengagement from his paintings, including the *Mona Lisa*. This view of Leonardo also relates to our emphasis here on the development of the *melancholy self*. When Freud wrote his monograph on Leonardo, the issue that especially concerned him was Leonardo's slowness in completing his paintings. For example, his difficulty finishing the *Mona Lisa* probably explains why the painting was still in his possession when he immigrated to France at the invitation of King Francois I to become a member of his court. Leonardo gave this and other paintings to the king, which also explains why it eventually ended up in the Louvre in Paris. Freud attributed this characteristic of Leonardo's, which he referred to as his "inhibition," thus suggesting that there were psychological conflicts relating to his identity as an artist, to the fact that Leonardo had an investigative mind, and his passion for investigation took precedence over the creative act itself. In Freud's view, what interested Leonardo "in a picture was above all a problem; and behind the first one he saw countless other problems arising" as he had earlier done in his "endless and inexhaustible investigation of nature." Thus, "he was no longer able to limit his demands, to see the work of art in isolation and to

4. Ibid., 160.
5. Ibid., 161.

tear it from the wide context to which he knew it belonged. After the most exhausting efforts to bring to expression in it everything which was connected with it in his thoughts, he was forced to abandon it in an unfinished state or to declare that it was incomplete." In effect, "the artist had once taken the investigator into his service to assist him; now the servant had become the stronger and suppressed his master."[6]

Freud traces Leonardo's investigative proclivities to his early childhood, to the curiosity of small children that manifests itself in their untiring love of asking questions, and particularly to the period in which they engage in "infantile sexual researches."[7] But Leonardo had particular reason to sublimate his expressions of love into an investigative, inquisitive mind. After all, his was an illegitimate birth, and he was probably cared for by his birth mother for three to five years, and then became a member of his father's household. And then, if Eissler is correct, he was shuttled back and forth between the two families. If emotional separation from one's mother is the precipitating cause of the development of a *melancholy self* in a small boy, this loss may result in one of two kinds of quests, the quest for someone to take her place in his affections, or the quest for explanations as to why this loss occurred at all.

Freud's Leonardo belongs to the second type (although it is certainly possible that he turned to this quest after an unsuccessful bid to find in his stepmother what he had lost in the case of his biological mother). Viewed retrospectively, Leonardo's scientific mind—his inquisitiveness, his effort to unravel the mysteries of the natural world—may be traced to the emotional loss of his mother in early childhood. When he took on the *Mona Lisa* commission, he returned to the locus of his original hurt and its inevitable repressions. To cope with this return of the repressed, the scientific investigator would eventually "suppress" the artist who, after all, was emotionally invested in the subject matter—indeed, the subject herself—of the painting. Central to his difficulty in completing a painting—or declaring that it was in fact completed—was the internal struggle between the emotionally invested artist and the emotionally disinvested scientist.

However, there may be another factor in the specific case of the *Mona Lisa* painting that inhibited Leonardo from declaring that the painting was finished. This factor arises from the very fact that, whereas Vasari claims that

6. Freud, *Leonardo da Vinci and a Memory of His Childhood*, 27.
7. Ibid., 28.

the painting was unfinished, the painting certainly appears to be finished.[8] This being the case, Leonardo may have used the claim that it was unfinished as a basis for keeping it in his possession, thus precluding a secondary loss of the maternal object. If, as Freud argues, this particular painting had succeeded in "representing the boy, infatuated with his mother,"[9] it makes psychodynamic sense that he would be reluctant to part with it. To hand it over to Lisa's husband, Francesco, would replicate the loss of the mother that occurred when his father took *him* away from Caterina and installed him in the house occupied by his father and his stepmother. Because the painter, not the patron, decides when a painting is finished, he can declare that the painting is unfinished and the patron has little recourse but to accept his claim. Since his failure to deliver a finished painting in a reasonable period of time would inevitably raise questions about his reliability (and risk the loss of future commissions), the very cost to his reputation testifies to his emotional investment in the painting itself. Still, Leonardo's scientific curiosity represents one of the ways in which a man may "work through" his ambivalent feelings toward the lost love object. In a sense, it represents the more gradual therapeutic approach that Freud identifies in "Mourning and Melancholia" as it works by indirection—in Leonardo's case, the withdrawal of emotional affect from the lost love object by employing the scientific curiosity he developed in the "endless and inexhaustible investigation of nature" in his vocation as a painter. There may, in fact, have been an association between his endless and inexhaustible scientific efforts to unravel the mysteries of nature and his declaration that he had not, as it were, completed his efforts to unravel the mystery of the woman—Lisa Gioconda—who was a stand-in for his mother.

THE THEFT OF *MONA LISA*

I would now like to turn to some of the ways in which *Mona Lisa* has evoked irreverent reprisals emanating from the *melancholy self*. I will begin with the theft of the painting on August 21, 1911. Freud could not have anticipated when he wrote his monograph on Leonardo that the painting would be stolen from the Louvre the following year. It remained in the possession of the thief, Vincenzo Peruggia, a thirty-year-old Italian painter-decorator, until early December 1913. Since Freud's "Mourning and Melancholia" essay was

8. Sassoon, *Becoming Mona Lisa*, 181.

9. Freud, *Leonardo da Vinci and a Memory of His Childhood*, 68.

published in 1917, it is not inconceivable that the theft of the *Mona Lisa* had some influence on his theorizing about the lost loved object, especially his suggestion that unlike the case of mourning, in which the absence of the lost object is due to physical death, the lost loved object in the case of melancholia "is usually to be found among those in his near neighborhood."[10] Until Peruggia arranged to hand the painting over to an Italian art dealer, which led to its recovery, it remained in his apartment in Paris, in the "near neighborhood" of the Louvre.

As Sassoon discusses at length, the theft inaugurated a new phase in the iconization of the *Mona Lisa*.[11] The numbers of visitors to the Louvre increased dramatically in the wake of the theft. In *Stealing the Mona Lisa* Darien Leader, a British psychoanalyst, quotes the following from a French newspaper account published when the Louvre reopened a few days after the *Mona Lisa* was discovered missing: "[The crowds] didn't look at the other pictures. They contemplated at length the dusty space where the divine *Mona Lisa* had smiled only the week before. And feverishly they took notes. It was even more interesting for them than if the *Gioconda* had been in its place."[12]

Sassoon adds that comments on the *Mona Lisa* "began to sound like obituaries," as they made claims in regard to "the dear departed" that "would previously have appeared excessive." For example, "the writer and Leonardo-idolater Josephin Peladan lamented the disappearance of what he called 'The Painting', as the Bible is 'The Book.'"[13] If "The Book" was central to the iconoclasm of ancient Judaism—descriptive words replacing graven images—then "The Painting" challenges this iconoclasm. On the other hand, its disappearance nonetheless fostered obituaries whose very excessiveness may well reveal the ambivalent feelings toward the lost loved object that we have associated with the emergence of the *melancholy self* in early childhood.[14]

Leader acknowledges but resists the view that the "lost object" is the boy's mother and that the *Mona Lisa* is therefore evocative of maternal ambivalence. Instead, he follows "the Lacanian argument" that "the crowds

10. Freud, "Mourning and Melancholia," 173.

11. Sassoon, Becoming *"Mona Lisa"*, 195–219.

12. Leader, *Stealing the Mona Lisa*, 66.

13. Sassoon, *Becoming Mona Lisa*, 183.

14. In this regard, the obituaries may be viewed as expressions of *ekphrasis* as discussed in chap. 1. See Heffernan, *The Museum of Words*, 1.

that flocked to the Louvre after the theft of the *Mona Lisa* demonstrated the true function of the work of art: to evoke the empty place of the Thing, the gap between the art work and the place it occupies."[15] The "Thing" for Lacan is the void or empty space that designates the horizon of our desires and, as Leader explains, "it cannot be represented as a positive, empirical object since, at the level of representations, it is less an object than a place: and when objects go into this place, they take on new and peculiar properties." Therefore, there is "a difference between the object and the space the object finds itself in, the special, sacred place of the Thing."[16] The importance of this distinction between the space and the object is supported by the fact that large crowds went to the Louvre to gaze upon the empty space that the object had occupied.

It is noteworthy, however, that it was the painting of a woman that had been stolen from the Louvre, and that it was a thirty-year-old man—exactly Pater's age when he wrote his famous lines about the *Mona Lisa*—who tucked her under his coat and carried her out of the museum. Moreover, he was an Italian living in Paris, and his ostensible reason for stealing the *Mona Lisa* was his mistaken belief that the French had stolen *her*—as the spoils of military victory—and he would be the one who secured her release from exile and returned her to her rightful home.

I suggest, therefore, that the thief was attempting, in a symbolic manner, to reverse the loss that he and other young boys experience in early childhood when they are emotionally separated from their mothers. As if to acknowledge that this act *was* symbolic—that he really couldn't have his mother back—Peruggia put the painting in the bottom of an old chest and didn't take it out again until he made arrangements to hand it over to the Italian art dealer. Meanwhile, he placed a small postcard of the *Mona Lisa* on his mantel. This very action seems odd and went against the popular fantasy that a wealthy art connoisseur had arranged the theft so that he could gaze on the *Mona Lisa* whenever it pleased him to do so. However, from the perspective of the *melancholy self*, this was not so strange, as the *melancholy self* has learned to be content with replicas and vestiges of the lost object. After all, it does not believe that it can repossess the original. In fact, Peruggia's act of secreting the painting into an old chest reenacts the

15. Leader, *Stealing the Mona Lisa*, 66.

16. Ibid., 61.

internalization of the lost object that Freud describes in "Mourning and Melancholia."[17]

From what is known about Vincenzo Peruggia, he seems to fit the profile of the melancholy male described in Freud's essay. Sasoon notes that when the identity of the thief became known, there was a collective sense of disappointment: "Instead of the sophisticated international art thief celebrated in popular novels he was, quite clearly, a classic loser. Even his criminal record was trivial. Once he tried to rob a prostitute. Incompetent to the last, he failed miserably. She resisted (he was only five feet three inches tall), and he was arrested and jailed for a week."[18]

We can imagine, therefore, that if he had been a patient of Freud's, he would have engaged in the "self-abasement" common to melancholy males, and Freud's caveat that the question of whether these self-reproaches are justified in the opinion of others is beside the point would have been applicable to him. As Freud points out, the point is that "he is correctly describing his psychological situation in his lamentations. He has lost his self-respect and must have some good reason for having done so." Equally relevant would have been Freud's observation: "In the clinical picture of melancholia dissatisfaction with the self on moral grounds is far the most outstanding feature; the self-criticism much less concerns itself with bodily infirmity, ugliness, weakness, social inferiority; among these latter ills that the patient dreads or asseverates the thought of poverty alone has a favored position."[19]

As noted earlier, the very nature of these self-reproaches and the fact that they are exaggerated is, for Freud, evidence that they are directed toward the internalized lost object, and that the melancholic patient is largely unconscious of this psychological fact. However, this does not mean that the symptoms pointing to this underlying dynamic are irrelevant, and it is therefore significant and revealing that Peruggia would have reason to reproach himself on moral grounds—after all, he is an art thief—and that his rationale for having stolen the painting would have had to do with thoughts of poverty. Few contemporaries believed that he stole the painting for purely patriotic reasons; after all, he handed over the painting only after having been assured—falsely—that he would be paid a large amount of money for it.

17. Freud, "Mourning and Melancholia," 170–73.

18. Sassoon, *Becoming Mona Lisa*, 187.

19. Freud, "Mourning and Melancholia," 168.

Thus, Vincenzo Peruggia was not only "a classic loser," but a "classic" melancholic as well. Even the fact that he had not originally planned to steal the *Mona Lisa* but changed his mind when he realized that the painting he *was* planning to steal (Andrea Mantegna's *Mars and Venus*) was too large— it was ten times larger than the *Mona Lisa*—may be related to his melancholia, for this would suggest that unconscious motivations were at work, and that these were not unlike his attempt to steal money from a prostitute. As Freud notes, in some melancholic patients, there is a regular alternation of melancholia and mania, while in others "signs of mania may be entirely absent or only very slight."[20] Surely, there is a manic element in the act of stealing a painting of a woman who reminds the thief of his mother (an Italian woman). Freud compares mania to instances "when a man finds himself in a position to throw off at one blow some heavy burden, some false position he has long endured," and notes that all such situations "are characterized by high spirits, by the signs of discharge of joyful emotion."In "complete contrast to the dejection and inhibition of melancholia," mania "is nothing other than a triumph," but one in which the real victim of this triumphant act remains hidden from the perpetrator.[21] There is no evidence to suggest that Peruggia was aware, truly conscious, of the deeper reasons why he stole the *Mona Lisa*. After all, there were many other paintings in the Louvre that were small enough to hide under his coat.

Sassoon discusses the various theories that were put forward by the public concerning the identity of the thief or thieves, why he or they did it, and so forth. He also devotes several pages to the public's imaginative "theories" as to why Mona Lisa allowed herself to be stolen or took it upon herself to come down off the wall and walk out of the museum. One "theory" was that she was pregnant and had gone away to bear her child. A popular postcard at the time depicted her sitting in a horse-drawn carriage driven by her husband and holding a baby in her lap. A popular interpretation of the painting also emerged at this time, one suggesting that the woman in the painting is pregnant, which explains her enigmatic smile (her secret), the way she is sitting, and the manner in which her hands are folded over her abdomen.[22] As we saw in chapter 1, this view was reaffirmed by

20. Ibid., 174.
21. Ibid., 178.
22. Sassoon, *Becoming Mona Lisa*, 178–80.

Kenneth D. Keele in 1959 and is supported by recent infrared photographs of the painting.[23]

The theory that she voluntarily left the museum to bear her child is also relevant to the emergence of the *melancholy self* in early childhood, as it suggests that the mother is not a helpless victim in the emotional separation between herself and her son, but has, it would seem, abandoned him. A mother going off to the hospital to bear another child is an event that is likely to evoke such feelings of abandonment. A postcard depicting three figures in the horse-drawn carriage—the expectant mother, her husband, and a small boy sitting next to or between them—would be a very different scenario. In any event, the "theory" that Mona Lisa was not stolen but took it upon herself to come down off the wall and walk out of the museum, where her husband was waiting for her in his horse-drawn carriage may have been more ostensibly comforting than the more likely theory that she had, in fact, been stolen. But it too could well have evoked repressed emotions relating to the experience of emotional separation from the mother in early childhood. In fact, the idea that she was taken away against her will would have been easier for the unconscious to accept, providing, of course, that she did everything in her power to resist it. But perhaps this is precisely where her enigmatic smile is especially relevant: for unlike the prostitute who resisted Peruggia's attempt to steal money from her, can one know for certain that the woman in Leonardo's painting would put up a similar fight? After all, if she is not Peruggia's prostitute, neither is she the Virgin Mary![24]

23. Ibid., 270.

24. I have argued that *Mona Lisa* serves as an iconic focus of the religious sensibilities that develop in response to the experience of emotional separation from one's mother in early childhood, but in noting her potential rivalry with the Virgin Mary I have indicated that her appeal was primarily to men of Christian background. The 1987 play *Gioconda* by Wolf Mandowitz bears on this point. He has the Paris chief of police going to consult with Sigmund Freud in Vienna about the personality of the thief. The policeman asks: "Do you think it possible, Herr Professor, that the culprit would be a Jewish intellectual?" "I doubt it," Freud snaps, biting his cigar, "The *Mona Lisa* is essentially a Christian mother. Jewish mothers are distinctly different" (see Sassoon, *Becoming Mona Lisa*, 204). Herr Professor Freud may simply be implying here that a Jewish thief would not mistake *Mona Lisa* for a representation of his own mother and would therefore not be disposed to steal the painting. There might also be the implication that a Jewish mother would not allow herself to be smuggled out of the museum under the coat of a thief for surely she would not have hesitated to call out to the guards and, if they were not around to hear, she would have turned on the thief and shamed him, "What would your mother think if she saw you stealing a painting from a museum?" In any event, the assumption is that the thief stole it because of its association with his own mother. Also, because she is a Christian mother, the religious sensibilities for which she serves as a symbolic

THE STONING OF *MONA LISA*

Peruggia's theft of *Mona Lisa* may be viewed as a symbolic attempt to reverse the effects of the small boy's emotional loss of his mother. In this sense, the theft may especially address the sadness that results from the loss, seeming to say that an ingenious boy can recover the lost mother. However, in order to do so, he must violate the very civilizing process that the emotional separation is designed to foster—his identification with his father and the social world his father represents—for theft, after all, is a criminal act. Yet, as Sassoon points out, Peruggia's defense lawyer "quite shrewdly explained that, in the end, no one had lost anything. The newspapers and postcard peddlers had boosted their sales. The Louvre had acquired even more renown. The return of the picture had improved the hitherto tense diplomatic situation between France and Italy." His appeal was largely successful, for Peruggia was treated leniently: "The prosecutor had asked for a sentence of three years; he got twelve and a half months."[25] This is some sixteen months less than the *Mona Lisa* herself languished at the bottom of an old chest. Had the painting been damaged, it would, of course, have been a very different story.

But Sassoon alludes briefly to an episode in which the *Mona Lisa* did suffer damage, and this episode reflects the darker side of male melancholia, that of anger and rage against the lost object for having abandoned her lovesick son. On December 30, 1956, Hugo Unzaga Villegas, a forty-two-year-old Bolivian, threw a stone at the *Mona Lisa*, slightly damaging her elbow. Two weeks later, a psychiatric report on Villegas found that he was suffering from a psychotic illness and heard strange voices. It added that he had intended to murder the Argentine dictator Juan Perón, but instead attacked the less well-protected *Mona Lisa*. Thus, as it had been in Peruggia's theft, *Mona Lisa* was a substitute for the original target.[26]

This event was, of course, less newsworthy than Peruggia's theft. After all, whereas the theft evoked fears that the painting might be permanently lost, Villegas's act merely damaged it. Nonetheless, seven years later Salvador Dali, as Sassoon puts it, "provided his own 'Freudian' interpretation"

---

representation of the boy's mother are essentially Christian, not Judaic or any other of the world's religions. Thus, while it is true that *Mona Lisa* has become a global icon, my interests here center on her function and role as an icon with particular relevance for Christianity in general, and men of Christian heritage in particular.

25. Ibid., 187–88.
26. Ibid., 220.

of Villegas's act of vandalism.[27] As Sassoon summarizes Dali's interpretation: "Imagine, he wrote, a naïve Bolivian visiting the Louvre. He perceives the museum as a whorehouse full of naked, shameless statues—these Rubenses, this naked flesh. He notices, hanging on a wall, the portrait of his own mother. What is she doing in place like this? She too must be a whore. What's more, she's smiling ambiguously at him. He has two options: the first is to run away with the portrait and hide it, piously, where it cannot be found; the second is to assault it."[28]

In effect, Dali's "Freudian interpretation" also provides an explanation for why Peruggia did what he did. He took the first option while Villegas adopted the second. Sassoon comments concerning Dali's interpretation of Villegas's action: "Dali has a point. It is difficult to imagine an attack on Raphael's *Baldissare Castiglione* (though he could look like someone's father). Usually, men who attack pictures attack those representing women." However, what Sassoon misses is Dali's explicitly "Freudian" suggestion that Villegas noticed "the portrait of his own mother."[29] Additionally, the very fact that he was mentally ill, suffering, it appears, from paranoid schizophrenia, means that he could act out the rage he felt against his mother—or her visual representation—that saner men, more inhibited, could not.

If so, Freud's argument in his essay on Dr. Daniel Paul Schreber that the delusions of a paranoid schizophrenic are "an attempt at recovery," is especially relevant to Villegas's stoning of the *Mona Lisa*. As Freud points out, while the delusions are bizarre, they are the sufferer's own attempt at self-recovery by undoing "the work of repression" and bringing back "the libido again to the people it had abandoned." In paranoia—which is almost certainly Villegas's form of schizophrenia—this is accomplished through projection, that is, "what was abolished internally returns from without."[30] By stoning the woman he took to be his mother, he undid the work of repression that was integral to his melancholia, which has taken the form of excessive self-reproach because he cannot bring himself to reproach his mother, especially in the form of the lost loved object who has, he feels, abandoned him.

27. Dali, "Why They Attack the 'Mona Lisa.'"

28. Sassoon, *Becoming Mona Lisa*, 221.

29. Ibid., 221.

30. Freud, "Psychoanalytic Notes upon an Autobiographical Account of a Case of Paranoia (Dementia Paranoides)," 147.

The link that we earlier saw between melancholia and mania in relation to Peruggia's theft also applies to Villegas's stoning of *Mona Lisa*. He
too found "himself in a position to throw off at one blow some heavy burden, some false position he [had] long endured," and the act of throwing a
stone at *Mona Lisa* was a triumph over the costly "expenditure of [psychic]
energy in repression."[31]

MONA LISA AS OBJECT OF HUMOR

Sassoon argues that prior to the theft, Leonardo's *Mona Lisa* belonged
largely to the cultural elite, but following the theft she became an icon for
the masses. This has, in turn, led to the development of *Mona Lisa* into
a commodity, one which the advertising industry has eagerly exploited.
Conversely, this popularization of *Mona Lisa* among those who have little
appreciation for art has prompted a backlash among the cultural elite, who
have claimed that the painting is of modest if not trivial significance.

Marcel Duchamp's *L.H.O.O.Q.*, which is now in the Philadelphia Museum of Art, is exemplary of this backlash. In 1919 he took a postcard of the
Mona Lisa and drew a moustache and a goatee beard on her face, then added
to the "sacrilege" (Sassoon's term) by naming it *L.H.O.O.Q.*, letters which in
French make the sound *elle a chaud au cul* ("She is hot in the arse"). According to Sassoon, this remains the most famous of *Mona Lisa* send-ups.[32]

If Villegas's assault on the *Mona Lisa* was direct and overt, more covert
and subversive forms are those, like Duchamp's *L.H.O.O.Q.*, that alter her

---

31. Freud, "Mourning and Melancholia," 175. It is possible that Hugo Villegas was familiar with the story in the Gospel of John (8:1–11) of the woman caught in adultery. Men
had gathered to stone her but were dissuaded from doing so when Jesus said to them, "Let
him who is without sin among you be the first to throw a stone at her" (v. 7). This statement is usually taken to mean that, after all, we are all sinners, so no one has a right to cast
a stone at another person. However, it may have a meaning that is more directly related
to the issue of adultery. We know, of course, that the woman could not commit adultery
all by herself and that a man had to be complicit in the act. It is also possible that this very
man was among the group of her accusers for his absence could be taken as evidence that
he was this man. Also, quite possibly, there were other adulterers among the men who had
gathered there. If so, Jesus was counting on their need for group solidarity on this occasion; splitting the men into two groups (the innocent and the complicit) would not be in
their own best interests. Being mentally ill and therefore isolated, Villegas was not under
the same sorts of constraints as these men were. Thus, he is free to cast a stone at *Mona
Lisa*. But the biblical story may shed light on his motivations for doing so.

32. Sassoon, *Becoming Mona Lisa*, 211.

appearance, or otherwise make her the object of a sort of rebellious, school-boy humor. I suggest that this too is an expression of the *melancholy self* and reflects the fact that the most effective such humor is that in which the victim is the mother figure and not, for example, a man whose appearance betrays the symptoms of melancholia. An especially witty example is the 1992 portrayal of *Mona Lisa* by the British cartoonist Steve Best with the caption, "Mona was trying not to smile as she waited for her silent fart to reach Leonardo."[33] In light of my proposal that the *Mona Lisa* allows for a displacement of the ambivalent feelings that boys and men experience toward the lost loved object, Best's humorous assault on the dignity of *Mona Lisa* may be a more effective way of undoing the repression than Villegas's more direct assault. In any event, it is noteworthy that it expresses one of the religious sensibilities associated with the *melancholy self—the sense of humor*—for as Jim Dawson points out, "farts and religion go way, way back together." In fact, the woman who farts recalls the ancient Egyptian goddess Let Pet, who "was the personification of a natural function."[34]

However, Salvador Dali's "Freudian interpretation" of Villegas's direct assault on the *Mona Lisa* may be an even more effective example of this religious sensibility precisely because it is more subtle and less overtly offensive. In imagining what was going on in the mind of Villegas, Dali managed to malign the object of Villegas's attack in the process. First, he made the association of *Mona Lisa* with the mother explicit, and then suggested that this mother was something less than the ideal mother, for she was a not-uncomfortable resident of a virtual whorehouse. This is a far cry from the Virgin Mary, the idealized mother of traditional Christianity.

Freud's own writings on humor help to explain how this religious sensibility of the *melancholy self—the sense of humor*—actually works. In *Jokes and Their Relation to the Unconscious*, he concluded that humor saves in the expenditure of painful emotions, costly inhibitions, and difficult thinking.[35] In his essay "Thoughts for the Times on War and Death" he noted that the demands of living in a civilized society require that we are forced, "psychologically speaking," to live "beyond [our] means."[36] If this is so, then humor, a savings in the expenditure of our limited psychological resources, is like money in the bank.

33. Ibid., 264.
34. Dawson, *Who Cut the Cheese?*, 93.
35. Freud, *Jokes and Their Relation to the Unconscious*, 293.
36. Freud, "Thoughts for the Times on War and Death," 217.

In his essay on humor, originally published in 1928, Freud pointed out that in his earlier book on humor he had considered the subject "from the economic point of view alone," and that, in doing so, he was able to show that the pleasure derived from humor "proceeds from a savings in expenditure of affect." But here he seeks to go beyond his economic theory of humor and relate humor to his theory of the mind. Thus, he contends that humor is "the ego's victorious assertion of its own invulnerability," its refusal "to be hurt by the arrows of reality or to be compelled to suffer." Humor, he notes, "is not resigned; it is rebellious," and thus "signifies the triumph not only of the ego, but also of the pleasure principle, which is strong enough to assert itself here in the face of the adverse real circumstances." The ego is able to achieve this victory because this rebellious reaction has the approval of the superego. Normally, "the superego is a stern master," but in the case of humor, the superego "winks" at "affording the ego a little gratification." And contrary to its usual function of enforcing social rules and regulations, the superego brings about the humorous attitude, and, in doing so, repudiates reality and serves an illusion. It seems to say, "Look here! This is all that this seemingly dangerous world amounts to. Child's play—the very thing to jest about." If, then, "it is really the superego that in humor speaks such kindly words of comfort to the intimidated ego, this teaches us that we have still very much to learn about the nature of that energy." One thing, however, is clear: "Finally, if the superego does try to comfort the ego by humor and to protect it from suffering, this does not conflict with its derivation from the parental function."[37]

This view that the superego, in its more kindly and nonpunitive guise, is the energy behind humor is relevant to *Mona Lisa*, especially her enigmatic smile. If Giorgio Vasari's account is accurate (that Leonardo employed mimes and flute players to keep the sitter entertained while she was being painted), then we may guess that her smile is neither seductive nor sinister, but the expression of a certain indulgent amusement, a mother watching the antics of her sons and saying, "Boys will be boys." This, I believe, is an essential aspect of *Mona Lisa*'s appeal to the *melancholy self* that inhabits every man. The Virgin Mary would neither invite nor countenance such antics in her presence. Nor would she allow her sons to get away with the jokes that have been played at the mother's expense in the case of the *Mona Lisa*. Sassoon indicates that the first Mona Lisa send-up was by the French illustrator Eugene Bataille, who, in 1887, placed a clay pipe in her

37. Freud, "Humor," 263–65, 268–69.

mouth.[38] Then, as we have seen, Duchamp contributed the moustache and beard. Is this not the rather juvenile mother-directed humor in which boys surreptitiously engage?

The obvious message here is that *Mona Lisa*, the archetypal mother, is not to be taken all that seriously. Thus, she herself becomes "the very thing to jest about," and through such jesting, the hurt and the anger associated with the emotional separation of the boy and his mother become relegated to the trash heap of unproductive emotions, and a comforting illusion takes their place. As Freud had ascribed to religion a similar illusory value the previous year in his monograph *The Future of an Illusion*,[39] it seems altogether appropriate that humor would be the religious sensibility that survives the iconoclastic assault on *Mona Lisa* that we have been examining in this chapter. As Sassoon points out, "Iconoclastic behavior requires, by definition, that the icon to be destroyed is widely revered and known."[40] Clearly, the religious sensibilities of honor and hope had raised *Mona Lisa* to the status of an icon. Now, the religious sensibility of humor was intent on undoing what the other religious sensibilities had done. But even as Peruggia's theft and Villegas's assault could not destroy her iconic status, neither was the religious sensibility of humor successful in doing so. In fact, one cannot help but think that the purpose of all three iconoclastic behaviors was to preserve her iconic status by humanizing her. Twenty-eight months in an old chest, an injury to her right elbow, a pipe in her mouth, and so forth—for better or worse, this is no longer the woman Walter Pater described in his sentences of "revolutionary importance,"[41] words that nineteenth-century men committed to memory and recited as they stood before the painting and gazed upon her face, searching for the mother whom they had lost so many years ago.

WHERE MELANCHOLIA IS, LET MOURNING BE

In "Mourning and Melancholia" Freud discusses two possible scenarios in regard to how one may deal with the loss of the loved object. One is the manic overthrow of the lost object in a single blow. The other is the gradual decathexis through a mourning process in which one relinquishes

38. Sassoon, *Becoming Mona Lisa*, 209.

39. Freud, *The Future of an Illusion*.

40. Sassoon, *Becoming Mona Lisa*, 209.

41. W. B. Yeats as quoted in ibid., 133.

the loved object in order that one may go on living.[42] Due to its liberating role in the relieving of painful emotions and costly inhibitions, humor may contribute to the work of mourning, but it is unlikely to be the final step in the mourning process itself. In the case of the lost maternal object, this final step is suggested in the pop hit of the 1950s, the song "Mona Lisa," written by Jay Livingston and Ray Evans. As Sassoon notes, Nat King Cole made it famous, singing in it the 1950 film *Captain Cary USA*. It received the Academy Award that year for best song.[43]

In his biography of Cole, Daniel Mark Epstein notes that the song, hastily written by Livingston and Evans, was originally titled "Prima Donna." But when they were informed (mistakenly, as it turned out) during the film's production that it had a new title, *After Midnight*, they were instructed to revise the lyrics to fit this title. So the first line—"Prima Donna, Prima Donna"—was changed to "After midnight, after midnight." However, when Evans's wife heard it, she felt the words weren't good enough, and being an art lover, she "thought the song should be about da Vinci's masterpiece, and on a lark the composers humored her, cooking up another set of lyrics."[44] When the demo was prepared, there was still a half hour of recording time on the disk, so Livingston and Evans asked the singer to do a rendition of the song with the "Mona Lisa" lyrics. When the film title was changed yet again, they convinced the studio music chief to use the "more graceful" Mona Lisa version. The fact that "Mona Lisa" lyrics were written "on a lark" and "to humor" Evans's wife may suggest that they were, for this very reason, expressive of deeply repressed emotions.

All the big-name Italian singers—Frank Sinatra, Perry Como, and Vic Damone—turned it down. Epstein notes that Cole, who was contacted next, first turned it down. Perhaps reflecting the longstanding tradition of women's inability to appreciate or understand *Mona Lisa*'s appeal to men, his wife objected to his recording the song, "feeling that an 'off-beat thing about an old painting wouldn't go.'"[45] But perhaps because his wife had objected so strongly to his singing it, Cole was persuaded to reconsider, and he recorded the song, thereby resolving his financial problems at one stroke. In this way, *Mona Lisa* proved herself a potent rival to the Virgin Mary, the one to whom Christians over the centuries have prayed for help

42. Freud, "Mourning and Melancholia," 176.

43. Sassoon, *Becoming Mona Lisa*, 223.

44. Epstein, *Nat King Cole*, 208.

45. Sassoon, *Becoming Mona Lisa*, 223.

and deliverance. The fact that Italian singers turned down the opportunity to sing a song about Leonardo's *Mona Lisa* may also reflect an unconscious reluctance of Italian males to lend their creative abilities to an enterprise that implicitly dethrones the Virgin Mary—the true Prima Donna—from her central place in the hearts of Christian men.

Since then, many others have recorded the song—Bing Crosby, Pat Boone, Elvis Presley, and others—but Cole's has remained the classic version. Here are the words:

> Mona Lisa, Mona Lisa, men have named you.
> You're so like the lady with the mystic smile.
> Is it only 'cause you're lonely they have blamed you?
> For that Mona Lisa strangeness in your smile?
> Do you smile to tempt a lover, Mona Lisa?
> Or is this your way to hide a broken heart?
> Many dreams have been brought to your doorstep.
> They just lie there and they die there.
> Are you warm, are you real, Mona Lisa?
> Or just a cold and lonely, lovely work of art?

Two features of the song have bearing on the transformation of melancholia into mourning. The first is that the singer is in no mood to reproach her. Others have blamed her, but he is not one of them. He recognizes that while the strangeness in her smile may be designed to "tempt a lover," it more likely serves her need "to hide a broken heart." If, as Freud suggests, the primary psychodynamic in melancholia is the internalization and reproach of the lost object, a reproach that is then directed—misdirected—against the self, these lines of the song are noticeably devoid of such reproach. This young mother is not to be reproached for having abandoned the boy who loved her so. Instead, she is to be the object of understanding, for her smile is a façade designed to mask her loneliness, her own broken heart. In other words, the poet sees how she is suffering, and this affords him a convincing explanation for why she seemed to have abandoned him. The two of them were victims, as it were, of something over which they had no direct control. Lurking in the background of this scenario is, of course, the all-powerful Father. And somewhere in the middle of it all is the painter, Leonardo da Vinci, who may well have recognized that his mother Caterina's smile was her own way to hide a broken heart, for, after all, the very year that she gave birth to her son, the father of her child married another woman.

The second noteworthy feature is the singer's recognition that dreams brought to her doorstep "just lie there and die there." This painful realization is a manifestation of the transformation of melancholia into mourning. Whatever dreams the boy's relationship to his mother has engendered, they are given up as lost causes. In the final two lines, the speaker asks whether she is "warm" and "real" or merely "a cold and lonely, lovely work of art." While the melancholy man wants to continue to believe the former, the man who has undergone the mourning process knows that the latter is true.

Sassoon concludes his own study of the *Mona Lisa* with this confession: "When I started this work, I did not find the *Mona Lisa* a particularly beautiful painting," but "Now I do."[46] Perhaps this is because he has completed the process of the sublimation and displacement of his feelings for the *subject* of the painting through his own scientific investigations into the history of the painting, and through this process of decathexis, he can now admire the painting for what it is—a "lonely, lovely work of art." No, she is not warm and real, but she is lovely, just the same, and she is not, after all, a haughty and condescending Prima Donna. The lost object is irretrievable. However, it is the acceptance of this fact that enables us to recognize that the painting itself is uncommonly beautiful. Moreover, it is a painting that invites the one who gazes upon it to smile back. In smiling back he realizes that he, at least, is warm and real. We cannot ask any more of a painting than this.

46. Ibid., 275.

chapter three

Whistler's *Mother*: Object of Reverence

JAMES MCNEILL WHISTLER'S PORTRAIT of his mother was painted in 1871 when he was thirty-seven years-old. Even more self-evidently than *Mona Lisa*, the subject of Whistler's famous portrait is a maternal figure. But she is considerably older than the subject of *Mona Lisa*, she is not a young mother, and there is not a trace of sexuality about her. Nor is there any hint of a smile. In contrast to the scooped neck and silk texture of *Mona Lisa*'s gown, the dress that Whistler's mother is wearing is a plain black one that completely covers her, from neck to feet. In contrast to *Mona Lisa*'s long flowing hair, her hair is tightly drawn, and much of it is covered by a plain white shawl. Where one of *Mona Lisa*'s hands rests comfortably on the other, Whistler's mother's hands appear to be tightly folded. If the most vivid colors in the *Mona Lisa* painting are Lisa's face, neck, and hands, "the wall dominates the color" of Whistler's *Mother*.[1] And whereas Lisa is seated on a terrace with a panorama of hills and uncultivated vegetation behind her, Whistler's mother is seated in a stark and unlit room, her feet planted on a low stool, a small framed picture on the wall (one of her son's etchings) and a hanging drapery.

1. MacDonald, "The Painting of Whistler's Mother," 55.

James McNeill Whistler's *Arrangement in Gray and Black No. 1* or *The Artist's Mother*: Musée d'Orsay Paris. Photo credit: Réunion des Musées Nationaux / Art Resource, New York.

However, despite these substantial differences between the two paintings, the major difference is in the relation of the subject to the viewer and (by implication) to the artist. Lisa del Giocondo looks directly at the viewer, with no trace of the demure lowering of gaze that was the custom for female subjects in Leonardo's day.[2] In contrast, Whistler's mother, who is seated sideways, neither looks at the viewer nor seems to be aware of the viewer's presence. This absence of any awareness of the viewer is underscored by the fact that she was engaged in prayer for her son and his successful execution of the painting. As befits the fact that she was engaged in prayer, her demeanor is serious, suggesting that her portraitist knows that he dare not take artistic liberties that might evoke her own disapproval.

2. Sassoon, *Becoming Mona Lisa*, 33.

Whistler's decision to paint his mother in a seated position was an accommodation to his mother's physical frailty. As Frances Spalding points out, "She originally posed in a standing position, but, owing to a recent illness, found this too tiring, and after two or three days the seated pose was begun." The side-view seating arrangement was a new innovation in portraiture technique. Spalding explains: "Various sources have been suggested for the pose, but the originality that Whistler brought to his conception of it caused a great many other artists to experiment with the seated side-view." She adds that one of the first reviews of this painting "mentioned the artist's powerful intellectual grasp of the Protestant character," and the side-view seating arrangement clearly contributed to its Protestant character.[3]

Thus, like *Mona Lisa*, Whistler's portrait of his mother was highly innovative in its day for the way its subject addressed the viewer. In Leonardo's day, women were expected to avoid the gaze of the male artist. This was also true in eighteenth-century European, metropolitan society. As Angela Rosenthal points out:

> Eighteenth-century European, metropolitan society developed an elaborate ideal of femininity, constituted by notions of private, domestic virtues, and culturally regulated through literature, conduct books and other media. Within the discourses governing female behavior, dominant gaze politics were more rigorously defined along gendered lines. The ideal woman could not direct a prolonged, searching look at a man without impropriety. That is, women who did not conform to such cultural limits were excluded from polite society, and considered uncultured, unnaturally powerful or immoral.[4]

Rosenthal is concerned in her essay with the female portrait painter of male subjects, and Angelica Kauffman's portrait of the actor David Garrick especially interests her. But her point about the female gaze is no less relevant to the subject of the portrait itself. However, in Whistler's day, it was common for women to face the artist and, most typically, to assume a standing position—the position that Anna Whistler had taken prior to the decision to change her position from standing and facing forward to sitting and facing toward the wall.

The original title of the painting was *Arrangement in Grey and Black No. 1*. The subtitle *Portrait of the Painter's Mother* came later, and only after

3. Spalding, *Whistler*, 88.
4. Rosenthal, "She's Got That Look!," 147.

the public began to refer to it as a painting of Whistler's own mother. The original title seems to have been a deliberate effort on Whistler's part to depersonalize the painting. As Margaret F. MacDonald points out, "His titles emphasized color harmonies as being more important than the subject of the painting, even when that subject was his much beloved and highly respected mother." Furthermore, his own efforts to displace emotional feeling with scientific curiosity is reflected in the fact that there is a limited range of color in the painting, prompting MacDonald to comment: "By carefully arranging and controlling the colors, Whistler felt that he had arrived at a more realistic scientific truth than if he had increased and exaggerated the colors."[5]

What prompted Whistler to paint his mother's portrait? The decision was a spur-of-the-moment impulse, a reaction to his frustration that his sitter, Maggie Graham, the fifteen-year-old daughter of a wealthy Glasgow Parliament member who had commissioned the painting, complained of fatigue and illness and eventually refused to sit any longer. In his biography of Whistler, Stanley Weintraub describes Whistler's reaction to Maggie Graham's defection: "Whistler nursed his annoyance through what was left of the day, then late in the evening decided that the back of the canvas was a good surface for something else." So, although it was stained through from the abortive *Blue Girl* on the other side, he began preparing it for use, and "early the next day he surprised his mother by telling her that he wanted her to pose for him, that he had long wanted to do her portrait." Weintraub adds, "It was his revenge upon Maggie Graham."[6]

Weintraub also notes that Whistler had attempted his mother's portrait four years earlier, "possibly as a peace offering," after his return from an impulsive ten-month trip to South America. He had gone with a group of American expatriates living in London who, on the spur of the moment, decided to lend their support to Chile and Peru against the Spanish fleet, which had mobilized against them. The two countries had demanded reparations for debts incurred when they were Spanish colonies. When the Spanish fleet bombarded the port city of Valparaiso, the volunteers from London joined the Chilean citizens in fleeing to the hills. Whistler later claimed that he was the first to panic.[7]

5. MacDonald, "The Painting of Whistler's Mother," 58.

6. Weintraub, *Whistler*, 146–47.

7. Ibid., 119.

In Weintraub's view, Whistler's decision to join the group was motivated less by his desire to aid the Chileans and Peruvians, and more to gain emotional distance from his personal difficulties in London. Shortly before he left, there was a bitter scene in which his mother had attacked his liaison with Jo Hiffernan, who had been his model and mistress for three years prior to his mother's decision to leave America and live in London. Jo moved into other lodgings when his mother decided to live with him instead of with her stepdaughter and her family, but when his mother was away visiting her English relatives, Jo would move back until his mother returned. Weintraub notes, "Anna Whistler knew the risks of bringing up the unmentionable subject, but her son's career as a responsible artist was at stake." In response, Whistler "flung himself" out of the house: "He was ripe for a quixotic gesture."[8]

However, this earlier effort to paint his mother had come to nothing. Now, when Maggie Graham defected, and when Whistler proposed that he paint his mother's portrait, both were determined to see the project through. As we will see, their mutual determination was a testimony to the fact that her religious faith and his artistic ambitions could cohabit the same room, the simple unadorned studio in which he worked with single-minded devotion. It was an improbable collaboration, but this time it worked beautifully.

If Leonardo da Vinci's *Mona Lisa* became the *iconic* center for the religious sensibilities of the *melancholy self*, Whistler's *Mother* became its *devotional* center, functioning as an object of reverence. As such, she evokes in the *melancholy self* the emotions of filial piety that men's own mothers evoked in them when they were little boys.

I will develop this proposition in some detail in the following chapter, but to lay the groundwork for it, I want to make the case in this chapter that Whistler's relationship to his mother was crucial to the development of his career as an artist. As we will see, her role in this regard was a paradoxical one, for she was initially opposed to his becoming an artist; then, when his career as an artist had begun to lose its direction and purpose, she came to its rescue. In order to show the importance of his relationship to his mother for his career as an artist a brief review of his life leading up to the painting of his mother is essential.

8. Ibid., 118.

WHISTLER'S CHILDHOOD, YOUTH, AND YOUNG ADULTHOOD

The Formative Years (1834–1851)

James McNeill Whistler was born in Lowell, Massachusetts, in 1834. He was the son of Lieutenant George Washington Whistler, a West Point graduate and civil engineer with expertise in the building of railroad lines. Although he was his father's third son, he was the first child of his father's second marriage. Whistler's mother, Anna McNeill, was the closest friend of his father's first wife, who died in 1827. From the moment she was introduced to the dashing young West Point cadet, Anna secretly adored him. But she was no match for her friend, Mary Swift, whose beauty and gaiety took West Point by storm, and George and Mary were married in 1821. When Mary was on her deathbed six years later, she told her husband that if he ever married again, she hoped it would be to her friend, Anna.

For four years prior to their marriage, Anna spent a great deal of time with the Lieutenant and his three children, two sons and a daughter. They were married in 1831, and when their son James was born three years later, it was hoped that his arrival would provide an important link between the new mother and her stepchildren. This hope was only partially realized, as there was often great tension between her and her three stepchildren, especially with her stepdaughter. Anna gave birth to two more sons, the first of whom died when James was five years old.

"Little Jamie," as he was called, was the apple of his mother's eye. In their biography of Whistler, Ronald Anderson and Anne Koval observe: "His mother's diary reveals him often as a mischievous, spirited little boy who, on the point of reprimand, could melt his mother's heart with one innocent glance. He was a fidget, never appearing to stand still for a second, and needed and often demanded constant entertainment. Apart from this incessant activity, which frequently drove the exhausted family to distraction, they all without exception were devoted to him. He easily held his own, with a confidence way beyond his years."[9]

The family moved from Lowell to Stonington, Connecticut, when James was three years old. Years later, Whistler claimed Stonington, but also Baltimore and St. Petersburg, Russia, as his birthplace. As Anderson and Koval note, "Lowell, that bleak industrial town without any apparent

9. Anderson and Koval, *James McNeill Whistler*, 6.

history, was conveniently forgotten."[10] Yet, as biographer Avis Berman observes: "Whistler was prepared when a snobbish society woman turned up her nose at his real place of birth in Lowell, Massachusetts, 'Whatever possessed you to be born in a place like that?' 'The explanation is quite simple,' replied Whistler, 'I wished to be near my mother.'"[11]

When he was nine years old, the family moved to St. Petersburg, Russia, where his father had the position of chief foreign consultant on the St. Petersburg to Moscow Railway. Their departure was delayed when James contracted rheumatic fever just days before the scheduled date. According to Anderson and Koval, "The attack was to have a detrimental effect on James's health for the rest of his life. For Anna, the thought of losing her darling James so soon after the death of Kirk [his younger brother] was almost too much to bear, and all through this very testing time only her faith in God kept her from totally breaking down."[12] Once in St. Petersburg, he "became prone to fits of ill temper and displays of blatant insolence to all and sundry." His parents became concerned about his mood swings: "His mother would chide him for inconsiderate behavior by telling him that it was "in his powers to make his mother's heart rejoice.' Playing upon his seemingly incessant ill-health, James usually blithely ignored her reprimands."[13]

Nonetheless, his parents supported his interest in drawing, and arranged for him to have private lessons. He eagerly accepted the tutelage of his instructor, a senior student at the Imperial Academy of Fine Arts. This was in stark contrast to his other schoolwork, for which his attention span was very limited. Then, in 1848, James, together with his parents and younger brother, William, visited London, where his stepsister and her husband were living. While they were there, the decision was made for him to remain in London, live with his stepsister's family, and attend school there. During the family visit, his father commissioned a portrait of him, and the portraitist, Sir William Boxall, took his young sitter to see paintings by Raphael, the sixteenth-century Italian painter. As Frank Zöllner notes, Raphael had been a frequent visitor at Leonardo's workshop and, "on the basis of the *Mona Lisa*, created a form of portraiture that was to hold good for decades."[14]

10. Ibid., 5.
11. Berman, *James McNeill Whistler*, 7.
12. Anderson and Koval, *James McNeill Whistler*, 7.
13. Ibid., 9.
14. Zöllner, *Leonardo da Vinci*, 75.

Whistler's father had been advising him to choose a career and enter an American college, perhaps to study some branch of engineering or architecture. But having seen "the work of the greatest artist there ever was," he wrote to his father and "defiantly declared his future intentions." He wrote, "I hope, dear father, you will not object to my choice: a painter, for I wish to be one very much and I don't see why I should not, many others have done so before. I hope you will say 'Yes' in your next [letter], and that Dear Mother will not object to it."[15] His father's nonresponse was his own answer, but his mother responded immediately. Although her response was not as discouraging as he had expected, she advised him to follow his father's wishes and save his "fancy sketches" for his leisure time:

> And now, Jamie, for your future call! It is quite natural that you should think of all others, you prefer the profession of an Artist [for] your father did so before you. I have often congratulated myself his talents were more usefully applied and I judge that you will experience how much greater your advantage, if fancy sketches, studies, etc., are meant for your hours of leisure. I have hoped you would be guided by your dear father and become either an architect or engineer—but do not be uneasy, my dear boy, and suppose your tender Mother who so desires your happiness means to quench your hopes.[16]

When his parents were informed by his stepsister shortly thereafter that he did not return to school but would be receiving private tutelage at home, they greeted the news with serious misgivings. Although they gave their permission, his mother warned him "not to be a butterfly sporting about from one temptation to idleness to another."[17] Perhaps recalling his mother's warning, the butterfly became his own self-image in later years, and appeared near his signature in many of his paintings.[18]

In 1849, when James was fifteen years old, his father contracted cholera, and after appearing to recover, he died of a heart attack. When he was informed of his father's death, he wept for many days. His mother returned to London with his brother, William, to collect James and sail for America.

---

15. Anderson and Koval, *James McNeill Whistler*, 20.

16. Ibid., 20.

17. Ibid., 21.

18. Walden, *Whistler and His Mother*, 25. Edgar Degas who, according to Walden, was "a vastly superior artist," once remarked to Whistler, "It must be very tiring to keep up the role of the butterfly. Better to be an old bull like me? What!" (25).

They were met in New York by James's stepbrother, who had followed in his father's footsteps.

Why his mother chose to live in Pomfret, Connecticut, a small rural town in the northeast corner of the state, is unknown. But the town had a private school, Christchurch Hall, whose headmaster was the Reverend Doctor Roswell Park. A West Point graduate like her husband, he was a strict disciplinarian, and Anna felt that her two sons needed "the firm guidance of a male hand." James's cousin Emma, who stayed with Anna and also attended the school, described his impact at Christchurch Hall: "He was a great favorite with all the school, for his spirits were perennial, and he charmed alike old and young. No one could withstand the fascination of his manner, even at this early age, or resist the contagion of his mirth, inconsequent and thoughtless as he often was. He was so amiable under the reproof of his elders, so willing to make amends that it was impossible to be provoked with him long."[19]

But Anna was growing increasingly alarmed by his wayward behavior. Her diary recounts her annoyance with him on numerous occasions. He often stayed away from home after school. Moreover, "in the mornings, he was usually gone long before breakfast, thus missing prayers—an important part of the family ritual." Unlike his younger brother, William, he avoided all household duties "and was always the first to disappear at any hint of work to be done." But his interest in drawing continued unabated, and his forte became the art of caricature. This was often the cause of merriment among his friends but created difficulties at school and elsewhere. When Dr. Park discovered James's picture of himself, he sentenced him to "a few strokes," and this seemed to bring his career as a caricaturist to an end.[20]

The West Point Years (1851–1854)

As his school years at Christchurch were coming to an end, there was the question of what he might do next. He had not dared to mention his desire to be an artist in the wake of his father's death and his mother's financial struggles. Given his father's exemplary career in the US Army and other family West Point connections, admission to West Point as a subsidized cadet seemed the best, and perhaps the only, option. His brother, William, with his diligence and obvious academic skills, deserved a college education.

19. Anderson and Koval, *James McNeill Whistler*, 23.
20. Ibid., 24.

James, who had not excelled academically, did not. But he could receive a solid education at West Point and continue the family's military tradition.[21]

On the other hand, he should not have been admitted to West Point. His weak eyesight and record of bad health would normally have excluded him, but he was admitted on the basis of his family background. Within a few months, the War Department sent his mother a report of her son's "progress." As Anderson and Koval point out, "It made for sorry reading. In nearly every aspect of his training, from drill to dress, he had been reprimanded on dozens of occasions. Anna was horrified, and immediately wrote to him to tell him so. She cajoled him and pleaded with him not to disgrace the family or 'break a widowed mother's heart.'"[22] Over the next several months, he did only enough to scrape by; and his sole motivation for doing even this much was that in the second year he would be allowed access to the drawing class, which was offered at West Point because it provided grounding in mapmaking and mechanical and reconnaissance drawing. However, the fact that he was the top student in his drawing class could not offset his poor performance in the other subjects, and in the middle of his third year there were plans to dismiss him.

His mother's response to his explanation that he was suffering from homesickness was to promise that she would send a new photograph of herself. She also contacted his stepbrother in hopes that he could pull some strings to persuade the officials at West Point to give James another chance. Thus, family connections that were exercised without his knowledge gained James a brief reprieve, but his demerits due to his inability to conform to military discipline made it patently obvious that he was totally unfit for military service. He himself suspected that his days at West Point were numbered, but he did not want to be dismissed on the grounds of bad conduct. Such a dismissal would have remained with him for life, and was, in any case, unthinkable in terms of his family honor.

However, in the summer of 1854 he failed his oral chemistry exam. When he identified silicon as a gas, the examiner told him to stand down. After some deliberation, the Army finally gave up on him. Avis Berman thinks his failure on the chemistry exam may well have been deliberate. In any case, he would cheerfully explain in later years, "If silicon had been a gas, I might have become a major-general."[23] Throughout his life,

21. Ibid., 25.
22. Ibid., 27.
23. Berman, *James McNeill Whistler*, 19.

he admired Edgar Allan Poe, who remained at West Point for only eight months before being discharged by court-martial for gross neglect of duty and disobedience of orders. At least Whistler was able to claim that he was dismissed on academic grounds.

Learning of his dismissal, his mother "finally vented her anger and frustration on him," but he defended himself, "claiming he had been unfairly treated by both the disciplinary and examination boards."[24] Seeming to believe him, she told him to write to Jefferson Davis, the Secretary of War, asking permission to retake the chemistry examination, and to have a reconsideration made of his disciplinary record. The letter was passed on to Robert E. Lee at the Academy, and he turned down the request, a decision that was upheld by the War Department.

Anderson and Koval suggest that despite his failure at West Point, his West Point years afforded his first taste of independence:

> The longer he stayed at the Academy, the further he seemed to distance himself from his mother. He rarely wrote to her, nor did he seem interested in what was happening at Pomfret or Scarsdale [where she had moved a few months prior to his dismissal]. On many occasions during these periods of silence, Anna wrote to him expressing her concern. She even sent some stamps on one occasion, but it made no difference. While he still needed her comfort from time to time, it now seemed he no longer needed or wished for her maternal guidance. James felt the burden of family tradition lift from his shoulders.[25]

Also, nothing had changed as far as his desire to be an artist was concerned. In fact, "his dreams of being an artist had merely been reinforced."[26]

Marking Time (1854–1855)

When he left West Point, he was twenty years old. He would have to wait until he turned twenty-one to receive the small inheritance from his father that would enable him to strike out on his own. The year of marking time was spent first in Baltimore, where he lived in the palatial mansion and worked in the mechanical drawing office of the firm of one of his father's old engineering friends. His work was desultory at best, and when his

24. Anderson and Koval, *James McNeill Whistler*, 31.
25. Ibid., 31.
26. Ibid.

mother learned of his increasingly flippant attitude toward his work, she came to Baltimore to see the situation for herself. She rented rooms in a small, modestly furnished boardinghouse. She confronted her son, berating him for his idleness and poor behavior, and demanded that he leave the palatial mansion immediately. Then she coerced him to visit another old friend of his father, who was attached to the United States Survey Department in Washington DC.

On the strength of his mapmaking course at West Point he was hired to work in the drawing office. But within days of assuming his new responsibilities, he began arriving late and leaving early, and within weeks, he was hardly there at all. In February 1855, he resigned his position and made plans to sail for Europe, where he could, at last, embark on the career he had envisioned for himself at age thirteen. He was never to return to his native land.

As we reflect on Whistler's childhood, youth, and young adulthood, it is evident that his mother played a dominant role in his life, and that their relationship was one in which the *melancholy self* which develops in all young boys would, in his case, have a rather central place among the various selves that made up his composite *Self*. As her firstborn, he had a special place in her affections. However, this meant that she was also very ambitious for him and constantly pressuring him to live up to her—and his deceased father's—expectations of him. She unquestionably loved him, but her love was not the sort of unconditional love that a boy may enjoy in the earliest months of his life. Rather, it was a love that had various conditions attached to it. She was forgiving when he failed to meet these conditions, but it was clear that these conditions mattered a great deal to her, and that she was willing to go to great lengths—and distances!—to exercise her parental influence, guidance, and authority. And there is no doubt that she expected that he would one day uphold the family's honor.

If he had been asked the question, are you a religious man?, he probably would have laughed and said, "Ask my mother! She would be the first to tell you that I am not." But this very denial would have been based to a large extent on the fact that he would have defined religion as she understood and practiced it. In my view, his religious sensibilities were those that had their genesis in the *melancholy self*, the *sense of honor* that originates in a boy's desire to win back his mother's love; the *sense of hope*, which derives from his effort to deal with the loss of his mother's unconditional love and admiration by redirecting these desires to some segment of the external world; and the *sense of humor*, which enables him to treat with a certain

lightheartedness the frustrations and disappointments that inevitably occur in his pursuit of the other two religious impulses. By treating these other religious sensibilities with a degree of disrespect, he actually preserved
them, as humor enabled him to avoid the deep cynicism to which he might
otherwise have been susceptible.

When we consider his formative years with these three religious sensibilities in mind, we can readily see that young Whistler was caught in the
conflict between his *sense of honor*, especially the desire to make his mother
proud of him and not bring disgrace on his family (especially his father's il-
lustrious legacy), and his *sense of hope*, which was directed toward his desire
to be an artist. This conflict became apparent when he was thirteen years
old and declared his desire to become an artist, a declaration to which his
father did not respond at all, a nonresponse that may have been worse than
overt rejection, for overt rejection may at least have indicated that his father
would be willing to discuss the matter. The fact that his father died shortly
thereafter, and that there had been no reconciliation between them would
certainly have weighed heavily on him. It is not inconceivable, in fact, that
he entertained the thought—if only to dismiss it—that his announcement of
his desire to become an artist may have had contributed to his father's death.

Whistler's *sense of humor* became, in a sense, his salvation. He could
joke about his failure to uphold the family honor, and he could even poke
fun at his desire to become a serious artist by drawing caricatures of the
adults who were displeased with him. Without his *sense of humor*, he may
well have succumbed to cynicism and despair, especially during the long
period in which his desire to become an artist was placed on hold.

WHISTLER'S MELANCHOLY STATE AND HIS MOTHER'S PORTRAIT

The Preportrait Years (1858–1871)

As has been noted, Whistler resigned his position in the United States
Survey Department in 1855 and set sail for Europe. He lived in Paris for
three years. Then, in 1858 he decided to move to London, and from that
time until his death forty-five years later (in 1903) he made London his
permanent home. This decision was influenced by the fact that his painting
At the Piano, which was rejected by the jury of the Salon, an official French
exhibition of paintings, was accepted by the Royal Academy of Arts annual

exhibition in London. His *The White Girl*, painted in 1861–1862, with his mistress, Jo Hiffernan, as the model, was rejected by the Royal Academy. But when it was shown later that year in a London gallery, it "caused much excitement in artistic circles,"[27] and was a major turning point in his art. As a contemporary critic put it, Whistler, in this painting, "found the road he was destined to tread."[28] Although he was still very much influenced by the latest currents in French art, he was moving in his own direction.

However, toward the end of 1863 he had a falling out with his stepsister's husband, a medical doctor of high social standing and an accomplished amateur painter, who came from a distinguished family of medical doctors. As a result, he was not allowed to visit their home, and he retaliated by forbidding his stepsister to visit him and Jo at the house they were renting. It was at this time, when family relations were already strained, that his mother announced that she had decided to leave the United States to make London her permanent home. As Anderson and Koval note: "At a stroke, his world was turned upside down," and in a letter to a friend in Paris he exclaimed, "General upheaval!! I had to empty my house and purify it from cellar to eaves."[29] Within a week's time, he had to find a place for Jo to live, an apartment for a male friend who had been living with him temporarily, and travel to Portsmouth to meet his mother.

His mother lived with her stepdaughter and her family for a month. But she had known from the outset that she could not stay with them indefinitely, so she decided to move in with her son instead, who had already found alternative lodgings for Jo. After all, "Jimmy was an authentic son, and in her Scotch Presbyterian fashion Anna Whistler was going to save her son from himself."[30]

The effect of her presence on his lifestyle was immediate. She began to censor his extravagant lifestyle, and on Sundays he would at least escort her to Chelsea Old Church, a short walk away, and leave her at the door. It was a small church, but, as she noted in a letter to a minister friend back home, "I think in the small Churches there is a more Evangelic spirit."[31] He never complained about her strict Sabbatarian ideas, but a friend noted that "he used to give a queer smile when he mentioned them."[32] Despite

27. Spalding, *Whistler*, 44.
28. Berman, *James McNeill Whistler*, 37.
29. Anderson and Koval, *James McNeill Whistler*, 141.
30. Weintraub, *Whistler*, 89.
31. Ibid., 91.
32. Walden, *Whistler and His Mother*, 71.

the enormous cultural differences between his mother and his friends, he also began to show her off to them, and they were gracious toward her. She especially warmed to the poet Algernon Swinburne, "perhaps sensing his vulnerability," and he reciprocated her affection, becoming "in a sense another son." When Swinburne "occasionally failed to keep a social appointment with her, she chastised him mercilessly." She "also lectured him endlessly on the sins of alcohol, and though Swinburne paid little heed he took great pleasure in her concern."[33]

As for Whistler himself, "after ten years' absence he found that he truly loved his mother in his own fashion and settled comfortably into the new domestic arrangements."[34] Also, her small pension helped with the household finances, and she established order, at least on the surface, in the Whistler household. As she wrote to a friend in New York soon after she moved in: "While his genius soars upon the wings of ambition the everyday realities are being regulated by his mother . . . I am thankful to observe that I can and do influence him . . . All those most truly interested in him remark upon the improvement in his home and health."[35]

On the other hand, the years between his mother's decision to move in with him and the painting of her portrait (1863–1871) were largely years of struggle. As Berman points out, he was riddled with self-doubt. His ambitions were much higher than his achievements to date, and he "had to keep testing himself, even if his experiments took him in the wrong direction or demoralized him." In addition, "the critics abused his paintings because he did not fit into any of their pigeonholes." Moreover, his "touchiness and pride" and physical combativeness—he physically attacked a critic who had condemned one of his paintings—were having a negative effect on the British public, and they "seized on their fear and dislike of the man as an excuse to dismiss his art." In a word, "he felt as if he were banging his head against a brick wall."[36]

Furthermore, in 1869 he had an affair with a parlor maid, and in 1870 she gave birth to his son. He called the boy "an infidelity to Jo," but Jo herself took charge of the baby. While the child was still an infant, he and Jo "separated for good, yet Jo became the boy's guardian."[37] She raised him,

33. Anderson and Koval, *James McNeill Whistler*, 143.
34. Weintraub, *Whistler*, 91.
35. Ibid., 114–15.
36. Berman, *James McNeill Whistler*, 47, 50, 54.
37. Ibid., 58.

presumably with support money from Whistler. As Sarah Walden observes, "his personal life—always unstable—was descending into chaos and farce." But just then, "in the days of his greatest despondency," he had the inspiration to do the portrait of his mother.[38]

The Portrait Accomplished (1871)

Since he was a slow worker, it was not unusual for Whistler to require seventy or eighty sittings for a portrait. And despite the fact that his mother was now in her sixties and physically frail, she was up to the challenge. Berman writes: "She stood for two or three days without complaint. Finally, she asked if she might sit down for awhile. Whistler, suddenly ashamed at his thoughtlessness, put his mother into a chair and pushed the footstool under her feet. And there it was—the pose he had been looking for."[39]

Even so, it took him the whole summer to complete the painting, and when he would cry out, "No! I can't get it right! It's impossible to do it as it ought to be done," she "would lift her eyes heavenward and pray that the crisis would soon pass." There were many such outbursts, "but at the end of the summer she heard him say, 'Oh, Mother, it is mastered, it is beautiful!' Anna then saw herself—sober and dignified, but without any nostalgia or tearful emotion . . . Whistler was unaware that his likeness of his mother would become one of the most famous portraits in Western art, but he knew he had succeeded in his task."[40]

However, the portrait was considered dull by the hanging committee of the Royal Academy of the Arts, and although it was accepted for the spring exhibition, it was placed in a very poor location. This prompted William Boxall, the artist who had painted Whistler as a young boy and had encouraged his artistic interests, to threaten to resign if it were not moved to a more prominent location: "In other words, Boxall's influence was the reason Whistler's painting was done some justice, and everyone, including Whistler, knew it. Moreover, Whistler was counting on the portrait to get him elected to the Royal Academy. But this did not happen, and the denial of membership "deprived Whistler of much potential income."[41]

38. Walden, *Whistler and His Mother*, 38, 43.
39. Berman, *James McNeill Whistler*, 56.
40. Ibid.
41. Ibid., 56–57.

Also, although he was pleased with the painting as a painting, he made a very conscious effort to play down the fact that the subject of the portrait was his mother. As noted earlier, he named it *Arrangement in Grey and Black* No. 1. Walden points out, "The 'Mother' was Whistler's most personal painting, as well as his finest," then adds:

> For anyone else but him, there would be no conceivable contradiction. Yet Whistler fiercely resented any suggestions that the portrait was chiefly or even partly an emotional homage to his own mother. He made an issue of artistic principle over the matter, which became the subject of a running controversy with friends and critics alike. However perverse or excessive this may have seemed, perhaps it was a natural defense mechanism against the very intensity of his affections. The remark in response to praise for the beauty of the portrait—"Yes, one does like to make one's mummy just as nice as possible"—may be seen among other things, as a typically evasive and humorous piece of understatement.[42]

However, Walden goes on to suggest that more than ambivalent feelings toward his mother were at stake here, for "the conflict over the importance of 'content' and 'feeling' in the portrait of his mother went to the heart of his concept of painting."[43] In a lecture delivered in London in 1888 and reproduced in his *The Gentle Art of Making Enemies*, published a year later, he proclaimed his aesthetic creed.[44] Walden points out: "He insisted that painting was 'the poetry of sight' and should be entirely independent of subject matter. Themes were unimportant; what mattered were 'celestial harmonies.' Art should stand alone without 'emotions entirely foreign to it, (such) as devotion, love, pity, patriotism, and the like.'" Walden adds that he cited his portrait of his mother as the prime example of art misunderstood: "Take the picture of my mother, exhibited at the Royal Academy as an 'Arrangement in Grey and Black.' Now that is what it is. To me it is interesting as a picture of my mother; but what can or ought the public to care about the identity of the portrait?"[45]

42. Walden, *Whistler and His Mother*, 86–87. In light of our focus in this book on the emotional separation that occurs in early childhood it is noteworthy that Whistler uses a small child's name for mother—"mummy"—in joking about his painting of his mother. See Agnes, *Webster's New World*, 947.

43. Walden, *Whistler and His Mother*, 87.

44. Whistler, *The Gentle Art of Making Enemies*, 135–59.

45. Walden, *Whistler and His Mother*, 87.

Hardly anyone agreed with him on this point, including his longtime friend, Algernon Swinburne, who, as we have seen, had a special affection for Whistler's mother. In a published commentary on Whistler's lecture,

> Swinburne praised him for the "Mother" and his portrait of [Thomas] Carlyle that came immediately after—but in a way Whistler found intolerable. Describing Whistler's "arrangements" as "lovely and effective," Swinburne teasingly adds that it would be quite useless for the painter to protest that his portraits did not appeal to the emotions as well as to the aesthetic sense, and he talks of the "intense pathos of significance and tender depth of expression (in) the portrait of [Whistler's] own venerable mother."[46]

Walden adds that anyone else but Whistler "might easily have forgiven Swinburne for discerning traits of filial affection in the portrait," but Swinburne's article had "impugned the artist's aesthetic code; his religion of art had been traduced," and in "a reaction which would have been more normal had Swinburne insulted Anna Whistler, he immediately severed his relationship with the poet." In Walden's view, however, Swinburne was "even more right than he supposed," for present in the portrait there is not only "pathos" and the "tender depth of expression," but "everything Whistler vehemently denied was there: devotion, pity, love, and patriotism." Furthermore, "It was quite natural that they should be; these were the emotions the artist must have instinctively associated with his mother."[47]

In my view, this controversy gets to the very heart of the *melancholy self*. Walden is certainly right in her contention that the emotions that Whistler must have instinctively associated with his mother are present in the painting, and that these are emotions that Whistler did, in fact, experience in his relationship to his own mother. At the same time, a painting of his own mother reflects and represents the emotional distance that occurs between the boy and his mother from the age of three to the age of five. He has lost the closeness that he had experienced in his earlier years, and the spatial distance that exists between the portrait painter and the frail woman sitting across the room is symbolic of this loss. The sudden inspiration to have her seated horizontally to the painter—his innovation in portrait painting—may itself have been a reflection of his *melancholy self*, especially because it was immediately preceded by his realization that he was causing

46. Ibid., 88.
47. Ibid., 88-89.

her to suffer by making her stand for several hours, a realization that made him feel "ashamed."

This is much like the three- to five-year-old boy who understands that he has pained his longsuffering mother, and seeks to make amends by treating her with greater sensitivity and kindness. Thus, his protestations that this painting is especially illustrative of the artistic principle that the painting "stands alone," separate, as it were, from its "subject," is a reflection of the artist's own *melancholy self*. So whatever one might say about his view that the painting is independent of its subject—beautiful in its own right— as a theory of art, this view is certainly true in psychodynamic terms.

The *melancholy self* played a central role in the formation of Whistler's composite Self, and his very decision to become an artist, formed at an early age, was an unconscious recognition of this very fact. Through his art, he could displace the ambivalent feelings he felt toward the lost loved object: the desire to draw close, and the need to pull away. No doubt, his female subjects, especially Jo Hiffernan, had been of great assistance to him in this regard, for, as women, they were "stand-ins" for his own mother. But it was not until his mother herself became the subject of his painting that he could bring to bear the full emotional intensity and artistry that his *melancholy self* afforded.

As was noted in chapter 2, the lyrics of "Mona Lisa" popularized by Nat King Cole ask this question: "Are you warm, are you real, Mona Lisa? Or just a cold and lonely, lovely work of art?" The word *just* implies that the art is *less* than the woman it depicts. But the *melancholy self* is more likely to feel that the depiction is so much *more* than the woman it depicts. As Whistler declared when he revealed the painting to his mother, "Oh, Mother, *it* is mastered, *it* is beautiful." (Note my italics.) I would add that *it* could not have affected him in this way were it not for the fact that he had long since experienced an emotional gulf between himself and his mother, one that was forever unbridgeable. In other words, the painting was the culminating act in a lifetime of mourning the loss of the love object and of the self who had internalized her unconditional love. It represented the successful displacement of the feelings that accompany such loss—of frustration, anger, and rage toward the lost loved object—into a work of art that he was the first to declare was truly "beautiful."

chapter four

Whistler's *Mother*:
Irreverent Reprisals

AS WE SAW IN the preceding chapter, Whistler contended that art should stand alone without emotions that are entirely foreign to it, such as devotion, love, pity, and patriotism, and he supported this contention with a reference to his painting of his mother.[1] With regard to the emotions that he specifically cites we can readily see that a painting of the artist's mother may evoke emotions of devotion, love, and even pity among its viewers. On the other hand, patriotism, and he does not come immediately to mind when one thinks of the emotional responses one might associate with a painting of one's own mother or someone else's mother. Yet, as we will see in this chapter, Whistler's *Mother* was to evoke very powerful patriotic feelings among Americans, and this applied as much or more to American men as it did to American women.

In this chapter I will focus on two of the religious sensibilities associated with the emergence of the *melancholy self* in early childhood: the *sense of hope* and *the sense of humor*. First, I will consider the emotional impact of Whistler's *Mother* when it toured the country during the Great Depression and will show that it was a symbol of hope for American men. Second, I will discuss the irreverent reprisals against Whistler's *Mother* and the devotion that it had evoked, thus expressing the religious sensibility of humor that pokes fun at the other religious sensibilities but, in doing so, saves them from cynical rejection.

---

1. Whistler, *The Gentle Art of Making Enemies*, 127–28.

WHISTLER'S *MOTHER*: SYMBOL OF HOPE FOR AMERICAN MELANCHOLY SELVES

The Melancholia of Dislocation

In her chapter on "The Portrait as Patriotism," Sarah Walden provides a detailed account of the fact that Whistler's portrait of his mother was recognized as a distinctively "American" work of art.[2] However, it was the work of an artist who left his native land at the age of twenty-one, and never returned. For Walden, this raises the question: "Could the artist have painted the 'Mother'—or anything like it—if he had stayed in his own land? Or was it only as a self-exile from the 'vast far-off-ness' of America, as a restless cosmopolitan, that Whistler could recapture the peculiar spirit of the place—a spirit Henry James once described, in a phrase that could almost have been used about the 'Mother,' as that 'thin, empty, lovely, American beauty.'"[3] Commenting on Whistler's work, Henry James, himself a self-exile from America, described its "charm of a certain degree of melancholy meditation."[4]

As Walden quotes James in her chapter on the portrait of Whistler's mother as patriotism, she strongly implies that Whistler's own *melancholy self* was related not only to his mother but also to his motherland. If so, his mother's decision to come to London to live would have been a continual reminder and representation of the land from which he had also sought emotional distance in order to pursue his hope of becoming an accomplished artist.

Whistler's occasional comments about his native land reflected the same ambivalent relationship that he had with his mother. He once said that if he ever went back, "it would only be to sail around Baltimore Harbor before coming straight back to Europe."[5] In other words, he would view America from a safe distance. At the same time, an American art critic, Louis Gillet, wrote in his 1907 book on Whistler that "in his personality as in his painting, the artist was 'furiously American,'" and added that it was impossible to look at his painting of his mother "without thinking of the word puritan."[6]

2. Walden, *Whistler and His Mother*, 90–149.
3. Ibid., 107.
4. Ibid., 108.
5. Ibid., 109.
6. Ibid., 106–7.

Walden suggests that Whistler's American personality was reflected in his flamboyance or "thoroughly American blend of self-confidence, self-publicity, and sheer gall," but alongside all of this "ran the deeper and more sober side of his character: his pietistic commitment to his work, a certain insecurity and isolation as an individual and as a painter, and the strain of moralistic Puritanism in some of his pictures as well as in his personality were all American qualities too, which in one way or another are brought together in the 'Mother.'"[7]

No Honor in His Own Country

Unlike the paintings of John Singer Sargent, also an American self-exile, Whistler's work was very slow to catch on in America. The portrait of his mother was shown at the Pennsylvania Academy of Art in 1881, exactly ten years after it had been painted, and the following year it was shown at the Society of American Artists in New York. It received virtually no attention. He had to get the painting out of hock in order to display it in America, and although the asking price was $1500, he would have taken $500 for it. Ten years later the French government bought it for $1000.

When Whistler died in 1903, there was no American representation at his funeral. The *New York Times* obituary summarized comments from obituaries of newspapers around the country, noting that they emphasized his "unique personality" and suggesting "that it is a question for posterity to decide his exact position as a painter," though "it is generally conceded that he was a consummate etcher." It observes that Whistler studied under the French painter Charles Gabriel Gleyre, "who was a painter of classic and early Christian subjects in the Neo-Greek style," adding, "Needless to say, one looks in vain in Whistler's work for any trace of Gleyre's teaching." The obituary's single reference to his portrait of his mother associates it with his portrait of Thomas Carlyle as two portraits painted during the decade following the rejection of *The White Girl* for the Salon in France. It identifies the painting as *The Portrait de Ma Mere*, and suggests that it "was only poetical justice that the picture should have been bought for the Luxembourg Museum." [8]

7. Ibid., 110.

8. *New York Times*, "James McN. Whistler Dies in London: Celebrated American Artist Unexpectedly Passes Away." Obituary, July 18, 1903.

The obituary makes several positive remarks about his work, referring to his *The White Girl* as "exquisite," and noting that his failure to pass his examination at the Military Academy "was extremely lucky for the art world." And in the concluding paragraph, it suggests that memory of his irascible personality would eventually be forgotten, and that "his work will remain." But, as a whole, it is cautious in its assessment of his work, preferring to leave this to the judgment of future generations of art lovers and critics. Although it asserts that he has been vindicated in the twenty-five years since John Ruskin condemned his work, it adds:

> And yet, even now, there are no standards by which one can judge his work, by which one can form an estimate of his true place in the ranks of the world's great artists. That he is among them is not doubted; just how high up among them is not so clear. It is only once or twice in a century that the originator of a new style in art or literature appears, and it takes at least a century for the world to recover from the dazed condition into which it is thrown by such a man's work.[9]

It is noteworthy that the writer of the obituary can unequivocally praise Whistler's skill as an etcher while expressing uncertainty as to his accomplishments as a painter. No less noteworthy is its assertion that the quality of Whistler's work will be difficult to assess as long as his personality is etched in the memories of those who appreciate art. It quotes the *Daily Telegraph*: "It may safely be prophesied that the light of his genius will but burn the brighter when his self-asserted individuality has been a little forgotten or, at any rate, obscured."[10]

The irony, of course, is that Whistler would have made the same point, but even more vehemently, for, in his view, art stands—or falls—on its own merits, irrespective of the identity of the painter. On the other hand, the very fact that he was considered a disagreeable person may well have enabled other men, like Algernon Swinburne, to focus on the fact that the subject of the painting is a mother. It is almost as if Whistler's own attempt to dissociate himself from the subject of the painting enabled other men to identify with the painting. Thus, despite the conflict that Whistler's effort to dissociate himself from the subject of his painting created between himself and his friend Swinburne, this very dissociation makes it possible for other men to claim the painting for themselves and to feel, somewhere

9. Ibid.
10. Ibid.

deep inside themselves, that the subject is the very personification of their own mothers. It appeals, in other words, to their *melancholy selves.*

The Reassuring Mother amid the Great Depression

At the time the *New York Times* obituary appeared in 1903, Whistler's *Mother* was hardly known in America. As has been noted, it was largely ignored on its initial trip to the United States in 1881. But by the time it made a return visit in 1932, it had become widely familiar through prints. It was loaned that year to the New York Museum of Modern Art by the Louvre, where it had been moved from the Luxembourg Museum, and was later transferred to the Musée d'Orsay, where it remains to this day. In a gesture of national goodwill, the Louvre had agreed to break its rule against lending works of art.

Walden notes that the *Mother* subsequently "toured the country with all the pomp and circumstance of a visiting dignitary." During its year-and-a-half-long tour, it was seen by two million people in twelve American cities; in all, thirty cities had asked to exhibit it. The American newspapers carried numerous stories "recording its triumphal progress," and the extraordinary security measures—including a platoon of federal troops who escorted it from Chicago's Union Station to the Art Institute—were themselves "seen as a mark of honor." There was even the suggestion in *Art News* (October 15, 1932) that the portrait really belonged in America, not France: "Whistler's Mother is an honored and carefully guarded guest in the land which might have been her home."[11]

Appropriately, the portrait was in Boston on Mother's Day, and a three-cent stamp "in memory and in honor of the mothers of America" commemorated the occasion. Throughout its tour of the United States, Boy Scout troops posed with their scoutmasters beneath the painting, thus underscoring the fact that the mother, Anna Whistler, who was the subject of the painting, was the mother of boys (only two of whom had survived into adolescence).

In his article on Whistler's *Mother*'s American tour, Kevin Sharp notes that after months of sleepless nights, Alfred H. Barr Jr., the thirty-year-old founding director of the Museum of Modern Art in New York, who arranged for the loan of the painting, had, in effect, "sought a mother to answer doubts about his leadership and to quell his lingering insomnia."

11. Walden, *Whistler and His Mother*, 117–19.

It was clear that his "fledgling museum needed a mother to push visitors through its doors, evidence of legitimacy to Park Avenue constituents, and of solvency to its trustees." Sharp asks: "Can it be that in moments of crisis all we want, all we really need, are our mothers?" He answers his own question by noting that in 1932, the year of the museum's financial peril, the nation as a whole "pined for a reassuring mother figure to guide it through the dire days and nights of the Great Depression." He adds, "Few could have guessed, however, that the mother who would console them all was no flesh and blood, no womb and succoring breast, but rather oil on canvas."[12]

Sharp notes that in the first feature article on the return of Whistler's *Mother* to America (*The New York Times Magazine*, October 23, 1932) a large reproduction of the painting was framed between the headline "Whistler's 'Mother' Comes Home Again" and the caption "Symbol of the dignity and patience of motherhood." A syndicated story picked up by dozens of small town papers across the country praised Whistler for creating a "symbol of mother of all ages and in all lands." Sharp observes: "Such an expansive, global understanding of Whistler's *Mother*'s iconic reach would not last long, however. By the time the painting landed on the walls of MoMA [Museum of Modern Art] the press had refined its interpretation considerably, transforming Whistler's *Mother* into a symbol of American motherhood."[13]

And so she remains to this day. Leonardo's *Mona Lisa* retains her iconic status as the archetypal mother who "is older than the rocks among which she sits," but Whistler's *Mother* is "America's Mother." And because she came home when the country—like the self-exile who painted her—was in the depths of despondency about its future, she is the reassuring mother who, like Anna Whistler herself, prays for the nation's recovery and success. Furthermore, as Sharp points out, the elaborate security measures that were employed throughout the country, and widely reported in the press, were themselves symbolic of the nation's profound longing for security:

> In such uncertain times, security filtered poignantly through the public discussion and debate of the issues that affected the country most: the economy, unemployment, farm and home foreclosures, the mounting crime rate and the threat of war in Europe and Asia. Recognizing that anxiety had become an almost collective second nature by 1933, newly elected President Roosevelt reminded

12. Sharp, "Pleasant Dreams: Whistler's *Mother* on Tour in America, 1932–4," 81.
13. Ibid., 85.

Americans in his first inaugural address: "The only thing we have to fear is fear itself." Roosevelt purposefully inserted "security" in the titles of his most dramatic legislative initiatives and recovery agencies, hoping to comfort a nation stalled as much by uncertainty and worry as by poverty.[14]

The president's own mother, wearing black satin with purple and white orchids, and looking remarkably similar to Whistler's mother, posed beneath the painting at the occasion of the painting's departure.

If the nation was stalled by uncertainty and worry, so had its painter been. Yet, with the vital assistance of his mother, he had painted his way out of it. As Sharp notes, it would be years before President Roosevelt's programs significantly altered "the social, economic and diplomatic landscapes or recast America's doubtful consciousness of them." Nonetheless, "if personal security, job security, economic security and national security were too much to hope for in such a perilous epoch, at least Americans could go to sleep knowing that Whistler's *Mother* was safe somewhere, protected by armed militia, watched over by savage dogs."[15] (In point of fact, despite these elaborate precautions, the painting was slightly damaged in transit from Kansas City to Baltimore, but this fact was withheld from journalists, and when the painting was returned to the Louvre, the damage was not disclosed to Louvre officials, and they apparently did not notice it.) Clearly, Whistler's *Mother* was the very symbol of hope, the same hope that kept Whistler himself at his task throughout the summer of 1871.

Sharp uses the word "reverent" to characterize the visitors who came to view the painting, a word that supports the idea that Whistler's *Mother* was the *devotional* center of the religious sensibilities evoked by the *melancholy self*. But, as Sharp also notes, there was an undercurrent of amusement in American press reports as well, such as the story of the young boy who waited patiently for the woman in the painting to whistle.[16] And this brings us to the fact that Whistler's mother has also helped to foster the third of the religious sensibilities of the *melancholy self*, that of the *sense of humor*.

14. Ibid., 91.

15. Ibid.

16. Walden, *Whistler and His Mother*, 42.

HUMOROUS TREATMENTS OF WHISTLER'S *MOTHER*

From Reverent Devotion to Irreverent Caricature

In effect, Whistler himself initiated this humorous response of the portrait when he made his oft-quoted response to a viewer who was impressed by the painting, "Yes—one does like to make one's mummy just as nice as possible."[17] If making one's mummy "nice" (which could be taken in a couple different ways) is central to the religious sensibility of honor, to joke about this very effort is equally central to the religious sensibility of humor. Thus, for Whistler, it was the religious sensibility of honor rather than of hope that was the target and victim of his humor. He showed little, if any, disposition to subject his hopes, especially as they concerned his artistic ambitions, to a similar humorous assault.

Also, in response to a critic who said that the painting was too severe, and that an artist as talented as Whistler could have "thrown in a few details of interest without offense," Whistler proposed, facetiously of course, that he might have included "a glass of sherry and a Bible."[18] Sarah Walden points out that in America Whistler's response "came close to being fulfilled," as the designer in the United States stamp commemorating the painting's tour in 1932–34 added a bowl of flowers, apparently so that Whistler's mother would have something to look at.[19]

But Whistler was not alone among his contemporaries to make jokes about the painting. There was an early French cartoon depicting an old woman wearing a black dress and heavy shoes, sitting glumly on a straight-backed chair in an empty room, with the caption, "A poor old lady left alone in a room with a smoking chimney," and a reviewer suggested that this was a posthumous painting of the old woman.[20] Most of the humor, however, has originated in the United States. Whatever else it may mean, it reflects the need of American males—for virtually all of the humor has been the work of male cartoonists and illustrators—to poke fun at the painting, at the mother whom it depicted, and, by implication, at all mothers. Such poking fun at the mother was part and parcel of the nation's corresponding desire to pay her homage and treat her with reverent devotion.

17. Spalding, *Whistler*, 88.
18. Walden, *Whistler and His Mother*, 120.
19. Ibid.
20. Ibid., 104.

Martha Tedeschi points out in her article on Whistler's *Mother* and popular culture that "Whistler's *Mother* continued to linger in the hearts and minds of Americans long after the painting had been returned to France in 1934," adding,

> References and images dating from the years of World War II in-
> dicate that "Whistler's Mother" was by now a household phrase,
> and with familiarity came a less reverent form of appropriation. A
> new plane, the Douglas A-26 bomber, was nicknamed "Whistler's
> Mother" when it was introduced in July 1942, presumably because
> of the whistling sound made by the bombs it released. "The Whis-
> tler's Mother-in-law" was a popular dance hit of the war years, re-
> corded by Woody Herman. From this point on, cultural references
> to Whistler's most famous painting are increasingly lighthearted
> and wide-ranging. Where once the painting's iconography was
> more narrowly defined as a respectful tribute to motherhood or to
> the greatest achievements of fine art, pop culture now began to tease
> out the humorous potential of Whistler's inscrutable old mother.[21]

As Tedeschi's comment suggests, some of the humor derived from the name of the painter. Boys who grew up in the 1940s and '50s would some-times refer to themselves as "Mother's little Whistler," and many boys at the time were aware that whistling was what a boy did when he was attempting to get away with some misdemeanor, often one committed in violation of one of her household rules.

The Inscrutable Old Woman

As Martha Tedeschi also notes, however, most of the humor has been di-rected toward the "inscrutable old woman" who is the subject of the paint-ing. In this regard, "a persistent form of humor explores what Whistler's Mother might be looking at, an obsession directly related to the pose and gaze in the original."[22] In 1964, she is watching television, still a relatively recent addition into many households. In 1982, she is sitting in front of a computer monitor with the caption, "Home is where the computer is." Tedeschi notes: "These two examples indicate not only the way in which Whistler's *Mother* has come to function as a visual synonym for 'home,' but also for how the image has been re-appropriated for the changing issues of

21. Tedeschi, "The Face That Launched a Thousand Images," 130, 132.
22. Ibid., 133.

each generation. In both of these instances, the juxtaposition of new technology with the archaic figure of Whistler's *Mother* speaks volumes about the 'shock of the new.'"[23] Again, she is the reassuring mother, this time communicating to those who are facing the challenges and dislocations created by new technologies that they will somehow manage to adapt.[24]

A second form of humor that focuses on the subject herself involves conjectures about what she might be thinking. The original Anna Whistler was thinking of her son's success and praying that the painting would help him to fulfill his ambitions and realize his talents as a painter. Although the earliest art criticism failed to discern that she was praying for the realization of her son's ambitions, it, nonetheless, as Tedeschi points out, "attributed only the most honorable maternal thoughts to the respectable Mrs. Whistler." On the other hand, "the early reading of the sitter's character as typically Protestant and puritanical has paved the way for recent lampoons in which her prudishness is only skin deep. 'Come on sonny boy, this picture would be a lot more interesting if I posed in the nude!' she quips in a postcard of the 1980s."[25] This quip has a certain irony, for the original Mrs.

23. Ibid.

24. In the concluding paragraph of *Jokes and Their Relation to the Unconscious*, Freud suggested that humor saves in the expenditure of painful emotions, costly inhibitions, and difficult thinking (293). Judging from the jokes he tells, her seems to have had primarily in mind the difficult thinking involved in philosophical, scientific, and relational matters. However, his point about humor saving in the expenditure of engagement in difficult thinking is also applicable to new technologies. As Christie Davies suggests in his chapter on stupidity and rationality in *Jokes and Their Relation to Society*: "The reason for the enormous popularity of jokes and stupidity in Western industrial societies must be sought in the antithesis between the attitudes and behavior displayed by the member of the 'stupid' minority in the joke on the one hand and the intensely and increasingly 'rational' character of industrial society on the other. Modern industrial societies are dominated by a belief in technical and economic efficiency, by the view that all institutions should be 'rationally' organized via the interplay of the key impersonal forces of the marketplace, bureaucracy and modern science so as to maximize the stated goals if these institutions from the means as their disposal." He adds, however, that in order to provide a full explanation for the popularity of these jokes, "it is necessary also to consider the negative impact of rational social organization on the individual" (65). The high degree of specialization and division of labor imposed by the market, bureaucracy and modern science creates an anxiety among individuals because they know that they are highly dependent on other specialists whose work they cannot reproduce or perhaps even comprehend: "Under these circumstances even the most knowledgeable and skilled person is aware of how little he or she knows and how little he or she can do in a world that puts enormous emphasis on skill and knowledge" (66).

25. Tedeschi, "The Face That Launched a Thousand Images," 134.

Whistler once entered her son's studio unannounced to bring refreshments, only to discover that his female sitter was nude. She quietly excused herself and never again entered the room without knocking first.

Other images show her smoking a cigarette, blowing a party horn, or stripping down to her lacy underwear in a card that proclaims, "It's your birthday. Don't just sit there! Show 'em stuff!" Tedeschi comments, "Her very immobility, it seems, is provocative; we feel compelled to help Whistler's *Mother* loosen up, as well as stand up and stretch her legs occasionally"—another irony, of course, in light of the fact that she is seated precisely because standing was so tiring.[26]

In a third form of humor that focuses on the subject herself, the inscrutable old woman serves as an icon of old age, prudishness, old-fashioned viewpoints, and conservative politics. Born in 1804, Anna Whistler was sixty-seven when her portrait was painted, which, in our own day, is still relatively young. Nonetheless, she seems to epitomize old age, and her iconic status in this regard has been exploited in various ways. A portrayal of Ronald Reagan's face grafted onto the prim figure of Mrs. Whistler accompanied a 1984 *Herald Tribune* article titled, "Is 74 Too Old to Be President?" In a 1997 *Washington Post* news story about a sixty-three-year-old woman who had just given birth, there was an accompanying portrayal of Whistler's mother doctored up to look pregnant, thus quite unintentionally creating an association between Whistler's *Mother* and Leonardo's *Mona Lisa*. Tedeschi also notes that the prudishness of Whistler's *Mother* "is frequently called upon to register disgust at vulgar or licentious behavior, as she does, for example, in a Little Annie Fanny comic when a beauty contestant removes her clothes during the talent portion of the contest."[27]

A fourth form of humor that focuses on the subject herself is her association with Mother's Day. This association, which began with her visit to the United States in 1933–34, is given a humorous twist in greeting cards with "her long-suffering profile perfect for instilling guilt in even the most attentive of children." For example, a greeting card replaces the framed etching on the wall with a sign reading, "Call Your Mother," and in the Mother's Day cover for *The New Yorker* in 1996 "an irritated Mrs. Whistler glares at the telephone, waiting, one presumes, for her negligent progeny to call."[28] Here, again, contemporary humorists are probably unaware of the

26. Ibid., 134.
27. Ibid., 134–35.
28. Ibid., 135.

fact that the original Mrs. Whistler was similarly able to instill guilt in her own attentive son.

A fifth form of humor replaces Whistler's original subject with someone else who is seated in the same pose, with the same wall and small framed painting as backdrop. This form of humor began as early as 1891, when the English artist and illustrator Aubrey Beardsley depicted himself as Whistler's Mother. But it has especially flourished in the United States, where "such eminent personalities" as Donald Duck, Bullwinkle the Moose, Tigger, Wile E. Coyote, the Muppets, and the Barbie doll "have struck the upright pose made famous by Mrs. Whistler."[29] Then there is Ken Brown's 1985 picture of *Whistler's Brother Ernie from Duluth*, a young male with a slightly bulging stomach, who slumps in a straight-back chair facing a TV set with a remote control in his right hand. His left arm hangs loosely at his side, his hand barely touching a newspaper with the headline, "Psychic's Head Explodes," that he has dropped on the floor. The framed picture on the wall, hung sideways, depicts a featherless chicken.[30]

Ken Brown's *Whistler's Brother Ernie from Duluth*, 1985.

29. Ibid., 137.
30. Walden, *Whistler and His Mother*, 80.

Finally, when Rita Hayworth, the Hollywood actress, was asked by *Look* magazine how she would cast herself, she chose Whistler's *Mother*. Consequently, the article features a picture of Hayworth assuming the same pose, but with her legs in full view, with the picture on the wall displaying her lying on a bed clothed in a two-piece bathing suit. The article explains that "Rita Hayworth, a mother herself, longs to portray Whistler's Mother with emphasis on the whistle."[31] The whistlers, of course, are men, who are likely to be less interested in the fact that she is a mother than that she is an attractive woman. The allusion to the male habit of whistling at an alluring woman (a far cry from the woman in the original portrait) brings us back, full-circle, to the humorous connotations of the painter's name.

Symbol of Defunct Values

Sarah Walden, who was commissioned to restore the painting several years ago and has therefore spent more time viewing Whistler's *Mother* than perhaps any other living person, expresses considerable regret over the cumulative effect of the humorous portrayals of Whistler's *Mother*. While acknowledging the indirect tribute in the fact that this painting "must surely hold the record" among paintings that have been caricatured, she contends that "the affectionate side of the picture, which was so obvious to earlier generations, has drained from the modern perception." To the children of the sixties "Anna Whistler is no longer a mother: she is a matriarch, a figure of almost risible severity, a symbol of defunct values."[32]

Walden also notes that unlike the *Mona Lisa*, "whose sensuous, teasing smile lends itself to playful sexual jokes, it is difficult to caricature the *Mother* without making a serious and occasionally complex point, however inadvertently," for "even at their most trivial or outrageous, cartoons of the *Mother* are often instructive and sometimes disturbing."[33] Of greatest concern to Walden is the fact that the humor takes on a moralizing tendency of its own: "In exchange for what seems to us the painfully constricted, joyless Puritanism, with its intimidating sobriety and gaunt moralism, we get wildly exuberant, 'life-enhancing' laughter, as perpetual youth is superimposed on the somber reality of age and approaching death. But in exchange other, more positive and arguably 'life-enhancing,' qualities of the original

31. Tedeschi, "The Face That Launched a Thousand Images," 138.
32. Walden, *Whistler and His Mother*, 125.
33. Ibid., 126.

have gone too: the impression of endurance in the face of isolation and adversity, of selfless devotion to family, and, above all, of a comforting faith."[34]

Walden takes particular note of what may seem to us one of the more benign and unobjectionable caricatures of the original painting:

> To an irreligious world with neither time nor inclination for the practice of contemplation, the mother in the portrait seems to be gazing at nothing. Because of our experience of seeing lonely old people seated with a vaguely disapproving but transfixed and immobile gaze before the ungodly screen, cartoons showing the *Mother* watching TV can make a disturbingly convincing joke, which blends rapidly into poignancy. The addition of the TV becomes an act of kindness to the old lady; it makes us feel better now that she has something to do. Instead of the bowl of flowers today she can have something animated to rest her old eyes on. Yet it is not just the incongruity of the TV that robs the *Mother* of her iconic status; *she is diminished as a person, deprived of the dignity of solitude together with the focus of her life—faith.*[35]

Walden contrasts the real mother who is secure in her solitude with the ersatz brother Ernie of Duluth, who "slouches with his remote controlled TV and his newspaper in easy permanent touch with the 'real' world," while, in fact, "he is staring into a void, too, and this time the joke is not on the *Mother*, but on Ernie."[36] Ernie, it seems, is the quintessentially American melancholy male, and there is nothing in his immediate surroundings—or the surrounding culture—to sustain his hopes or offer reassurance.

Walden also cites examples of the less amusing caricatures of the painting where, as she puts it, "the desacralization is crude, witless, and ugly."[37] For example, there is Richard Bobler's "Stories My Mother Never Told Me," in which Anna Whistler "is converted into a ferociously grumpy mother with a repulsively weird child, with a skull dangling suggestively from the brim of his hat. The artist seems to be making a heavily ethical point by typically trenchant twentieth-century means; an allegory perhaps of nineteenth-century bigotry giving birth to twentieth-century freakishness and violence."[38] She concludes that the best that can be said for these crude

34. Ibid.
35. Ibid., 127–28 (italics added).
36. Ibid., 128.
37. Ibid.
38. Ibid., 126–27.

caricatures is that "the portrait is such a powerful nexus of symbols that it can sometimes invite a single, annihilating riposte," and adds: "Something that has to be challenged, explained, mocked or destroyed so frequently must have its own renewable sources of strength."[39] Thus, if Martha Tedeschi appears to enjoy the humorous portrayals of Whistler's *Mother*, viewing them as good-natured kidding of the woman who, over the past century, has become "inscrutable," Walden finds many of these caricatures disturbing; for, in her view, these ostensibly humorous portrayals subject Anna Whistler and the values she represents to ridicule, mockery, and desecration. Walden contrasts these portrayals with the humorous treatments of the *Mona Lisa*, which, to her, are fundamentally playful.

Why the difference? I believe that the difference lies in the emotions that the mother evokes in the young boy who no longer experiences her as warm and tender and who finds her feelings toward him difficult to decipher. Significantly enough, Mona Lisa too may be inscrutable, but in a way that draws the viewer to her, and even, as the Livingston and Evans lyrics suggest, evoke in the viewer his own protective feelings toward her. If she is lonely, he truly wants to assuage her loneliness. Something about her appeals to the male desire to accommodate himself to the woman.

In contrast, Whistler's *Mother* is almost impossible to warm up to, and one needs to make a deliberate effort to remain in her presence for any length of time. The viewer senses that she will not accommodate herself to him and expects little accommodation in return. There seems to be no basis for compromise between her moral sensibilities and those of the viewer, so the viewer exaggerates the gulf that lies between them. Something about her evokes the more negative emotions that originally emerged with the emotional separation between mother and son in the early childhood years. As I noted in the introduction, the boy does not understand the causes of this emotional separation, and his attempts to understand it result in mistaken interpretations, including inappropriate forms of self-reproach.

So, in effect, the very inscrutability of the subjects of both paintings evokes deep, repressed melancholic reactions. But in the case of Whistler's *Mother*, the reactions are far more likely to be those of irritation and frustration—the mother, after all, is looking away from him and does not acknowledge his presence—and also of anger and retaliation, as she appears cold, unbending, and not in the least disposed to make herself available, emotionally speaking, to the viewer.

39. Ibid., 128.

However, this means that Whistler's *Mother* can be more fully therapeutic than Leonardo's *Mona Lisa*, who does not evoke such a full range of
melancholy emotions. At one extreme, she can be treated as a sex-object
(Anna Whistler becomes Rita Hayworth). At the other extreme, she can be
transformed into a ferociously grumpy mother who brings out the worst in
her boy and does so under the guise of being a woman of impeccable mor-
als and good breeding. Her therapeutic value, therefore, lies partly in the
fact that she invites these emotionally cathartic responses, thereby releasing
long-repressed feelings toward the viewer's own mother.

On the other hand, her therapeutic value is also due to the fact that,
as Walden suggests, there is something about her that enables her to withstand these emotional responses and to survive these attacks. As we saw in
the introduction, Freud envisions two scenarios in which one relinquishes
one's emotional attachment to the lost loved object, the one being a manic
attack on the object that disposes of the attachment in a single blow; the
other being a gradual process of withdrawal of emotional feelings toward
the object that is akin to mourning: "Just as the work of grief, by declaring
the object to be dead and offering the ego the benefit of continuing to live,
impels the ego to give up the object, so each single conflict of ambivalence,
by disparaging the object, denigrating it, even as it were slaying it, loosens
the fixation of the libido to it."[40]

In this way, it is possible for the process in the unconscious to come
to an end, "whether it be that the fury has spent itself or that the object is
abandoned as no longer of value." Freud acknowledges the difficulty of de-
termining "which of these two possibilities is the regular or more usual one
in bringing melancholia to an end, nor what influence this termination has
on the future condition of the case." But what is clear is that ego enjoys "the
satisfaction of acknowledging itself as the better of the two, as superior to
the object."[41] The self-reproach that is so much a part of melancholia (which
is actually a reproach of the object itself) is consequently abandoned.

Freud is reluctant to identify, in any unequivocal way, the ultimate
effects of this release of fury by means of the denigration of the object on
the future condition of the case of melancholia or, as I would put it, the
degree to which the *melancholy self* plays either a commanding or a more
peripheral role among the selves that make up the composite Self. I think,

40. Freud, "Mourning and Melancholia," 178.
41. Ibid., 178–79.

however, that the ultimate prospects are better if the object of the denigration is considered capable of enduring the denigration inflicted upon it.

As D. W. Winnicott suggests in his article on the use of an object, it
is vitally important that the object is able to "survive" the attack and that
its survival does not involve retaliation.[42] Winnicott is concerned in this
article with the patient-analyst relationship and the patient's need for the
analyst to survive the patient's attack. Otherwise, the patient will not be able
to "use" the analyst therapeutically. However, his understanding of "object
use" is also applicable to our consideration here of how Whistler's *Mother*
may play a therapeutic role for viewers who have unresolved issues relating
to their own mothers, issues that go back to the emotional separation that
occurred in early childhood.

I believe that Sarah Walden is exactly right when she suggests that
"something that has to be challenged, mocked or destroyed so frequently
must have its own renewable sources of strength."[43] In fact, Winnicott's idea
of "object-use" would suggest that those who challenge, mock and "destroy"
her know—and need to know—that these attacks will not really destroy
her. They also need to know that she will not retaliate, that, in fact, the need
to retaliate is not integral to who she is. She may be "inscrutable," but there
is nothing about her inscrutability that suggests she is sitting there plotting
revenge against her attackers. She may be rather severe in appearance, but
she is not one to get riled, upset, or furiously angry. The steady look of her
eyes expresses the steadiness of her mind and heart, and such steadiness is
the ultimate source of her strength. This very strength can, in fact, help to
bridge the gulf between the subject of the painting and the viewer of the
painting. As we have seen, when the painting toured the United States in
the early years of the Great Depression, it evoked in its viewers the awareness of their "own renewable sources of strength." They saw in her something that they felt within themselves.

To be sure, she appears even more dated to us than she did to members
of Whistler's own generation. And, as Walden notes, the acts of "desacralization" that the painting has provoked are "explicable only by reference to
the sociologist's lexicon: rejection of authority, age, family, God, national
allegiance—it scarcely matters what."[44] But for this very reason, I think it
is a tribute to James Whistler and his artistry—as well as to Anna Whistler

42. Winnicott, "The Use of an Object and Relating through Identifications."
43. Walden, *Whistler and His Mother*, 128.
44. Ibid., 128.

herself—that they found a way to traverse this very boundary between his own way of life and hers. As noted earlier, he could not bring himself to enter Chelsea Old Church with her. Instead, he escorted her to church and returned later to escort her home. But he *did* escort her. And, conversely, she accepted his invitation to cross the threshold of his studio. As Walden notes:

> On the face of it, anything further removed from the Quaker-like simplicity we think of as the natural habitat of Anna Whistler than an artist's studio in Chelsea would seem hard to conceive. Yet there is a curious and not entirely fortuitous concordance between the two . . . His mother herself had once compared his single-minded devotion to his painting with her own religious convictions, and the frugal, almost Shaker-like purity of the studio, relieved only by the wispy Chinese matting and the black framed prints, recreates a puritanical atmosphere out of foreign materials.[45]

Here, in this quiet space, a mother's prayers and a son's ambitions were in accord, and her faith was itself justified when he declared, "Oh, Mother, it is mastered! It is beautiful!" She did not disagree, and neither should we, for its beauty rests in the fact that it is a symbol of hope offering reassurance that the success for which a man so desperately longs is within view. Because it *is* such a symbol of hope, it is eminently qualified to serve as the *devotional* or *reverential* object of the *melancholy self's* religious sensibilities, and especially the *sense of hope.*

45. Ibid., 52.

chapter five

Rockwell's *Shuffleton's Barbershop*:
On the Outside Looking In

KARAL ANN MARLING BEGINS her book on Norman Rockwell with the declaration that "Norman Rockwell is America's best-loved artist." She notes that "his works have been reproduced on greeting cards, calendars, figurines," and that "his magazine covers for the *Saturday Evening Post*— over 300 of them in all—have been collected and cherished by its millions of loyal readers, their children, and their grandchildren." But then she adds: "And yet, his portraits of America and Americans have been overlooked or openly denigrated by critics of the fine arts."[1]

In Marling's view, the reason for this denigration is that Rockwell is considered an "illustrator," and an "illustration" seems to imply "some lesser branch of image-making, excluded from serious consideration by its own popularity and the commercial venues in which it appears." She notes that this is rather ironic, for "he hardly ever painted a picture that wasn't intended to be an ad, a cover, a calendar, a gloss on a magazine story, or a Christmas card," and thus "the for-profit context in which Norman Rockwell labored so successfully may make him the most American of all artists in a period that both witnessed and celebrated the primacy of American commercial enterprise." Thus, the "essential paradox" of his life is that "he was America's best-loved and most famous artist but, according to the gate-keepers of the institutional world of art, he wasn't an artist at all."[2]

Another charge against Rockwell was that of falsity or fakery: "His America is too neat, too sweet, and entirely too rural and old-fashioned, his

1. Marling, *Norman Rockwell, 1894–1978*, 7.
2. Ibid.

detractors say." For example, "smiling kids ride to a one-room schoolhouse on horseback, the most serious crime in Rockwell-land occurs . . . when three fresh-faced country boys (and their dog) disobey a sign that forbids swimming in a nearby pond and find themselves pursued by the local sheriff," and "Santa's biggest worry . . . is how to squeeze enough money out of his annual budget to deliver presents to absolutely everybody."[3]

The painting I will focus on in this chapter—*Shuffleton's Barbershop*—challenges these charges against Rockwell. This *Saturday Evening Post* cover (April 29, 1950) displays Rockwell's ability to paint in the style of the seventeenth century Dutch interior painters (Jan Vermeer and Pieter de Hooch). It also reflects the sense of melancholy that is discernible beneath the neat and sweet appearances of his paintings. On a more personal level, I will make the case that it is an expression of his own *melancholy self* and thus a displacement, through art, of his ambivalent feelings toward the lost love object—his mother—who was nonetheless "to be found among those in his near neighborhood."[4] In addition, this painting may be viewed as illustrative of Freud's observation in "The 'Uncanny'" that the home that men associate with their mothers has become uncanny—no longer home-like or familiar.[5] Thus they are faced with the challenge of finding that home in another location or place. Although *Shuffleton's Barbershop* appears to be such a place, the viewer is on the outside looking in.

To see the relevance of *Shuffleton's Barbershop* to Rockwell's own *melancholy self,* we need to give some attention to his personal life, focusing especially on his relationships with his three wives. These relationships reflect the religious sensibility of the *sense of hope,* which is especially reflected in the quest for an alternative to the lost love object.

Given Rockwell's identification with traditional values, we would anticipate that his search would express itself in the desire for a warm and loving woman whom he would marry and with whom he would settle down and raise a family. What we would not have anticipated, given his public persona, is that this search was filled with disappointed hopes and personal tragedy. I will draw extensively on Laura Claridge's excellent biography of Rockwell for this discussion.[6]

3. Ibid.
4. Freud, "Mourning and Melancholia," 173.
5. Freud, "The 'Uncanny,'" 152–53.
6. Claridge, *Norman Rockwell.*

SON OF A SELF-CENTERED MOTHER

Rockwell was born on February 3, 1894, in New York City. The Rockwell family—which included his parents, older brother Jarvis, and Norman himself—lived on the Upper West Side until 1907, when the family moved to Mamaroneck, a small commuter village of 2500 residents on Long Island. He begins his autobiography *My Adventures as an Illustrator* with an account of his memory of sitting at the dining room table in his family's apartment in New York City on a winter evening. His head is "scrunched down on one elbow, a pencil clutched in my fist, drawing a picture of Mr. Micawber while my father reads *David Copperfield*." His mother is sewing, "her chair drawn up to the table to catch the light from the gas lamp with the large green glass shade fringed with red silk ribbons which hung above the center of the table," and his brother Jarvis is "doing his homework beside me."[7]

An idyllic family scene, perhaps, but, in Claridge's view, the very fact that he began his autobiography with a reference to Charles Dickens's *David Copperfield* is significant because this "story of a fatherless boy tended by the Micawbers [is a] wonderfully humane projection of Dickens's own desires for substitute parents."[8] She suggests that Rockwell's later portrayal of the city in which he lived the first thirteen years of his life as unpleasant, sordid, and unsettling was a form of displacement: "It was safer to blame the city than his parents for his failure to receive the family warmth and validation he craved."[9]

Claridge attributes much of this failure to receive family warmth and validation to the fact that Rockwell's mother, Nancy, suffered from neurasthenia, a diagnostic term first employed by an American electrotherapist, George Beard, in an article published in the *Boston Medical and Surgery Journal* in 1869. Neurasthenia was a type of mental disorder involving such symptoms as irritability, fatigue, weakness, anxiety, and localized pains, none of which had apparent physical causes but were thought to result from weakness or exhaustion of the nervous system.[10]

Claridge notes that Rockwell's mother, who was born in Hoboken, New Jersey, in 1866, was deeply affected by the death of her brother and that "she appropriated the theme of suffering for the rest of her life as a way

7. Rockwell, *My Adventures as an Illustrator*, 15.

8. Claridge, *Norman Rockwell*, 56.

9. Ibid., 67.

10. Shorter, *From Paralysis to Fatigue*, 221. Interestingly enough, Alphonso Rockwell, apparently no relation, was Beard's associate.

to be recognized." Also, as the youngest girl in the family, "she learned early to whine effectively and often in order to gain attention from her volatile household." On the other hand, she encouraged "in her own children an openness to excitement, reserving her highest praise for accomplishments that marked her sons as intrepid men of the world, like her brother and her father before them." She herself "could be an invalid" while "they would be the outlet for her needs that went otherwise unaddressed."[11]

In Claridge's view, Rockwell's mother's invalidism and neediness invoked very ambivalent feelings in him. She suggests a strong connection between his "ambivalence toward his mother—the cost to others of her vanity, her desire to be tended, her physical weakness, and her unattractive if enviable ability to get what she wanted—with his longtime championing of the cultural or economic underdog." In effect, his paintings reflect "his lifelong identity with the outsider, stemming from the mixed messages Nancy gave him as he grew up."[12]

Rockwell's own portrayal of his parents in his autobiography suggests that he would have tacitly agreed with Claridge's association of his mother's imperious ways with his lifelong championing of the underdog—in this case, his longsuffering father. For example, he notes that whenever he thinks about his parents,

> a certain scene invariably presents itself, a scene which was repeated day after day during my childhood. It is late afternoon. I am playing on the stairs or in the hallway of the apartment house. The front door opens and closes and my father comes up the stairs, worn out from his day at the office and his hour ride on the trolley. He goes into the apartment and I can hear him ask my mother: "Well, now, Nancy, how are you?" "Oh, Waring, I've had such a hard day. I'm just worn out." "Now, Nancy, you lie down on the couch there and I'll get a cold towel for your head." And then he'd shut the door and all I could hear would be my mother complaining, interrupted at long intervals by my father in tones of gentle sympathy and concern.[13]

The neighbors, he adds, would tell him that his father is "a saint" and "a wonderful, wonderful man," and he agreed.

11. Claridge, *Norman Rockwell*, 19–20.
12. Ibid., 133.
13. Rockwell, *My Adventures as an Illustrator*, 36–37.

He notes that it was soon after his father married his mother that she fell ill: "That was the beginning of a long series of illnesses continuing through her whole life (she lived to be eighty-five years old)," but "whether or not this almost constant sickness was a way of drawing attention to herself, I don't know." However, the doctors "often said there was nothing wrong with her" medically speaking, and he suspects that her psychosomatic illnesses were due to her feeling "that my father was lowering himself when he married her, the daughter of a wild impoverished artist." In any event, his "father's life revolved around her to the exclusion of almost everything else" and he "cared for her constantly and with unflagging devotion."[14]

Although he admired his father for his devotion to his ailing mother, he didn't feel that he had much of a relationship with him: "Dignified, holding to the proprieties, gentle and at the same time stern; but distant, aware of Jarvis and me, but always, even when we were children, treating us as sons who have grown up and been away for a long time—that's how I remember my father. I was never close to him." He adds, "I was never close to my mother either," and tells of the occasions when his mother "would call me into her bedroom and say to me: 'Norman Percevel, you must always honor and love your mother. She needs you.' Somehow that put a barrier between us."[15]

This emotional barrier may well have been due not only to his mother's tendency to call him by his first and middle names (he hated the name Percevel) and to her demand that he always honor and love her, but also to the fact that her expression of her need for him occurred in her bedroom, thus arousing anxieties concerning her sexual neediness. As we will see, this bedroom scene foreshadows the oedipal themes in his wife Mary's relationships with their sons, and most overtly in Mary's request of their son Peter to share her bed at a time when she was feeling especially lost and lonely.

On the other hand, Rockwell learned to keep his thoughts and emotions relating to his mother to himself. For example, in 1911, when he was seventeen years old and embarking on his career as an illustrator, he was upset that the family moved back to New York City from Long Island mainly to indulge his mother. As Claridge notes: "He was furious at his mother, but he let his anger simmer rather than express it. He blamed her for the family's entrenchment in the down-at-the-heels midtown boardinghouse." Convinced that his mother was incompetent and selfish, he

14. Ibid., 37.
15. Ibid., 37–38.

"believed that choosing a boardinghouse over a place of their own was damaging self-indulgence on Nancy's part." It was convenient for her to have nothing to worry about—cooking, grocery buying, cleaning, the laundry—because the boardinghouse took care of everything, all for one payment each month. "But other women provided their families with a normal home; why was she special?"[16]

In later years, he supported his mother with monthly checks, and after her death, he sent a weekly check to his mother's relatives as compensation for their having cared for her the last few years of her life. Thus, it would seem that he made every effort to be a good and honorable son. But he concludes his reflections on his parents, city life, and the summers he spent in the country with this observation:

> Maybe as I grew up and found that the world wasn't the perfectly pleasant place I had thought it to be I unconsciously decided that, even if it wasn't an ideal world, it should be and so I painted only the ideal aspects of it—pictures in which there were no drunken slatterns or self-centered mothers, in which, on the contrary, there were only Foxy Grandpas who played baseball with the kids and boys fished from logs and got up circuses in the back yard. If there was sadness in this created world of mine, it was a pleasant sadness. If there were problems, they were humorous problems. The people in my pictures aren't mentally ill or deformed. The situations they get into are commonplace, everyday situations, not the agonizing crises and tangles of life.[17]

Rockwell's use of the word "unconsciously" in reference to his decision to paint only the ideal aspects of the world suggests that before he entered psychoanalysis with Erik H. Erikson in the 1950s, his underlying motivations for doing so were largely unknown to him, or, if known, went largely unexplored. Also, his observation that he had painted a world "in which there were no drunken slatterns or self-centered mothers" is an especially revealing choice of words, for although "drunken slatterns" is ostensibly a reference to women he had encountered on the streets of New York when he was a boy, while "self-centered mothers" is a reference to his experience of his own mother as he was growing up, both phrases also have relevance to his later years of married life, especially with his second wife Mary, who succumbed to alcoholism and displayed a deep neediness

16. Claridge, *Norman Rockwell*, 104–5.
17. Rockwell, *My Adventures as an Illustrator*, 46–47.

for her own sons, a neediness that the youngsters found it impossible to assuage or effectively counter.

Also, his observation that the people in his pictures "aren't mentally ill" is not only a veiled reference to his mother's neurasthenia but also to his first wife, Irene, who was a patient at McLean Sanitarium in Somerville, Massachusetts, and eventually drowned in her bathtub in 1934, a probable suicide[18] and to his second wife Mary, who was a residential patient at Austin Riggs Center in Stockbridge, Massachusetts, and at the Institute for Living in Hartford, Connecticut. The untimely death of his wife Mary occurred when he was dictating his autobiography.

As we review Rockwell's early relations with his mother, it is not especially difficult to identify the psychological roots of his *melancholy self*. Due to his mother's neurasthenia, she was emotionally detached from her sons. He himself refers to the "barrier" that existed between them. On the other hand, this comment refers to a later stage in his development, not to the years between ages three and five when the initial emotional separation is most likely to occur. Can we point to anything that might have exacerbated this emotional separation?

Although this is purely conjectural, I wonder if his mother was disappointed that her second child was a son instead of a daughter. In her account of his mother's decision, years later, to live near Rockwell and his family, Claridge observes that she "was looking forward to spending Christmas among her three young grandsons, 'even though,' as her niece remembers well, 'she preferred girls instead.'"[19] Although this preference for girls related to grandchildren, it may also reveal feelings about her sons as well, and especially the fact that Norman, her second and last child, was not a girl. The very fact that Rockwell struggled throughout his life with self-doubts as to whether he was a "real man," doubts exacerbated by his decision to become an artist, may reflect his awareness, largely unconscious, as a small boy, that he was a disappointment to his mother because he was not a girl. He may even have felt—unconsciously—that her disappointment in this regard may have been a contributing factor in her neurasthenia which, as we have seen, manifested itself in the absence of the usual maternal attentions that very young children receive from their mothers.

18. Claridge, *Norman Rockwell*, 253.
19. Ibid., 273.

HUSBAND OF A SELF-CENTERED WIFE

Rockwell married Irene O'Connor in 1916 when he was twenty-two and she was twenty-five years old. They had met when she took a room in the boardinghouse where he had been living in New York City. They were married in Potsdam, New York, at Blessed Sacrament Catholic Church, but in the priest's study and not the sanctuary because he was not a Roman Catholic. He later mentioned that her family kept trying to convert him, but that it didn't matter much because Irene hardly ever went to church herself. It was also evident that she had rather expensive tastes which Rockwell, a struggling illustrator, attempted to gratify. They settled in New Rochelle and began hobnobbing with its social elite.

Although early in their marriage rumors began to circulate about her flirtations, Claridge believes that she "behaved conventionally in public for at least the first five or six years."[20] However, she also notes that Irene advocated an "open marriage," and that Rockwell's son Peter (his third son by his second wife Mary) told her that his father had confessed to him that during his marriage to Irene he had had a brief affair with the young widow of a friend and fellow illustrator for the *Saturday Evening Post* who had died of kidney failure at the age of forty-seven.[21]

In 1922, Irene's father died, and because he had made no arrangements for the financial future of his wife and his three unmarried children, Rockwell soon "found himself supporting them all under his own roof."[22] He was both amused and repulsed by Irene's brother Hoddy, a decorated war hero who suffered from nightmares that caused him to fall out of bed at least once a night, hitting the floor with a loud thud that reverberated through all three floors. He also felt himself entitled to whatever Rockwell could provide. Rockwell's son Tom, his second son by Mary, told Claridge that his father also had to finance two abortions for Hoddy, and his tone of voice suggested that his father "thought the situation morally shaky."[23]

Within a couple years of sharing his home and wife with her mother, sister, and two brothers, Rockwell had had enough. But when he asked Irene to agree to their finding a place to live by themselves she responded, "And leave my family?"[24] So he decided to move out of his own home and

20. Ibid., 140.
21. Ibid., 194–95.
22. Ibid., 175.
23. Ibid., 185.
24. Ibid.

went to live in the Salmagundi Club in Manhattan, a temporary home for artists. Then, when he was hospitalized several weeks later, either he or Irene seized the opportunity for a reunion, and as soon as he agreed to her demands for an expensive new house, she kept her part of the deal by convincing her family to return to Potsdam.

The illness for which he was hospitalized was a severe case of tonsillitis. Noting that his tonsils had been removed when he was a little boy, Claridge suggests that "his use of the pseudo-illness probably substituted for a less seemly ailment."[25] The phrase "less seemly" appears to imply a sexually transmitted disease owing, perhaps, to their "open marriage." However, it seems more likely that he was resorting (unconsciously?) to his mother's method of dealing with her emotional conflicts through psychosomatic symptoms, hoping that Irene would respond with genuine sympathy, much as his father had responded to his mother's physiological complaints.

Perhaps because their reconciliation was essentially a negotiated settlement, it did not last. In 1929, Irene announced that she wanted a divorce because she had fallen in love with another man. Rockwell tried to talk her out of it but she was adamant and he finally agreed. Contributing to the humiliation of a highly publicized divorce was the fact that Irene had rendezvoused with the other man while Rockwell was touring Europe. She had declined to accompany him. Claridge notes that he "had to feel that his wife's new object of affection was everything that he was not," for "machismo, not drawing skills, was the key to Irene's heart." Moreover, his rival was a war hero who possessed enormous "masculine prowess," and was a "genuine he-man."[26]

25. Ibid.

26. Ibid., 212. Rockwell's pseudo-illness of tonsillitis may have had symbolic significance in that he was very much aware that Irene was attracted to men with machismo. In *Norman Rockwell: The Underside of Innocence*, Richard Halpern notes that among Rockwell's most embarrassing physical endowments, "the one he mentions most often and most self-consciously is his large Adam's apple, which makes repeated awkward appearances in the memoirs. The Adam's apple is by nature a troubled signifier of masculinity. Because women and eunuchs don't grow one, the presence of the Adam's apple points to the fact that its bearer enjoys a working set of masculine endowments below. And yet a prominent Adam's apple sprouts most often not on the thick necks of bruisers but rather on the pencil necks of thin, gawky men. Rockwell had no trouble reading it, along with his pale complexion, narrow shoulders, and jelly arms, as a sign of effeminacy. It marks him as a man, but unmanly. It specifies his gender, but also renders it inadequate, lacking somehow. The prominent Adam's apple is not so much a phallic symbol as phallic satire, its massiveness in mockingly inverse proportion to its owner's masculinity" (64–65). It is possible that when Rockwell had his tonsils removed, he made an association between

By the time Irene broke the news that she had fallen in love with another man, Rockwell, in Claridge's judgment, "was a solid product of the emotional template laid down throughout his childhood, especially by his mother," and now, "at this juncture of an adult crisis, his boyhood lessons guided his response." Observing his parents' marriage had prepared the way for his acceptance of Irene's self-centeredness: "If a wife chose not to accompany her husband on his first—or on any—trip abroad, in spite of his entreaties otherwise, that just seemed like the natural progression set in place by Nancy Rockwell, who was encouraged to think of herself before anyone else in the family." He had grown up "expecting no one but himself to satisfy his deepest emotional needs, which he finessed through his work."[27]

A WIFE BESET WITH INSECURITIES

Five days after their divorce was granted, ending a fourteen-year marriage, Irene remarried (January 23, 1930). Two months later (March 27, 1930) Rockwell became engaged to Mary Rhodes Barstow, whom he had met in California on a blind date only two weeks earlier. Raised in Alhambra, a suburb of Los Angeles, and fourteen years his junior, Mary taught mathematics in a grade school in nearby San Gabriel. They were married three weeks later (April 17, 1930).

Noting that Irene had also been a schoolteacher when Rockwell met her, Claridge suggests that Rockwell was undoubtedly "smitten with the outgoing, enthusiastic, and intelligent young schoolteacher he so quickly asked to become his wife." However, she adds that deeper psychological needs also played a role, for he "was also transparently relieved to meet someone to replace Irene, the first schoolteacher spouse meant to substitute for his mother and father."[28] Indeed, both his personal and his professional life reflected

> the complicated dynamics set into motion by Nancy's critical, self-centered—yet, at some level, loving—mothering, and Waring's distant, authoritarian, but well-intended fathering. Rockwell's pithy

---

his enlarged tonsils and his large Adam's apple, as the neck region would be implicated in both, so that when he was in danger of losing Irene to a more manly male, his psychosomatic symptoms of tonsillitis were a disguised acknowledgment of his effeminacy (as well as an unconscious identification with his mother and her resort to psychosomatic illnesses when she was unable to cope with life).

27. Claridge, *Norman Rockwell,* 213.

28. Ibid., 225.

self-pronouncements reveal much about his motivations. When, for instance, he said, as he did frequently, that one reason he became an illustrator instead of risking a life in "fine arts" was to please his parents, he told the truth. What he did not assess until much later, under the auspices of psychoanalyst Erik Erikson, were the ways he kept trying to compensate for the childhood he lacked, by positioning his wives to play out the roles for which his parents had only auditioned.[29]

The newly married couple occupied the same house in New Rochelle, New York, where he and Irene had lived before their divorce. His father died a year later (in August 1931), and their first child, Jarvis Waring, named for his brother and father, was born the following month. Claridge notes that Rockwell "joyfully took on the role of father" and "far more uncomfortably" agreed to underwrite, financially, his mother's move to Kane, Pennsylvania, to live with his older brother.[30] Two years later (March 1933) their second son, Thomas, was born.

The following year he was faced with having to find a place for his mother to live because she had worn out her welcome with his brother's wife. The initial arrangement was for her to live in a boardinghouse in Providence, Rhode Island, near her cousins, but she expressed the desire to be near one of her sons, which, under the circumstances, meant that Rockwell was the chosen one. So, with Mary's encouragement, she moved to New Rochelle. Mary believed that she could make her happy through "thoughtfulness," but he found her presence a distraction from his work, and in time, Mary's "enthusiasm, endless as it seemed, dissipated under the pressure of her mother-in-law's relentless requirement for 'thoughtfulness.'"[31] So she was sent back to Providence in 1936.

The year that Rockwell's mother came to New Rochelle (1934) was also the year that his first wife, Irene, died. She was found dead in her bathtub, a probable suicide. For the previous two years she had been a patient at McLean Sanitarium in Somerville, Massachusetts, but had been released to attend her mother's funeral. As the majority of McLean's patients were suffering with manic-depressive (now called bipolar) disorder, Claridge believes that this would have been her official diagnosis, especially in light of accounts

29. Ibid.
30. Ibid., 230.
31. Ibid., 231.

of her behavior by those who knew her well: "a personality that alternated between extreme melancholy and wild bursts of energy and activity."[32]

The effect of her death on Rockwell is impossible to determine because he avoided talking about her, going so far in later years as to feign to forget that he had ever been married to "that pretty girl who lived in my boardinghouse."[33] The fact that her death was probably a suicide was the kind of publicity that he would certainly have abhorred.

In 1936 Mary gave birth to their third son, Peter. Two years later, Rockwell's mother returned to New Rochelle. Meanwhile, Mary was becoming nervous about the attention other women showed her husband at social gatherings in New Rochelle and increasingly uncomfortable with the fact that they had continued to live in the house where he and Irene had lived. So they decided that it would be a good thing for them to move to New Arlington, Vermont, where they had earlier purchased a summer home. In time, it was winterized, and in 1943 they sold their home in New Rochelle. They settled Rockwell's mother in nearby Bennington, and Mary played the important role of protecting her husband from his mother's intrusions, her requests for better accommodations despite the fact that she was living in an expensive boardinghouse, and continual suggestions that she would be much happier if she could live in New Arlington instead.

Among their relatives and friends, no one seemed to remember when Mary began drinking too much. However, in early 1948 she was showing signs of mental fatigue. She was just forty years old. Her two oldest sons were spending most of their time away from home at a Quaker boarding school in Poughkeepsie, New York, and her youngest son was only six years away from entering college himself. Claridge notes that it was time for her to reestablish herself outside the roles of mother and wife, and she began taking in local writing classes. Claridge writes, "At this stage, Mary's sons sometimes wondered why their mother worried so much; but, looking back, Jarvis [their eldest son] recalls seeing her hunched next to a visiting teacher on their living room couch several years before, earnestly talking to the other woman about her own unfulfilled ambitions and fears of inadequacy."[34]

It would be all too easy, Claridge notes, to associate Mary's subsequent years of alcohol abuse and mental illness with her husband's career and growing emotional distance, to surmise that "the talented woman, forced

32. Ibid., 255.
33. Ibid., 256.
34. Ibid., 348.

to play second fiddle to her famous husband, languished in the wake of his fame." And, in fact, she did "dedicate herself to ensuring that her husband's work could always proceed unimpeded, from cooking the food he preferred to keeping the hours he worked best by to spending her days taking care of his professional and domestic needs."[35] Moreover, her role as his financial manager was certainly a cause of anxiety, especially when the IRS conducted audits of their taxes in 1942 and again in 1945. But Claridge questions this rather easy explanation by noting that Rockwell was not averse to hiring people to do the chores Mary performed instead:

> He had admired her brains and competence and social extraversion from their first meeting, and nothing suggests that he enjoyed her sacrificing any of them on his behalf. He just didn't want her needs to stand in the way of his career, and she knew no other way to meet such a requirement than through making herself indispensable to him. What is saddest about such a tale is the evidence suggesting that he found indispensable what was in fact easiest for her to give—emotional support, belief in his talent, and honesty in her criticism. The rest—the running of errands, the housekeeping, the answering of fan mail, the tending of his mother—all this he found easy to replace with professional help, when Mary finally had no more ability to provide it.[36]

By the fall of 1948 crying scenes had begun occurring within their youngest son's hearing. One evening, when his older brothers were away at boarding school, Peter sat on the top of the stairs and listened to his parents down below. His mother was sobbing and his father, obviously bewildered and upset, said, "Why don't you just stop drinking?" to which she replied, "Because I can't."[37] Records from a doctor in nearby Bennington indicate that she had been seeing a psychologist, and a neighbor, Joy Edgerton, later recalled that one day when she went to visit her, Mary was all excited about a book that she had been reading, *The Art of Loving,* by Erich Fromm. Mary urged Joy to read it, and she did. But when Joy returned the book and tried to discuss it with her, Mary "became distant, even defensive, and that was that."[38] Claridge suggests that her confusing reaction to Joy's desire to discuss the book was itself a manifestation of the problem—severe mood swings—that only worsened over time.

35. Ibid.
36. Ibid.
37. Ibid., 352.
38. Ibid., 353.

Joy Edgerton also recalled that during the dinner parties the Rock-wells hosted in the late 1940s, Mary would sneak next door to get a drink from the Edgertons' liquor cabinet to "settle her nerves." Also, Rockwell's mother had begun telling tales in Providence of how Mary would reach down to the space between the car seat and the door when she was driving her mother-in-law back to Rhode Island, and swig quickly from a flask.[39]

However, on her own initiative Mary began driving to Stockbridge to receive psychiatric treatment from Robert Knight, the director of Austen Riggs Center. She would usually schedule her appointments in order to be home before Peter returned from school, but a few times she arranged to take him from school so that he could join her on the drive to Stockbridge for her appointment. Then they would drive to Poughkeepsie to see her two oldest sons and return to New Arlington later in the day. On some occasions, she felt too nervous to drive to Stockbridge, and her neighbor Clara Edgerton would take her there. The fact that a few of the trips included a visit to her sons suggests that she was mourning their absence, and it seems likely that her difficulties stemmed more from her loss of their everyday presence than from her husband's tendency to work long hours in his studio located a hundred yards or so from the house.

As winter approached, Rockwell had lost patience with Mary's drinking, and he left for one of his regular winter retreats to California, telling her that she could follow with Peter when she had her drinking under control. To Peter, this was tantamount to desertion. Years later, he mentioned to Claridge in an interview that he was only twelve years old at the time, noted that his father "left me alone with a mother who was falling apart," and added, "It doesn't seem to me to have been a very responsible thing to do."[40] The affront would seem to have been all the greater for the fact that Mary was from California, and that he would be staying near her own family.

On their way back from the train station where they had seen her husband off, Mary suggested to Peter that they go to a movie, something the family rarely did. Then, when they returned home, she invited him to sleep with her in his parents' bed to ward off their mutual loneliness and because she was afraid of the noises outside. Peter later observed that this "wasn't exactly the wisest thing to do, for a mother to put her pubescent son in bed with her," and although he has "no memories of anything untoward,"

39. Ibid., 353.
40. Ibid., 352–53.

it nonetheless "makes me cringe. She was just so lonely, and I guess it made her feel less abandoned."[41]

A month or so later, Mary and Peter were on the train to join his father, and Peter recalls the occasion when he returned to their compartment and found porters and attendants swarming around his mother. He wasn't sure what had happened, but suspected that she had collapsed after having gotten drunk for the first time in a month or so. When they arrived in Los Angeles, neither told Rockwell what had happened on the train, but Mary began seeing a psychiatrist in Los Angeles, and, according to various family reports, this did more harm than good. Her sister Nancy told Claridge that the psychiatrist advised Mary that she needed the space to become "self-actualized" instead of living her life as a mere extension of her husband. But Nancy felt that Mary's problems were rooted in their mother's treatment of her when she was a young girl, and that everyone in the family "wanted her to blame my mother."[42]

Claridge suggests that Rockwell's comments to his sons and friends, as well as his extant correspondence, indicate that he "was interested most of all in what could be done to help his wife, not in why she was troubled." He agreed that his absorption in his work was detrimental to his family, but "he also continued to believe that Mary could get well if she figured out what would make her happy."[43] With this in mind, he arranged for his oldest son Jarvis to come to California and enroll at Hollywood High, and he began to encourage Jarvis's interest in becoming an artist himself.

When the family returned to Vermont a few months later, he decided to create a summer artists' colony as an inducement for Jarvis to stay at home where he could be a comfort to his mother. He asked the Art Students League to send him several of their best students, one of whom, Don Winslow, decided he would like to stay after the others had gone. He continued to live for several more years in the abandoned schoolhouse that Rockwell had secured for the students. The two had formed a special bond, one that surprised the other students, because Winslow exhibited signs of manic-depressive illness (or bipolar disorder). But Rockwell tried to help him with his mood swings by giving him "pep talks, telling him to pick himself up, get moving."[44] In turn, his young protégé helped ease his studio demands.

41. Ibid., 355.
42. Ibid., 356.
43. Ibid., 357.
44. Ibid., 375.

However, Mary tried to get Winslow to leave because she "disliked the way the young man's kinetic presence cut into the spousal intimacy she gained from being indispensable to her husband's work," and deprived of this role, "she wasn't sure what she was supposed to do with her life." Before long, she became a voluntary resident at Austen Riggs. As for Winslow, Rockwell "tried hard to help him deal with his mood swings, which sadly, before the decade was over, would lead to suicide."[45]

When Mary moved to Austen Riggs, she decided, for reasons that were unclear to her sons, that she would only allow Peter, the youngest, to visit her. She also suggested to Rockwell that they should get a divorce. In response, he wrote her a plaintive letter, assuring her of his complete love and devotion, acknowledging that he is "extremely difficult at times due to my absorption in my work," but expressing his conviction that even as they "have come a long way," he was certain that they would "as a team go further and higher."[46] One hears echoes in this response of his father's efforts to mollify his wife with expressions of "gentle sympathy and concern,"[47] and evidently the letter had its intended effect, for Mary did not bring up the issue of divorce again.

In August 1952 Rockwell wrote to the director, Robert Knight, inquiring about beginning therapy himself. Because Mary and their son Thomas were already seeing him, Knight was uneasy about treating yet another family member, so when he met with Rockwell he recommended that he begin therapy with Erik H. Erikson, who had recently moved to Stockbridge from the University of California in Berkeley to join the staff at Austen Riggs. He was deemed by Knight to be ideally suited to be Rockwell's therapist because he himself had attempted to become an artist in his late teens and early twenties. Mary returned to New Arlington and became involved in a writing workshop.

By the end of 1953, the Rockwells decided to leave New Arlington and relocate in Stockbridge. This move had the advantage of eliminating the frequent trips that Mary was taking to Stockbridge for therapy, and Rockwell himself wanted to increase his own treatments with Erikson. He also justified the move on the grounds that he had used up all the New Arlington model pool, having employed two hundred town residents over the past decade, but Claridge suspects that the move was also prompted by

45. Ibid.
46. Ibid., 376.
47. Ibid., 36–37.

the fact that many New Arlington residents were aware that the Rockwells were having their problems.

Jarvis Rockwell recalls how impressed his father had been at the time by Shirley Jackson's short story, "The Lottery," published in 1948 in *The New Yorker*. The story was about a small New England town's yearly ritual of drawing lots to see who would be the sacrificial victim stoned to death by the villagers. The publication of the story provoked such outrage that hundreds of readers had cancelled their subscriptions; but Claridge notes that "when the citizens are shown passively accepting the evil annual sacrifice of an innocent townsperson, readers are forced to reevaluate what lies beneath the tranquil surfaces of their communities."[48] Rockwell's interest in the story at this time may have reflected his feeling that he had become the town's sacrificial victim, and may also have prompted him to reevaluate "this created world of mine," with its pleasant sadness and humorous problems, and begin to give much greater attention to "the agonizing crises and tangles of life."[49]

However, Mary's condition did not improve with the change of scene. Although she produced abstract canvases from art classes at Austen Riggs, she continued to have severe bouts of depression, and would walk for hours around Stockbridge trying to shake the depression and suicidal urges. During the summer Rockwell worked on the *Saturday Evening Post* cover for September 25, 1954, titled *Breaking Home Ties,* which depicted a dressed-up, college-bound young man sitting on the running board of an old truck and waiting eagerly for the train, his farmer father hunched over beside him, and a collie resting its head on the boy's knee.[50]

Years later Rockwell acknowledged that the dispersal of his own family and his own relocation at the time had inspired this painting, and he noted that the disconsolate dog symbolized what the father was unable to say. As Claridge notes, he

> was struggling with the exits his sons were making, and the scary challenge of starting life anew, in Stockbridge, with only Mary. His willingness to move for her treatment was a sign of his own developing awareness that he played no small part in her troubles, and he did not flinch, whatever image the American people maintained of him as patriarch of the perfect and happy family they all desired,

48. Ibid., 388.

49. Rockwell, *My Adventures as an Illustrator*, 46–47.

50. I discuss this painting in *Striking Out*, 140–43.

from aggressively seeking help for her and for himself. But his own life was unfolding in ways that were far afield from any of the ideal pictures he had created for himself of what happiness looked like.[51]

In a handwritten letter, Erikson asked Knight to do what he could to support his own efforts to persuade Rockwell to take a vacation to Europe with Tom's fiancée's parents by encouraging Mary to forego the trip herself. He was certain that Mary was not up to the trip herself but was also aware that she had been insisting to her husband that she was well enough to make it. He added that his own patient was very depressed and was entertaining suicidal ideas because he believed that his wife "would probably never be well enough to live with as a reasonable person, nor sick enough to reside in an institution," and that he was also struggling, as she was, "with the same adjustment to missing his children."[52] For whatever reason, Rockwell's trip to Europe did not take place. Instead, he remained home, and the summer of 1954 he worked not only on *Breaking Home Ties* but also on *The Art Critic*, using Mary and his son Jarvis as his models.[53]

Two years later, in a decision suggesting that Mary may have tried to kill herself, the staff at Austen Riggs acknowledged that she was too ill for them to treat and recommended her admission to the Institute for Living in Hartford, Connecticut, for electroconvulsive therapy. She began treatments that extended over six months, during which she was able to attend their son Tom's wedding. Rockwell continued to invest himself in his work, prompting Claridge to suggest that he "was trying to do everything he could devise to help his wife, short of what might have made the most difference: turning away from his work and devoting himself to her." On the other hand, when Rockwell was on a month-long publicity trip, Erikson wrote him a letter intended to reassure him that Mary was doing well, adding that he had learned that Rockwell had phoned her regularly from overseas, and that she appreciated it "ever so much."[54]

At this time Rockwell's oldest son, Jarvis, was in San Francisco at Erikson's suggestion. As he explained to Claridge years later, "I was trying to define myself, and my father wasn't sure I should go on with art at this point, and Erikson encouraged me to, and told me to move to some place

51. Claridge, *Norman Rockwell*, 400.

52. Ibid., 403.

53. See Capps, "Erik H. Erikson, Norman Rockwell, and the Therapeutic Functions of a Questionable Painting."

54. Ibid., 412–13.

interesting and far away from my family like San Francisco." He added, "It was great advice." Because he was floundering, Jarvis was also in therapy, for which Rockwell paid the bills without complaint. He also wrote his son's therapist seeking advice as to ways he might help his son and expressing concern that his parenting had led to his son's problems, but "in one touching response from Dr. Wheeler, the artist is assured that he was a good father."[55]

Meanwhile Mary returned home to Stockbridge, and when she proposed that they move to a bigger house—one that did not look out onto a cemetery, a landscape too morbid for her to tolerate—they bought another house in Stockbridge Village. In February 1958 their son Peter was married, and Mary was in far better condition than she had been for a long time. Erikson attended the wedding. But although Mary and her husband had been keeping weekly appointments at Austen Riggs, it was clear by late summer that Mary's condition had worsened, and in the fall she needed more shock treatments. Rockwell drove her to Hartford for her weekly treatments, which continued for a year.

At this time, he reduced his work commitments and set to work on his autobiography. His oral dictations into a recorder were transcribed by his son Tom, who made stylistic changes. It was evident from the beginning that he had little interest in interpreting the anecdotes he recounted, and Tom and Mary had to convince him to mention his first marriage. As Michele Bogart notes, the "myth of comforting superficiality was sustained by Rockwell in the autobiography," and she specifically cites his "throwaway comments" about his depressions that "were followed not by introspection about their causes or significances, but by evasive statements about not knowing why they occurred."[56]

Since Rockwell had been in analysis for several years, we might imagine that Erikson would have hoped for greater evidence of his patient's introspective capacities. However, we should keep in mind that Rockwell called his autobiography *My Adventures as an Illustrator*, a title that not only emphasizes his professional role but also reflects his seeming acceptance of the fact that he was destined to occupy a different niche from that

---

55. Ibid, 416. Claridge identifies Jarvis's psychotherapist as a "Dr. Wheeler." I believe, however, that he was in fact Allen Wheelis, a close friend of Erikson's who had been on the Austen Riggs staff prior to moving to the San Francisco Bay Area. As Wheelis, like Erikson, was focusing on identity issues, it would have made sense for Erikson to refer Jarvis, who was "trying to define myself," to Wheelis. See Wheelis, *The Quest for Identity*.

56. Bogart, *Artists, Advertising, and the Borders of Art*, 76. Quoted in Claridge, *Norman Rockwell*, 422.

of other influential American painters. The dust jacket emphasizes that his work has "adorned over three hundred covers of the *Saturday Evening Post*" and that his "exacting technique and unfailing humor have endeared him to the hearts of millions." Had he written a deeply introspective autobiography he might well have jeopardized his reputation as "America's most beloved painter."[57]

Meanwhile, he was working on a painting titled *The Family Tree*, which portrays the generations of Americans from the beginning to the present, and his dictations indicate that "his absorption in the project is so complete that it sounds as if this is the first important painting he has ever done, not a late, and relatively minor, commission." In addition to consulting art historical sources and "knowledgeable friends," he drills Erikson, "who pops in every now and then during languid summer afternoons, all to see if each of the heads that he is painting to represent a generation of Americans interbreeding makes sense." Recalling that he had finally decided not to begin the family tree with a Puritan but with a "seafaring dog" of a pirate with a smile on his face and a "voluptuous gal beside him," he added that his "dear friend Erikson thinks that if I show ribald people I show myself to be healthier. So this is partly due to him."[58]

His dictations for the autobiography indicate that by August he was feeling much better about the painting. In addition, Jarvis had returned home for a brief visit, and "in spite of the awkward emotional distance between father and son, Rockwell felt good that they got along 'pretty well,'" noting that he had taken an afternoon off to mountain climb "in an effort to 'bond,' as he half laughingly, somewhat ironically recorded into the machine one night."[59] Also, his son Peter, a sculptor, and his wife Cinny had come to visit, and Cinny was helping Rockwell on a mural he was doing for *Berkshire Life.*

On August 25, 1959, he and Mary started the day as usual, having coffee together, a new ritual that, to Jarvis, was an indication that his parents "seemed to be enjoying being together, more bonded than before."[60] That afternoon when Rockwell went into the house to ask her something, he had to go upstairs to wake her, and she didn't respond. He ran outside the house

57. Rockwell, *My Adventures as an Illustrator*, dust jacket; Marling, *Norman Rockwell, 1894–1978*, subtitle.
58. Claridge, *Norman Rockwell*, 423–24.
59. Ibid., 425.
60. Ibid., 426.

and frantically called out to Cinny that something was wrong with Mary. When Cinny entered the bedroom, she knew immediately that Mary was dead. She fetched Peter, who was working in a rented workspace nearby, and called the doctor.

The family's initial assumption was that she had committed suicide, but there was no evidence to support this conclusion—no note, no missing pills, and no change in her behavior from preceding days. Claridge theorizes that the long-term abuse of alcohol and potent psychopharmaceutical drugs, in conjunction with electric shock treatments, probably triggered heart failure.[61]

Rockwell took her death exceedingly hard. Those who interacted with him said that he "walked around for the next year like a marked man." His son Jarvis took photos of him at this time and recollected later that "the results were so emotionally dark, even when his father was laughing, that it scared him."[62] But he continued his weekly therapy at Austen Riggs, and Tom recalled later "that Erikson at one point became worried enough about the possibility of suicide that he took away a gun Rockwell had in the studio," adding that his father "had never asked for it back."[63]

AN UNMARRIED SCHOOL TEACHER

After a few more months had passed, Rockwell accepted more projects than he could complete in order to stave off loneliness. Also, he began dating a woman, an urban artist and divorced mother of two children, who lived in Stockbridge and Manhattan. Claridge notes, however, that "he must have suspected they could not live together very successfully," and various friends, including Erikson, "suggested that Rockwell should meet another teacher they thought he might really like."[64] This teacher was Molly Punderson, a sixty-three-year-old unmarried woman who had grown up in Stockbridge and taught for thirty-eight years at Milton Academy, a boarding school near Boston. She had recently retired and returned to Stockbridge, and was in the process of figuring out how to spend the rest of her life. The two of them had in common the fact that their mothers had been

61. Ibid., 427.
62. Ibid.
63. Ibid., 429.
64. Ibid., 433.

semi-invalids, and, in Molly's case, she, the only daughter, "thought little of her mother as a result."[65]

Rockwell signed up for an adult poetry course that Molly was teaching during the evenings in the nearby Lenox Public Library. Pretending that he preferred the poetry of Edgar Guest to that of far greater poets, he was apparently a "naughty boy" at these sessions, not hiding his amusement at the class's "overly serious discussions" of Yeats and Eliot.[66] They were married in St. Paul's Episcopal Church in October 1961 and according to Claridge, their marriage was "extremely successful," thus supporting the old adage that "the third time proved the lucky charm."[67] They traveled extensively together, and when they were home, Molly protected his privacy so that he could maintain his productivity despite signs of aging and eventually ill health. He died on November 8, 1978 and Molly died six years later.

ON THE OUTSIDE LOOKING IN

I concluded *Men, Religion, and Melancholia* with the observation that the *melancholy self* "lives in the shadows of life, wistfully gazing through the lonely windows into the brightly lit room where mother and son frolic and sing in careless abandon, their hearts bursting with everlasting love."[68] Rockwell's *Shuffleton's Barbershop* is a painting that especially evokes this sense of wistfully gazing through the lonely windows. As Claridge notes, it was painted "during the first few months of 1950," which were "among some of the most trying personal times Rockwell had faced since the humiliation dealt him by his first schoolteacher wife." She adds that "many consider this painting his masterpiece," and suggests that its powerful impact lies in "the details that overwhelm in exactly the right way, in their potency." Also, "the final moment in which Rockwell compulsively adds the overkill to most of his paintings, pushing the portrait into caricature partly to avoid being judged as a serious artist, never occurred in this painting."[69]

65. Ibid.
66. Ibid., 435.
67. Ibid., 440.
68. Capps, *Men, Religion, and Melancholia*, 214.
69. Claridge, *Norman Rockwell*, 368.

Norman Rockwell's *Shuffleton's Barbershop*. Photo credit: Courtesy of the
Berkshire Museum, Pittsfield, Massachusetts.

Claridge draws particular attention to the detail of "the small black
cat that sits quietly near the front of the outer-room, observing the elderly
men in the distance as they practice their instruments after closing time,"
and suggests that it "controls the viewer's experience perfectly, refusing any
tendency for the onlooker to feel superior as the outsider who sees without
being seen." This painting is especially reflective of Rockwell's appreciation for what he called Vermeer's eye "for meticulously rendered, palpable
surface detail," which appealed to him as a similar painter of "practical
temperament."[70]

70. Ibid., 368. Quoted in Taylor, 1971.

Richard Halpern notes that this painting is something of an anomaly in Rockwell's work because his art is, in general, a highly narrative one: "It usually tells a story, or a joke," and although Rockwell exhibits pride in his technique, he believes that the success or failure of a given cover depends on the quality of the idea that animates it." But in the case of *Shuffleton's Barbershop*, "the pressure of the idea seems to recede," taking second place "to pleasure in representing light and space for its own sake." In Halpern's view, "Rockwell's technique has liberated itself from the merely anecdotal and revels in the nuances of visual texture and chromatic harmony. The image is, in a word, *beautiful*." This achievement "is made possible, in part, by the fact that its human figures are tucked away in a back room—central but miniaturized," and "the image is dominated instead by the empty barbershop, heated by a potbellied stove but uninhabited by anything but a black cat. By pushing people into the background, Rockwell allows the poetry of things to emerge, and the effect is luminous."[71]

Halpern's observations that the painting reflects Rockwell's *liberated* technique and that the resulting image is truly *beautiful* suggest that this painting has special meaning for Rockwell himself, a meaning that, as we will see, reaches back to his relationship with the lost love object.

Like Claridge, Halpern takes particular note of the fact that the painting draws attention to the viewer:

> The trompe l'oeil window does an especially good job of locating the viewer in space, and in so doing makes us aware of our own looking. We are standing on the sidewalk outside of Shuffleton's barbershop in East Arlington, Vermont, peering through its windows and past the empty shop into a room that we are able to observe only because its door has been left open. The occupants of that room are unaware of our gaze, but were they to notice it, and us, we would surely feel some embarrassment. Seeing and not seeing, exposure and the threat of it, are, as often in Rockwell, central to the experience of this image.[72]

Halpern adds that typically in Rockwell's work, the viewer peers at some sexual indiscretion or notices someone who is at work. But this is not the case with this particular painting. The men are engaged in a leisure activity after work. Thus, the painting harmonizes commerce (the front

71. Halpern, *Norman Rockwell*, 135–37.
72. Ibid., 137–38.

room) and art (the musical ensemble in the back room), an issue with which Rockwell was concerned throughout his life.

But more noteworthy is Halpern's suggestion that, like Rockwell's *Girl at the Mirror* this painting portrays "the same combination of nostalgia and wistful recognition of loss" and exemplifies "a certain melancholia," although in the case of *Shuffleton's Barbershop,* "the melancholy is largely self-directed on Rockwell's part." Halpern suggests that the locus of melancholy is in Rockwell's awareness that his "project of imitating the classic Dutch painters is thoroughly anachronistic."[73] I believe, however, there is something more deeply personal in the melancholy tone of the painting, deriving, in part, from the fact that it was painted at an especially trying personal time in Rockwell's life. Claridge's allusion to the humiliation he suffered from his first wife together with the fact that it was at this time that "Mary was beginning to reach out to friends in the community to regain her mental stability" recalls his resentment of the fact that when he was just embarking on his career as an illustrator, the family had to leave its familiar surroundings in Mamaroneck in Long Island and move to New York City to accommodate his "self-indulgent" mother, thus reawakening his early childhood experience of his mother's emotional unavailability to him due to her own illness.

His son Jarvis also made a significant point when he was commenting on the painting in his conversation with Claridge. She writes: "His art historian son explains that his father loved finding new challenges, and now he had taken on the problem of putting a small group of men playing musical instruments in an illumined inner cubicle at the back of a large darkened room, all seen through a plate-glass window."[74] If male companionship is one of the ways in which boys begin to compensate for the emotional separation from their mothers in early childhood, the painting suggests that the viewer, who is on the outside looking in, is probably aware of the fact that he will not become a member of the musical group that has gathered together in the back room. We do not assume that he brought along his instrument or even that he knows how to play one.

73. Ibid., 146–47. Marling notes that *Girl at the Mirror,* "one of Rockwell's most penetrating psychological studies . . . captures a moment of self-doubt on the part of a girl becoming a woman. Will she be as pretty as the movie star—Jane Russell—whose picture she holds? Her doll has been cast aside in favor of face powder, lipstick, and a comb. These are private doubts, but the mirror allows us to share them." *Norman Rockwell 1894–1978,* 75.

74. Claridge, *Norman Rockwell,* 368.

However, as Claridge suggests, the viewer identifies with the black cat. The fact that this identification precludes any possibility of the viewer assuming a superior attitude—as seeing without being seen—is not, however, the issue. For it is more likely, and more congruent with the painting's combination of nostalgia and wistful recognition of loss, that there is something in the viewer that would welcome being seen and invited in. After all, the men are in an interior space that appears cozy and inviting. There is nothing overtly maternal about this space, but it may well evoke memories of home, perhaps of entering the front door and seeing mother in the back room preparing the evening meal. And the fact that that the men are practicing their instruments may also evoke memories of when the viewer's mother sang to him or they even sang together in unison.

Finally, though, if Rockwell's *Shuffleton's Barbershop* reflects his admiration for Vermeer's interiors, it is noteworthy that the majority of Vermeer's interiors portray women and girls. The viewer senses that these are their customary surroundings. They are seated at a table, playing the virginal (a small harpsichord), or standing reading a letter near an open window. Occasionally, men are also present, but, for the most part, they give the appearance of being intruders in this space. This is especially apparent in Vermeer's *Soldier and Young Girl Smiling*.

She is sitting comfortably at the table, her hands resting on it, and she is smiling. He, on the other hand, is sitting upright, with his arm bent at the elbow, and his hand, with fingers bent, is pressed against his upper thigh. He is wearing a black hat that seems incongruously large. As Edward Snow says of the way that Vermeer has positioned him in the forefront of the painting, "The woman and the space she occupies appear to recede from the soldier, while he in turn becomes a dark, looming presence, alien and ominous in his place opposite her."[75]

Snow makes a similar observation regarding the man in Vermeer's *Couple Standing at the Virginal*. As he stands at her side, he seems "isolated in his desire, gazing with feelings he keeps secret at a woman whom he assumes to be his object" while she looks at him in the mirror that is placed above the virginal. Her viewing of him through the mirror suggests a detachment that can be read in many ways—"desiring, trying to draw the man's attention, observing him wistfully, furtively, or with cool detachment, perhaps even wishing to redeem him from his predicament."[76]

75. Snow, *A Study of Vermeer*, 82.
76. Ibid., 115.

Johannes (Jan) Vermeer's *Soldier and Young Girl Smiling,* The Frick Collection, New York. Photo credit: The Frick Collection.

Given the evident awkwardness of the men in these two paintings, it is significant that the solitary men in Vermeer's *The Geographer* and *The Astronomer,* both of whom appear to be occupying the same room that Vermeer used for his *Soldier and Young Girl Smiling,* do not exhibit the same awkwardness. The geographer is standing with a drawing compass in his right hand and is peering at a map on the table in front of him. The astronomer is seated at a desk and gazing at the portion of the globe that his right hand has marked out for him.

Snow draws a contrast between these two men and Vermeer's *Woman Holding a Balance.* He notes that the men "reach out through consciousness in an attempt to map, to encompass the limits of their world, to grasp the realm beyond as thought or image or microcosm; yet in doing so they instinctively tighten their grip on the material dimension that supports their speculations." In contrast, the woman "locates more intuitively (both in her measuring and by virtue of her presence) the center, the balance point, and, suspending it, gently touches down."[77] Nevertheless, the men are at home in the interior space they occupy because they are alone and engaging in work that employs and tests their competence. Rockwell, who spent long hours in his studio, would have understood these two men.

Vermeer's *Christ in the House of Martha and Mary* is rather exceptional in this regard because Jesus appears to be fully at ease in an interior space also occupied by women.

Johannes (Jan) Vermeer's *Christ in the House of Martha and Mary*, The Scottish National Gallery. Photo credit: The National Galleries of Scotland.

Martha, who is placing a basket of bread on a table with a white cloth, stands slightly above him while he is seated in a large comfortable chair to her left. Mary is sitting on a small overstuffed chair in front of him and

77. Ibid., 163.

looking up at him as he speaks to Martha. His whole demeanor is relaxed—his hands are open, his gown is loose fitting—and he and Martha meet one another's gaze. The fact that he is drawing a contrast between Martha being "anxious and troubled about many things" and Mary, who has "chosen the one thing needful" (Luke 10:38–42), is evident in the fact that the forefinger of his right hand points toward Mary as his face is turned toward Martha. But there is no awkwardness in his demeanor and he appears to be speaking to Martha in a manner that is calm and without any suggestion that he is scolding her. Like the woman holding the balance, he locates the center and gently touches down. He is on the inside looking out for the others.

I can imagine Rockwell deriving some comfort from this painting. He could not save the women in his life, but perhaps he, like Vermeer, can see that they are in good hands. But what about the man who stands on the sidewalk outside Shuffleton's Barbershop? And what of the little boy who lives inside of him in the form of a *melancholy self*? Does he stand at the window on the off-chance that one of the men will see him and go to the door and invite him in? More likely, he will move on, much as a museum visitor does after having lingered before a painting. But where will he go? To where he resides or somewhere else?

PART 2

The Maternal World

chapter six

Gifford's *Kauterskill Clove*:
The Mother Outdoors

IN THE PRECEDING CHAPTER, we left the viewer standing on the sidewalk in front of Shuffleton's barbershop peering into the window and observing a small group of men in the back room preparing to play music together. The darkened room in the interval is symbolic of his distance from the men. We imagined that if one of the men happened to look out and see him standing there, and had taken it upon himself to get up, go to the door, and invite him in, he would have welcomed this overture and entered the barbershop, and have found a chair for himself so that he might at least listen to them and perhaps join in their conversation.

A more likely scenario, however, would be that he would soon turn away and continue his walk. But to where? Back to where he resides? Or some other gathering place, a local tavern, perhaps, which he is free to enter and sit down and order a drink and perhaps find others with whom to talk about the events of the day? Or maybe he just keeps walking, out beyond the town limits and into the adjoining field. The latter course will be the focus of the following two chapters. But the fact that he may be considering these various scenarios in his mind before choosing one or the other reflects the ambivalent feelings that are integral to the *melancholy self.*

By focusing in this and the following chapter on the genre of the landscape, we will be able to explore the longing of the *melancholy self* for a place where he can be "at home" in the world—the longing that Freud ascribes to "homesick" men in his essay on "The 'Uncanny.'" In this chapter, I will give particular attention to Sanford R. Gifford's *Kauterskill Clove*. In the following chapter, I will focus on George Inness's *Sunrise*. To set the stage for our consideration of Gifford's painting, a brief discussion of the genre of still life paintings will be useful, for the still life underscores the point that the male is an awkward presence in the domestic space. Thus, still life represents the predicament of the *melancholy self*—its sense of exile from the maternal environment—which landscape art addresses and, hopefully, overcomes by creating a sense of being at home in the world to which the *melancholy self* has been consigned.

THE GENDER IMPLICATIONS OF STILL LIFE

In *Looking at the Overlooked: Four Essays on Still Life Painting*, Norman Bryson notes that in the case of still life "no theoretical body of work exists at a level of sophistication comparable to that found in contemporary discussions of history painting or landscape; it is to the higher genres, regarded as more intrinsically interesting, that modern art gravitates."[1] He asks: Why this ambivalent response to still life? He believes that it has something to do with gender and, more specifically, with the cultural construction of gender, for the still life has acquired an association with the female gender and, for that very reason, is considered to be less significant as a genre than history painting or landscape.

This, he believes, is an ideological issue. For although "the basic routines of self-maintenance" (cooking and eating, shopping, seeing to domestic chores, and keeping our creatural habitat in good repair) are objectively necessary for our welfare and respond to inescapable conditions of human life, the *value* that is placed on the life of creaturely routine is very much a matter of culture and of history: "Whether these activities are respected or dismissed, valued or despised, depends on the work of ideology."[2] He points out that the need to devalue the life of creaturely routine arises from the threat it poses for those who would regard another level of culture as affording access to superior or exalted modes of experience. As still life is centrally concerned with these routines, it, too, is subject to denigration.

But why would an art form that is concerned with such creaturely routines pose a threat? One possible reason, he suggests, is that the *forms* represented in still life are virtually indestructible. While bowls, vases, and dinner plates reflect the cultural values of their creators and manufacturers, their forms change very little over long periods of time because they serve

1. Bryson, *Looking at the Overlooked*, 136.
2. Ibid., 137.

purposes that do not vary. Thus, while their names seem demeaned—jug, jar, bowl, and pitcher—the very forms of still life have enormous *force*:

> As human time flows around the forms, smoothing them and tending them through countless acts of attention across countless centuries, time secretes a priceless product: familiarity. It creates an abiding world where the subject of culture is naturally at ease and at home . . . The forms of still life are strong enough to make the difference between brutal existence and human life: without them there is no continuity of generations, no human legacy, only an intermittent and flickering chaos; with them, there is cultural memory and family; an authentically civilized world . . . While complicated tools and technologies are subject to rapid change, simple utensils obey a slow, almost geological rhythm.[3]

Thus, what the still life threatens are the ideological assumptions that ascribe high cultural significance to historical events and low cultural significance to the routines of self- and household maintenance:

> This is not simply a formal choice between genres, but a genuine crisis in which painting is forced to contemplate two utterly different conceptions of human life: one that describes what is important in existence as the unique event, the drama of great individuals, the disruptions of creaturely repetition that precipitate as narrative; and one which protests that the drama of greatness is an epiphenomenon, a movement only on the surface of earthly life, whose greater mass is made up of things entirely unexceptional and creatural, born of need on a poor planet.[4]

This opposition, however, does not exist in a vacuum: "*It is over-determined by another polarity, that of gender.*"[5] With the exception of Christian monks, the "delegates" of still life are far more likely to be women than men, and in the case of seventeenth-century Dutch still life, "the interior of the house is regarded as intrinsically female space," for "it is women rather than men whose job it is to guard the moral and physical purity of households."[6]

Furthermore, when men occupy the inner space (as in the case of the soldier in Vermeer's *Soldier and Young Girl Smiling*), they seem awkward and ill at ease; and when men's cherished objects (helmets, swords, pistols,

3. Ibid., 138–39.
4. Ibid., 154.
5. Ibid., 157 (italics original).
6. Ibid., 157–58.

pipes truinpets, and coins) are depicted in a still life, they seem out of place, invasive, intrusive, as though the "man of the house" is bent on asserting a power which in this setting is not rightfully his. Thus, "when still life of the table sounds the theme of disorder, asymmetry of the sexes is an important factor in the emotional nuancing of the scene," for "in this littering of the table with masculine paraphernalia, there is signaled the male's inability or refusal to harmonize with the domestic space."[7]

Bryson also notes the tendency of the male artist to paint still life as an outside observer. For example, still-life paintings by Jean-Baptiste-Simeon Chardin reflect the desire "to enter the feminine space of domesticity gently and invisibly . . . to capitulate, to make himself and his canvas *porous* to the female space."[8] Yet even he "encounters an obstacle which is without equivalent in the other genres, and which must be negotiated. The asymmetry of the sexes with regard to domestic life constantly works to place the male painter of still life in a position of exteriority to the subject. Inevitably, still life's particular mode of vision bears the traces of this exclusion." The male painter of still life is highly focused, almost glaringly so, "as if the world of the table and domestic space must be patrolled by an eye whose vigilance misses nothing."[9]

Bryson suggests that the result of this patrolling eye "is often the production of the uncanny: although everything looks familiar, the scene conveys a certain estrangement and alienation."[10] To explain this phenomenon of estrangement, he cites Freud's essay "The 'Uncanny,'" quoting the passage where Freud, citing his melancholic patients, associates the uncanny with the female genital organs, the place, once familiar, that has become defamiliarized ("unhomelike").[11] Noting that Freud's remarks on the uncanny are "highly suggestive," Bryson discusses the separation from mother that every child needs to experience. He writes:

> In order to develop the individual identity the child of either sex must eventually leave the cocoon of warmth and fusion that is its mother's body. For within that earliest and deepest relation to another being, the subject cannot yet exist as subject: the boundaries defining self and other have not yet been drawn, and the infant

7. Ibid., 160.
8. Ibid., 167 (italics original).
9. Ibid., 169–70.
10. Ibid., 170.
11. Freud, "The 'Uncanny,'" 152–53.

remains an amorphous, undifferentiated bundle of sensations, bodily movements, and libidinal drives. This reign of fusion and commingling is destined not to last; both sexes lose the mother as site of imaginary plenitude.[12]

But "the manner in which the mother is lost differs in either case":

> The girl is enjoined to separate from the mother along the path of identification by modeling her being and her sexuality on the imago which the mother provides. She must pass from fusion to separation to imitation, in a triple movement of extraordinary complexity and difficulty. The boy is enjoined to refuse identification with the mother; the realm of the mother represents what he must give up, and if identification with the mother nonetheless occurs and persists, it is at the cost of running counter to the codes of masculinity that order him to internalize the imago of the father . . . Far more insistently than the girl, the boy must draw a line of separation between himself and the domain of maternal nourishment and warmth. In this later perspective, the persistence of his desire to remain within the maternal orbit represents a menace to the very center of his being, a possibility of engulfment and immersion that threatens his entire development and viability as a subject.[13]

He must escape, and "he can do so by no other means than by claiming as his another kind of space, away from that cocoon and its fascinations; a space that is definitely and assuredly *outside*, behind a protective barrier, a space where the process of identification with the masculine can begin and can succeed." Thus, "Still life bears all the marks of this double-edged exclusion and nostalgia, this irresolvable ambivalence which gives to feminine space a power of attraction intense enough to motor the entire development of still life as a genre, yet at the same time apprehends feminine space as alien, as a space which also menaces the masculine subject to the core of his identity as male."[14]

In this portrayal of the uncanny, Bryson notes the boy's desire to escape from the "maternal orbit," but the very sense that he needs to escape has been promoted by adults, including the mother. As Bryson puts it, "the boy is *enjoined* to refuse identification with the mother,"[15] and the reason for this refusal is essentially that his desire to remain within the maternal

12. Bryson, *Looking at the Overlooked*, 172.

13. Ibid., 172.

14. Ibid., 172–73.

15. Ibid., 172 (italics added)

orbit is a threat to his identity as male. This makes the male still life painter a radical of sorts, for he is the most willing of painters to place his male identity at risk.

Thus, still life represents one option for the *melancholy self*, which is to resist its exclusion from the interior environment and to make itself as "at home" there as it possibly can. I do not wish to question, much less denigrate, this option or the strategies that the *melancholy self* uses to achieve it. On the other hand, I think there is much to be said for the option of seeking in the external world—"a space that is definitively and assuredly *outside*"—what one has lost in the internal world, and this, in part at least, is what the landscape artist is attempting to realize.

In focusing in this chapter and the next on landscape painters, I am implicitly agreeing with Bryson that there is a large ideological gulf between still life and historical painting, but questioning whether this is true with regard to still life and landscape painting. As we will see, landscape shares with still life a protest against the conception of life represented by historical painting, that what is important in existence is "the unique event, the drama of great individuals, the disruptions of creaturely repetition that precipitate as narrative."[16] It, too, represents the unexceptional and creatural, as represented in birds and animals doing what they have always done, and humans engaged in routine acts of walking, mowing, fishing, and so forth. One could say that the subject of the landscape is the "still life" of the external world and that, in contrast to the history painter, the male landscape artist is no less willing than the still life painter to place his "male identity" as risk. He has simply chosen to do this in his adoptive world out of doors.

SANFORD ROBINSON GIFFORD: AMERICAN LANDSCAPE ARTIST

Sanford Robinson Gifford (1823–1880) is commonly referred to as belonging to the second-generation Hudson River School.[17] He was born in Greenfield, Saratoga County, New York, the fourth of eleven children of Elihu and Eliza Gifford. When he was an infant, his family moved to Hudson, New York, which is located on the eastern side of the Hudson River,

16. Ibid., 154.

17. The following sketch of Gifford's life is based on two sources: "Sanford Robinson Gifford" (http://wikipedia.org/wiki/Sanford_Robinson_Gifford); and "Sanford Robinson Gifford (1823–1880)" (http://www.questroyalfineart.com/artist/sanford-robinson-gifford).

south of Albany. The only painter among his contemporaries to be born and grow up in the heart of the Hudson River Valley, he had a special affinity for the mountains, valleys, and rivers of the region. His father operated iron foundries and a bank. The fact that Gifford came from a reasonably wealthy family allowed him the freedom to pursue his artistic endeavors unhindered by commercial incentives and trends.

He attended the Hudson Academy from 1830 to 1842 then went to Brown University in Providence, Rhode Island, for two years. In 1845 he moved to New York City to study art. He trained to become a portrait and figure painter by studying drawing, perspective, and anatomy, and also studied the human figure in anatomy classes at the Crosby Street Medical College. He developed solid skills at figure drawing, but during a sketching trip in 1846 to the Catskills and the Berkshires he decided that his future lay in landscape painting. He later explained the profound significance of this trip to a friend: "Having once enjoyed the absolute freedom of the landscape artist's life, I was unable to return to portrait painting. From this time my direction in art was determined." After this decisive trip, he returned every summer for the next nine years to experience the freedom of the Catskills and the White, Shawangunk, and Adirondack Mountains.

Gifford exhibited his first landscape at the National Academy of Art in 1847 and submitted work almost annually thereafter. He was elected an associate of the Academy in 1851 and a full Academician in 1854. Thus, he was well established as an artist in his mid-twenties. From the summer of 1855 to the summer of 1857 he traveled in Europe. In 1856 he rented a studio in Rome where he painted his largest, and one of his most famous works, *Lake Nemi*. This work, with its depiction of radiant sunlight and hazy atmosphere, marked the beginning phase of his mature style as an artist. He returned to America at the end of the summer in 1857 and rented a studio in New York City which he retained for the next twenty-three years, working in it in the fall, winter, and spring. He spent most of his summers traveling along the Delaware, Chenango, Susquehanna, Chemung, and Hudson Rivers.

He served in the National Guard during the Civil War and while stationed near Frederick, Maryland, where his regiment was positioned to protect the nation's capital, he painted a series of wartime scenes. Between his two stints in the National Guard he returned to his boyhood home in the Catskill region and in 1862 he painted *Kauterskill Clove*. His reputation grew rapidly during this period, but his professional success during these years was marred by personal tragedy. His brother Charles committed suicide in 1861 and his brother Edward was killed in the Civil War in 1863.

In the late 1860s Gifford traveled extensively, in Europe, the Middle East, and the Western United States; and in the 1870s he continued to travel around the northeastern region of America and into Canada. He married an old school friend, Mary Cecilia Canfield, in 1877, and three years later he contracted a respiratory ailment on a fishing trip at Lake Superior and died shortly thereafter in New York City at the age of fifty-six. He was buried in the Gifford family plot in Hudson, New York.

As we turn our attention to Gifford's *Kauterskill Clove*, we should keep in mind that it was painted between two stints in the National Guard during the Civil War. As noted, he continued painting during his military deployment. His painting *The Camp of the Seventh Regiment, near Frederick, Maryland, in July 1863* depicts the ordinariness of camp life in the foreground (men are shown writing letters, cooking, eating while standing, hanging wash, sleeping, talking, and cleaning muskets) and in the background is a host of Union infantry and wagon trains winding their way southward into the mountains. However, as Kevin J. Avery and Franklin Kelly point out in their book on Gifford's landscapes, above this depiction of the camp the "viewer witnesses the spreading of the sun's providential light over the landscape and its Union occupants, and, in the background, the registering of its glinting reflections on the host of Union infantry and wagon trains winding their way southward into the mountains."[18] The painting, in other words, is quietly, cautiously hopeful.

However, there were also the personal tragedies during this period in his life. The death of his brother Charles occurred the year before he painted *Kauterskill Clove*. The reasons for his suicide are not indicated in any of the available sources, but there can be little doubt that Gifford's emotional response to his brother's death would have involved the whole range of melancholy feelings that a death by suicide is likely to evoke. Also, there is a sense in which the very act of suicide exemplifies both the overt self-reproach of the *melancholy self* ("I do not deserve to live") and the desire to triumph over the lost object, the one who was principally responsible for the fact that he is, in fact, a resident of this world. We can well imagine that as one of the surviving sons, Gifford felt especially sad for his mother, and that these feelings also informed his work on *Kauterskill Clove*. When his brother Edward was killed the following year, we may imagine that the painting itself

18. Avery and Kelly, *Hudson River School Visions*, 160.

was a source of comfort to himself and to other family members, perhaps especially his mother, who lost two of her sons within a single year.

It is also noteworthy that Gifford married quite late in life, and that he married an old childhood friend. The fact that he had remained unmarried all these years is significant, for it suggests that unlike other males who, early in life, seek in a relationship with another woman what they sense they have lost in their emotional separation from their mothers in early childhood, Gifford was not inclined to take this avenue. Instead, his art became his life, and it is significant that he decided against becoming a portrait artist, a career that would have afforded the opportunity to express his melancholy feelings in portraits of women, as was the case, for example, of Thomas Eakins.[19] On the other hand, it is no less significant that when he married, it was to an old childhood friend, a woman associated with the times and experiences of his early boyhood in Hudson, New York.

In her study of American landscape artists, Angela Miller cites Worthington Whittredge's comment, in his address at the memorial in Gifford's honor at the Metropolitan Museum of Art shortly after his death, that Gifford was born in the Catskill Mountains and he "loved them as he loved his mother, and he could not long stay away from either."[20] This comment establishes an emotional link between his mother and the subject of his art, and invites us to explore how his art enabled him to make creative use of his *melancholy self*.

THE FEMININE ATMOSPHERE OF KAUTERSKILL CLOVE

Angela Miller concludes her study of nineteenth-century American landscape art with a chapter titled "Domesticating the Sublime: The Feminized Landscape of Light, Space, and Air."[21] In it, she contends that American landscape painting underwent a profound change during the midfifties to midseventies, for unlike their predecessors, notably Frederic Edwin Church, who were preoccupied with America's historic sense of mission, landscape painters like Sanford Robinson Gifford and John Frederick Kensatt were not concerned to create a narrative in which nature is undergoing domestication through cultivation. Rather, they sought to produce

19. Johns, *Thomas Eakins*, 167–68.
20. Miller, *The Empire of the Eye*, 285.
21. Ibid., 243–88.

landscapes "that answered the frequent critical call for breadth of treatment *guided by a unifying emotion.*"[22]

Church and his contemporaries had represented the landscape as having three dimensions: up front, a narrow space not yet domesticated (e.g., with wild trees and shrubs, a solitary hiker, a small group of natives); in the much wider middle section, signs of peaceful cultivation of the environment (e.g., homes, schools, churches, small factories, roads, plowed land); and, in the distance, hills or mountains that appeared to be presiding over the activity before them—"presiding" being the appropriate word, as the mountain peaks in northern New York State and New England were named for American presidents and thus had a distinctly patriarchal presence. These landscapes told a story, one about the peaceful settlement and cultivation of the land. The viewer's eye was directed toward the middle ground of the painting, the locus of human activity and enterprise.

However, Gifford, Kensatt, and their contemporaries did not divide space into three discrete aspects. Rather, as Miller notes, "resonant, light-suffused atmosphere melded topographic divisions into a visually seamless whole," and "space appeared as an undifferentiated continuum, a vessel or container, encouraging a sustained absorption in the image in place of an active movement through it."[23]

Miller refers to this emergent expression of landscape artistry as "atmospheric luminism." She cites, for example, Kensatt's *View on the Hudson*, which inverts the earlier compositional emphasis on natural mass and shape: "Light fuses the elements of the landscape, breaking down the spatial syntax of foreground, middle ground, and distance. *View on the Hudson* optically insists on instantaneous apprehension of the image as a whole, picking out random details here and there but in no particular sequence."[24] This alternative spatial mode "characteristically eliminated the foreground, the physical stage for the visual survey of the landscape, as well as the metaphoric stage for human activity. Without this spatial anteroom, the precise boundary between viewer and image was vitiated."[25]

22. Ibid., 243 (italics added).

23. Ibid., 243.

24. Ibid., 244.

25. Ibid.

Sanford R. Gifford, *Kauterskill Clove*, The Metropolitan Museum of Art collection. Photo credit: Art Resource, New York.

Also, in contrast to the landscapes of Thomas Cole, which "dramatized confrontation with the landscape and the vicarious feeling of danger," the aesthetic of atmospheric luminism was grounded "in an identification with nature rather than an insistence on one's physical separateness from it—a separateness confirmed by the organism's revulsion to danger. Instead of temporalizing space through planar divisions, atmospheric luminism spatialized time. In doing so it freed landscape art from its loyalties to a narrative or literary meaning."[26] This meant that the landscape of atmospheric luminism was difficult to survey and mentally organize, a difficulty due, in part, to the fact that its "appearance marked not only a stylistic and aesthetic shift but also a basic transformation in the ideological content of landscape art."[27] For example, Kensatt's landscapes only glancingly portray the world of labor, of tourism and transportation, of land divisions and ownership: "Given no particular order of importance, human actors, like motes in the light, drift imperceptibly into the frame and beyond it, leaving little or no trail. The quasi-military quality of visual command, the landscape as seen, ordered, and ultimately possessed by human vision, gives way here to a dreamlike absorption that confuses the boundaries between the viewing subject and the objects of sight."[28]

What has happened here? What accounts for this dramatic change in the aesthetics of landscape art? In Miller's view, the landscapes of the 1860s and early 1870s reflect a fundamental cultural change:

> The shift from the strenuous masculine associations of the romantic mountain sublime to an interest in space as a container of colored air marks a fundamental change in cultural preferences. The sublime as a category of experience did not disappear, but it was reformulated and extended. This redefinition emphasized subtle passages of feeling and mood associated with secondary attributes such as finely graded color rather than with the primary attributes of form. It coincided with, and was a part of, the appearance of a new language that couched social and moral formation in natural analogies, *framing both in the language of gender*. The new emphasis on feminine agency, signaled by the growing potency of sentimental language, had important repercussions for imaging both nature and society.[29]

In earlier landscapes, nature evoked "the fear of imminent annihilation" through the depiction of earthquakes, lightning and hurricanes, volcanoes and avalanches. The new landscapes reflected the view that too much visible motion in nature was in poor taste, like speaking too loudly in public. Thus, "The sublime now found its highest meaning in nature's generative potential. No longer threatening annihilation, nature appealed

26. Ibid.
27. Ibid., 244–45.
28. Ibid., 245.
29. Ibid., 248 (italics added).

through a deeper identification with the expansive soul of life itself. Nature's most profound meaning was to be found not in moments of destructive, elemental violence but in its invisible power."[30]

Noting that "the new sublime" was "as far removed from the old as the force of gravity from the thunder of the heavens," Miller cites an art critic at the time who suggested that the new interest in atmosphere was grounded in "a revelation of Nature's repose, of her permanent moods rather than . . . her fitful phenomenal display."[31] Another critic wrote of the beauty of nature's imperceptible internal adjustments: "Infinitely complicated though they [nature's forces] are, yet such is the precision of their movement that no jarring is felt, and no noise is heard, throughout the vast systems of infinite space."[32]

Miller concludes that the perception of and discourse involving natural agencies was clearly gendered and that this gendering was reflected in landscape painting:

> The transformation from catastrophic theories of earth change to gradualist uniformitarian models bears the discursive imprint of feminine process and indwelling agencies . . . Critics, writers, and artists wrote about the properties of light and air in both nature and art in specifically feminine terms. These same terms were also applied to women and their effect on society. New interests in landscape painting coincided with emerging definitions of women's social agency. Each development challenged or qualified the grounds of cultural authority and assumptions by revisualizing nature—and society—as a self-generating feminized space.[33]

An example of how nature was feminized in landscape paintings was the technique of "veiling" space by requiring the viewer to see nature "through layers of palpable and subtly radiant air . . . Such atmospheric veils not only softened contours but also moderated the sudden influx of

30. Ibid., 249–50.

31. Ibid., 251. Fourteen years after Gifford's death, Annie Payson Call advised her readers in her book *Power through Repose* to imitate "the work and quiet economy, the lack of strain and false purpose, in fine old Nature herself." In other words, she advocated the imitation of "Nature's repose," of "her permanent moods rather than . . . her fitful phenomenal display," 165. In his 1896 lecture to the graduating class of Boston Normal School of Gymnastics titled "The Gospel of Relaxation," William James said that Call's book should be in the hands of every teacher and student in America, 835.

32. Miller, *The Empire of the Eye*.

33. Ibid., 256.

sensation that had accompanied the experience of the sublime."[34] These atmospheric effects "not only domesticated the sublime; they threatened to displace it as a carrier of masculine will and to substitute a very different order of knowledge and causality symbolized by silent feminine influence rather than noisy manifestations of power."[35] Women, like the objects of nature in landscape paintings, were defined by their atmospheric veils: "Like air and space softening the rugged forms of nature, women were the medium or transparent screen that vitiated the harsh outlines of social life. The realization of this ideal social role, however, rested on the presumed selflessness of women, and on their renunciation of all 'narrowly' self-serving claims to autonomous identity or personal fulfillment."[36]

This new feminized aesthetic was also reflected in the artists' focus on more accessible landscape elements than the distant mountains. The vale became a favorite subject of landscape artists. For Miller, Sanford Gifford's *Kauterskill Clove* is an especially fine example of this shift in focus from mountains to vales. She writes:

> Instead of building the composition around the standard mountain-centered iconography of nature which had dominated earlier views of the Catskills, Gifford substituted a great light-filled spatial chamber in the center. Only Haines Falls in the remote distance resembles in any way a conventionally picturesque motif, yet this is so softened by veils of atmosphere that it is reduced to a glimmer of reflective light in the very center of the painting. What occupies the place normally reserved for a central motif is the radiating, impalpable glow of the sun whose light and heat hollow out a great well at the center of the composition with a force that seems to push the physical forms of the landscape to the margins of the painting.[37]

Miller adds that topographical elements lose their distinctive outlines in the opalescent haze which, in her view, is the real subject of the work: "Yet far from being empty, this womblike space seems fully animate, its generative force touched into life by the warmth and light of the sun." Moreover, the "well of space at the center appears to expand with unconscious creation."[38]

34. Ibid., 257.
35. Ibid., 259.
36. Ibid., 264.
37. Ibid., 281.
38. Ibid.

To be sure, *Kauterskill Clove* "never entirely renounces the discrete, anthropomorphized forms of the spatiotemporal mode, as is evident in the detailed foreground on the left." On the other hand,

> Only when one passes beyond this area are the true space-defining implications of light fully explored. The spectator seems nestled in the recesses of the earth, overwhelmed by nature's silent authority. The almost invisible figure of a hunter and his dog, who scramble up the foreground ledge, their vision blocked and their presence obscured by shadow, further suggests the incidental quality of the human presence. *Kauterskill Clove* places the viewer directly in front of the source of light. The effect is epiphantic. Access to knowledge is not through transformative labor, willful activity, or acquisitive vision, but through a direct identification with the source of power in nature.[39]

Miller suggests that perhaps Gifford's "boldest gesture" was "to substitute a cavity in place of a mountain," and cites in this connection the observation of a contemporary of Gifford's that the artist has "so bathed this vast unrelieved depression in the face of nature with broad yellow sunshine, and interpreted its giant distances by such curiously skillful gradations of distinctness in its forest lining from ridge to base, that one begins to admire a gorge as he does a mountain—in fact, *as the largest kind of mountain turned inside out.*"[40] If so, Gifford's *Kauterskill Clove*, "a womblike gorge filled with life-giving light, is the landscape equivalent of the feminine principle, nurturing through self-negation rather than summoning spiritual aspiration through sublime example." This womblike gorge, which appears as "a mountain turned inside out," is an inversion of "the traditional iconography of mountains as masculine-centered symbols of religious exaltation, patriarchal authority, and the crushing might of nature." Yet, in another sense, it is also "an image of feminine introversion, of nature as a form of inner space associated with the inception of life itself."[41] As for the viewer, Miller suggests that he experiences himself as "drawn in by a powerful force from within the painting." Thus, *Kauterskill Clove* "implies a new interdependence in which nature is not only activated by but in turn appears to activate consciousness," for the "resonant chamber is brought into focus, as it were, by the absorbed gaze of the male landscape painter."[42]

39. Ibid., 281.
40. Ibid., 281–82 (italics original).
41. Ibid., 284.
42. Ibid., 285.

Miller also notes that Gifford's *Kauterskill Clove* is deeply and profoundly communal. To be sure, it "neglects the heroic public meanings attached to older landscape views," but "it *is* communal in another sense, referring as it does to the common source of all life in the generative womb of nature, and the source from which the artist drew his creativity." She adds that the association of Gifford's paintings with the maternal source of life itself was pointed out by his own contemporaries. As indicated earlier, Worthington Whittredge noted that Gifford was born in the Catskill Mountains and that "he loved them as he loved his mother, and he would not long stay away from either."[43]

It is also noteworthy that his most intense engagement with the clove occurred just before, and between, his first two tours of duty with the National Guard during the Civil War. Several months before he painted *Kauterskill Clove* he wrote from Baltimore, where he was stationed, to friends who had described their recent trips into the Catskills. He said that their accounts "somehow made me think I have a right to be there, but when under the hallucination I go to the gate of the Fort and am rudely roused from my dreams by the sentry sharply bringing his musket to 'arms port!' and an abrupt 'Halt!'—'Your pass!' . . . I find myself obliged to right-about, and limit my walk to the round of the parapet, or mingle again with the busy-idle crowd in the quarters."[44] His suggestion that he experienced a sort of hallucinatory sense that he had every right to be there is perhaps reminiscent of the infant's sense that his mother's absence is an injustice, a feeling that may well evoke a hallucinatory perception of her actual presence. In fact, this anticipatory mental picture of her could well be the original source of the artistic imagination.

On the other hand, Miller's observation that Gifford's Catskill gorge "was not simply a spatial absence, for he imbued it with a different kind of presence," a "presence that leads "beyond communal memories to a more occult kind of presence,"[45] suggests that the painting represents the

43. Ibid., 285.

44. Avery and Kelly, *Hudson River School Visions*, 133.

45. Miller, *The Empire of the Eye*, 285. Erik H. Erikson suggests in his chapter "Seeing Is Hoping," in *Toys and Reasons*, that in the interplay with the *primal person*, which occurs in infancy, we develop two forms of vision, "the capacity to see what is before us, here and now, and the power to foresee what, if one can only believe it, might yet prove to be true in the future." He adds that the auditory sense especially assists in the latter "because it permits one to hear what is not in the visual field, and thus reinforces the hope that the voice heard will come 'around the corner' and be confirmed as the familiar

displacement of emotions associated with one's mother onto nature itself. The appellation "Mother Nature" may be something of a cliché, yet it expresses a profound truth, that nature is life-bearing, life-giving, and life-sustaining. However, in the final analysis, Miller believes that although the vision of the viewer seems to be met and drawn in by a powerful force from within the painting, there is also a sense in which something is missing—incomplete—with regard to the viewer's "subjective identification with the landscape." This is because the viewer remains outside the chamber: "Vision and space, the male observer-subject and the feminine object, remain discrete," and "in this sense, while the new atmospheric mode in midcentury landscape expressed belief in feminine agency, in the end it reconfirmed the objectification of feminine influence as a therapeutic resource."[46] That is to say, she is not a "subject" in her own right, but rather a "selfless" presence, one who has renounced "all 'narrowly' self-serving claims to autonomous identity or personal fulfillment."[47]

This very suggestion that "feminine influence" is objectified as "a therapeutic resource" also implies that the male painter and viewer is not in perfect emotional health; and this, in turn, invites us to consider the likelihood that the painting is a reflection of their *melancholy selves*. Miller's description of the gorge as "womblike" and her suggestion that this "womb-like space" is "far from being empty," that it "seems fully animate, its generative force touched into life by the warmth and light of the sun," recalls Freud's allusion to "womb-phantasies" in his essay on "The 'Uncanny,'" and his observation that it "often happens that male patients declare there is something uncanny about the female genital organs," and that this "*unheimlich* place, however, is the entrance to the former *heim* [home] of all human beings, to the place where everyone dwelt once upon a time and in the beginning."[48] Thus, for the male artist and viewer, the clove or gorge—especially as represented in Gifford's painting—is a beautiful expression of their sense of loss and longing.

As Avery and Kelly note, the painting that is commonly identified as *Kauterskill Clove* is more accurately titled *A Gorge in the Mountains*. This was its original title. The alternative title was a result of a confusion of this painting with two smaller sketches of the same scene that were the basis for

face" (46–47).

46. Miller, *The Empire of the Eye*, 286.

47. Ibid., 264.

48. Freud, "The 'Uncanny,'" 157, 152–53.

another painting titled *Kauterskill Clove, in the Catskills*.[49] This very confusion seems relevant to the *melancholy self*, for the word *clove* suggests a very benign setting, and invites associations with the phrase "in clover," which connotes a life of ease and luxury, as cattle in good pasture. In contrast, the word *gorge* suggests a deep, narrow pass between steep heights, and also has associations with the gluttonous or voracious ingestion of food, with a feeling of disgust. It is also the name traditionally given to the entrance from the rear into a bastion or projecting section of a fortification.[50] The fact that the word *gorge* may apply to the back entrance of a bastion as well as to a feature of the landscape seems especially significant for the artist himself because, as noted above, Gifford's paintings of the scene occurred between stints in the National Guard. In this sense, the very painting of the clove/gorge would have been therapeutic. As for the male viewer of the painting, there is a very real sense in which the two words express the *heimlich/unheimlich* ambivalences of the *melancholy self*. And this, in turn, raises the question, does this viewer see a clove, a gorge, or do the two views alternate in his mind's eye?

I would suggest that the alternation captures the full emotional resonances of the *melancholy self*. On the one hand, the scene before the male viewer is bathed in warmth and light and he can easily feel that he—the beloved infant baby—is the very recipient of a truly pleasurable bathing. On the other hand, it is difficult not to identify with the barely visible hunter and his dog who, as Miller points out, are scrambling up the foreground ledge, "their vision blocked and their presence obscured by shadow."[51]

Because it evokes feelings of security and well-being on the one hand, and threat and obscured vision on the other, the painting enables the male viewer to get in touch, so to speak, with the whole range of melancholic emotions associated with the mother and her generative force and silent authority. Thus, the painting is potentially therapeutic precisely because it is able to evoke the full range of feelings that are associated with the *melancholy self* and yet he is not engulfed either by them or by the feminine influence that evokes them. Nor, for that matter, does the painting—as would a patriarchal painting of a distant mountain—demand a heroically moral response. In effect, it turns such expectations inside out and allows him to be the man he is, not the man that he is expected to aspire—to

49. Avery and Kelly, *Hudson River School Visions*, 132.
50. Agnes, *Webster's New World*, 278, 612.
51. Miller, *The Empire of the Eye*, 281.

rise—to be. It is informed, we might say, by a *sense of hope* rather than the *sense of honor*. In this regard, the painting does its own therapeutic work, and therefore, not incidentally, releases the woman who lives outside of the painting—whoever this woman may be—from the obligation to assume the role of "therapeutic resource."

THE ETERNAL RHYTHMS OF NATURE

Miller concludes her chapter on the domestication of the sublime on a rather somber note. On the one hand, she points out:

> Landscape artists, magically materializing the most subtle proper-
> ties of light and air, evolved a new aesthetic language which ad-
> dressed the anxieties associated with the post-heroic generation,
> combining the best of masculine and feminine elements. Imbued
> with the new feminine properties of space and light, nature was
> transformed into an expansive and inexhaustible realm—precisely
> what this later generation of landscape painters wished to believe
> about a nature that appeared increasingly fragile and finite. The
> art of Kensatt and Gifford pays tribute to the feminine mystique
> of space, revealing a yearning to fuse male subject and feminized
> landscape object rather than pitting them against each other.[52]

On the other hand, there was the "deeply tragic import of Americans' will to inscribe nature with their own personal or national ambition" that was "embodied in Melville's Ahab, maniacally struggling to dominate a natural world of unfathomable, elusive meanings." It was against this "imperial quest for an expanded self acted out upon a passive nature" that the landscape painters of the later generation were implicitly reacting. Miller concludes: "The aesthetic brings us back inevitably to the social, for atmospheric luminism employed the displaced language of nature to explore a cultural yearning for immersion, for refuge, a resistance to the pull of history and to the demands of progress. Yet in the end this aesthetic attempt to revalorize nature, to posit a purely unconscious mechanism of reform, foundered on the hard rock of national conflict, one more failed effort to give nature an authoritative voice in the formation of cultural identity."[53]

Thus, from a cultural point of view, this generation of landscape artists was unsuccessful. And yet, they contributed to a new understanding

52. Ibid., 288.
53. Ibid.

of the individual in his or her relationship with the world, and, for many, this new understanding was life-changing. As we have seen, Miller locates this new understanding in discourses concerning the sublime in which the "imperceptible and sustained operations of natural law now carried a far more profound significance than the momentary if dramatic interruptions in the rhythms of nature."[54] As noted above, she cites the observation by a writer in the April 1861 issue of *The Crayon* that the newer interest among landscape painters in atmosphere is grounded in "a revelation of nature's repose, of her permanent moods rather than . . . her fitful phenomenal display." The writer went on to suggest that such scenes offered consolation and refuge from "the abortive tests of politics and commerce."[55] The association between childbirth and nature's generative acts is implicit in the use of the word "abortive" in reference to the tests of politics and commerce.

Miller also cites an editorial in the November 1848 issue of *The Bulletin of the American Art-Union*, which lauded the "sweet lessons breathed in all the works of Nature, when we are taught to understand and love them by the pictured canvas," and in a characteristic call for men and women to adjust their lives to the eternal rhythms of nature, the editorial continued, "Thousands have been taught lessons of beauty, of gentleness, of hope, of effort, and of endurance, by like silent but certain monitors." Thus, as Miller points out, landscape art and its appreciation "furnished a form of social instruction."[56] And prominent among the lessons the pictured canvas has taught us to understand and to love is *the sense of hope* that is among the religious sensibilities of the *melancholy self*.

54. Ibid., 250–51.
55. Ibid., 251.
56. Ibid., 253.

chapter seven

Inness's *Sunrise*:
The Anonymous Figure

WE SAW IN THE preceding chapter that Sanford Gifford, who was representative of the second generation of American landscape painters, sought to represent the feminine quality of the natural world. But we also saw that in the case of *Kauterskill Clove*, subjective identification with the landscape remains incomplete because we—as viewers—remain outside the scene. As Angela Miller notes, "Vision and space, the male observer-subject and the feminine object, remain discrete," She adds that although the new atmospheric mode in landscapes expressed belief in feminine agency, "it reconfirmed the objectification of feminine influence as a therapeutic resource."[1]

Given the focus of this study on the *melancholy self* of boys and men, my concern has more to do with the fact that the "feminine object," especially in its maternal guise, remains beyond the reach of the male viewer. The very use of the analogy of the veil is a reflection of the distance between them. To be sure, as Norman Bryson notes, the persistence of the male child's desire "to remain within the maternal orbit represents a menace to the very center of his being, a possibility of engulfment and immersion that threatens his entire development and viability as a subject."[2] On the other hand, as we saw in the preceding chapter, the very representation of the natural world as maternal represents a displacement of emotions associated with one's own mother to the natural world. In this sense, the very

1. Miller, *The Empire of the Eye*, 286.
2. Bryson, *Looking at the Overlooked*, 172.

accessibility of the maternal through engagement with the natural world would actually support the man's development and viability as a subject.

In this chapter, therefore, I will focus on George Inness's landscape paintings, giving particular attention to his pictorial device of "the anonymous figure." As Adrienne Baxter Bell, who coined the term, points out in her study of Inness, the anonymous figure in Inness's landscapes accentuates the implied presence of the artist and the viewer in the world that is the object of their vision.[3] She identifies his use of this pictorial device in various paintings, but I have chosen to focus especially on his *Sunrise* because this painting is one whose atmosphere conveys a deep sense of maternal presence. Also, in light of the fact that Bell sees profound connections between Inness's art and the writings of William James, I will conclude this chapter with James's own reflections on the natural world as a deeply sympathetic one.

GEORGE INNESS: AMERICAN LANDSCAPE ARTIST

The landscape artist George Inness (1825–1894) was born in Newburgh, New York, a few miles from where Sanford Gifford grew up, just two years after Gifford was born.[4] However, his family moved to Newark, New Jersey, when he was about five years old. He was the fifth of thirteen children born to John William Inness, a farmer and grocer, and his wife, Clarissa Baldwin. His father wanted him to become a grocer, but he wanted to be an artist.

When he was fourteen years old, he studied for several months with an itinerant painter, John Jesse Barker, and at the age of sixteen he served a two-year apprenticeship as an engraver with the New York mapmaking firm of Sherman and Smith. He received some instruction in painting from Regis Gignoux in 1843. At this time he was studying and being influenced by the paintings of seventeenth-century Dutch landscape artists. He was also attending classes at the National Academy of Design in New York City, studying the work of Hudson River School artists Thomas Cole and Asher Durand. He opened his first studio at the time, and by the late 1840s he was exhibiting his work regularly in New York.

3. Bell, *George Inness and the Visionary Landscape*, 118.

4. Sources for this sketch of Inness's life are ibid.; "George Inness" online: http://en.wikipedia.org/wiki/George_Innesss; and "George Inness (1826–94)" online: http://archive.com/artchive/I/nness.html.

In 1849 Inness married Delia Miller, who died a few months later. The following year he married Elizabeth Abigail Hart, with whom he had six children. In 1851 a patron, Ogden Haggerty, sponsored his first trip to Europe to paint and study. He and Elizabeth spent fifteen months in Italy, and on their way home, they stopped in Paris, where he visited an exhibition that included the work of Theodore Rousseau, an artist working in the Barbizon school. Barbizon landscapes were noted for their loose brushwork, dark palettes, and emphasis on mood. During a second trip abroad in 1853–1854, he embraced the Barbizon style and quickly became the leading American exponent of this style, which, however, he developed into a highly personal style of his own.

In the mid-1850s he was commissioned by the Delaware, Lackawanna and Western Railroad to create paintings that documented the railroad's growth, and his paintings of this period integrated technology and wilderness within the observed landscape. In time, he shunned the industrial presence in American landscapes and focused on bucolic or agrarian subjects, but he produced much of his mature work in the studio, drawing on his visual memory to recall scenes that were often inspired by specific places, yet concerned with formal considerations.

He and his family left New York in 1860, moving first to Medford, Massachusetts, and later to an estate near Perth Amboy, New Jersey. Around this time a fellow artist introduced him to the theories of the Swedish mystic Emmanuel Swedenborg, and these made a lasting impression on him. Throughout the 1860s, spent in rural settings, he sought to make his paintings convey the profound spiritual meaning he felt the landscape around him possessed. In an interview published in *Harper's New Monthly Magazine* in 1878, he said that "the true use of art is, first, to cultivate the artist's own spiritual nature." He also felt that spiritual and emotional considerations go hand in hand with scientific ones (Swedenborg was also a scientist with specializations in mathematics, geometry, chemistry, and metallurgy), and his scientific approach to painting was reflected in an empirical study of color and a mathematical structural approach to composition. As he put it, "the poetic quality is not obtained by eschewing any truths of fact or of Nature."

In the late 1870s Inness bought a house and a studio in Montclair, New Jersey, and shortly thereafter a major exhibition of his work secured his reputation as a leading figure in American landscape painting, a position he enjoyed for the rest of his career. During the last years of his life, he spent summers traveling and painting in Connecticut, New York, Massachusetts,

Virginia, California, and Florida. In 1894 he and his wife returned to Europe, and on the way home they stopped in Scotland and spent a few days in the Bridge of Allan, a small Scottish resort village. George Inness Jr., his son, who also became a landscape painter of note, reported that when his father was viewing the sunset there on August 23, 1894, he raised his hands into the air and exclaimed, "My God! Oh how beautiful!" Then he fell to the ground, having suffered a stroke, and died a few minutes later.

THE ANONYMOUS FIGURE IN INNESS'S LANDSCAPE PAINTINGS

In her study of Inness's work, Adrienne Baxter Bell emphasizes the influence of Emmanuel Swedenborg's views on Inness's understanding of the world of nature and his engagement with the natural world in his work. But she also makes a number of associations between Inness's painting style and William James's writings. For example, she notes that "in his late landscape paintings Inness used brushstrokes in ways that resonate deeply with William James's innovative description of consciousness as a 'stream of thought' or 'stream of subjective life.'"[5] She also observes that the world-views of these two men—Swedenborg and James—are profoundly compatible because James's father, the philosopher Henry James Sr., had written numerous books and articles on Swedenborg, and his son grew up in a home environment in which Swedenborg's ideas were not only regarded as legitimate and worthy of extended scholarly investigation, but were also capable "of providing a new and inspiring worldview based on the central role of the spiritual in nature."[6]

Bell indicates that it is unknown whether Inness read James's pre-1894 articles on consciousness or his landmark textbook, *The Principles of Psychology*, originally published in 1890. But we do know that James and Inness met on at least one occasion. In June 1863 James joined Inness on a sketching trip to Mount Desert in Maine. It is also possible that Inness came into contact with the James family in the mid-1850s through Samuel Gray Ward, a mutual friend of George Inness and Henry James Sr.

It is also noteworthy that William James had originally intended to become an artist. When he was fifteen years old and the James family was

5. Bell, *George Inness and the Visionary Landscape*, 53; James, *The Principles of Psychology* 1:224–90.

6. Bell, *George Inness and the Visionary Landscape*, 63.

living in Paris (1856–1857), he was accepted into the atelier of the painter Leon Cogniet. Two years later, when the family was living in Newport, Rhode Island, William went to the studio of William Morris Hunt and was preparing himself "for a life of art." Another student of Hunt's, John La Farge, who became a prominent painter, muralist, and stained-glass-window maker, later wrote that William had showed an "extraordinary promise of being a remarkable, perhaps a great painter."[8] But William decided against a life as an artist, largely because his father wanted him to enter a scientific field, but also because he had been developing eye trouble and nervous indigestion (a psychosomatic reaction?). In 1861 he enrolled in the Lawrence Scientific School at Harvard.[9]

In light of James's experiences as an artist, it is not surprising, in Bell's view, that he often used the language of art to describe psychological activities, or that he likened his text on the stream of thought to "a painter's first charcoal sketch on his canvas, in which no niceties appear."[10] She also notes James's discovery, when he was reviewing personal accounts of religious experiences, that some individuals became aware of a visionary quality greater than, *distinct from*, but potentially continuous with their own selves, and that he employed a pictorial analogy that nearly conjures one of Inness's later landscape paintings, describing how visionary experiences "soften nature's outlines and open out the strangest possibilities and perspectives."[11]

But perhaps the most compelling association Bell makes between James's writings and Inness's landscapes is her discussion of what she calls "The Anonymous Figure." She cites James's lecture on "The Reality of the Unseen" in *The Varieties of Religious Experience* in which he observed that the "adjective 'mystical' is technically applied, most often, to states [of mind] that are of brief duration," and that "unpicturable beings" are "realized with an intensity almost like that of an hallucination."[12] She suggests that Inness used a pictorial device that reflects this brief perception of unpicturable

7. Richardson, *William James*, 38.

8. Ibid., 39.

9. Ibid., 43.

10. Bell, *George Inness and the Visionary Landscape*, 141, citing James, *The Principles of Psychology* 1:225.

11. James, *A Pluralistic Universe*, 769, cited in Bell, *George Inness and the Visionary Landscape*, 57.

12. James, *The Varieties of Religious Experience*, 69, 72, cited in Bell, *George Inness and the Visionary Landscape*, 57.

beings that are realized with an intensity that resembles a hallucination. She notes that this device is "the representation of a single human figure in the landscape. The gender, character, and identity of this figure often remains ambiguous; in certain cases, particularly in Inness's late landscape paintings, only the head-and-body configuration signifies this figure's anthropomorphism. Depicted with the same vivid brushstrokes that Inness used for the rest of his landscapes, the figure can be difficult to discern, especially in reproductions. It rarely crosses the horizon line, remaining, instead, deeply embedded within the texture of nature."[13]

These "anonymous figures" rarely act. In this sense, they are quite different from the figures in Inness's landscapes whose activities confer on them known identities, such as fishermen, laborers, a woman with a calf, and a woman waving to two figures in a rowboat in the middle of a lake. According to Bell, "These active figures fulfill the traditional pictorial identity of *staffage*, or accessories to the scene. They participate in and corroborate the illusion of representation. There is little need to question the nature of their activities, much less their core humanistic identities." In contrast, "by assuming a wholly contemplative demeanor," the anonymous figures "nearly disengage from the pictorial representations in which they exist" and "tend, therefore, to stimulate the viewer's attention even more effectively."[14]

Over the course of Inness's career, the anonymous figure became more and more indistinct, and in his last several paintings (1891–1894) "the figure is so summarily depicted that its very existence seems to depend on the interpretation of each viewer."[15] Bell rejects the idea that these anonymous figures are intended as "phantasmagoric beings," for it is unlikely that Inness "would have condoned such a literal interpretation." On the contrary, "these anonymous, nearly ephemeral creatures correlate more closely to the elusive *character* of the visionary experience than to the region of the descriptive, even when the subject of the descriptive is the spiritual realm." Thus, the anonymous figure "gazes deeply into the landscape" and in this pose "he adopts our own position and renders us increasingly aware of our identity as contemplative beings." Thus, anonymous figures draw our attention not only to the artist's "generative role as inventor but also of our own role as interpreter of the pictorial forms and field."[16]

13. Bell, *George Inness and the Visionary Landscape*, 58.
14. Ibid.
15. Ibid., 58–59.
16. Ibid., 59.

In effect, they give us—as viewers—a locus within the painting itself so that we are no longer outsiders looking at the scene before us. Through this rather simple pictorial device, we become coextensive with the landscape. Or, as Bell puts it, these anonymous figures fuse the mysterious with the revealing: "Often incarnated with only two or three rapid brushstrokes, these figures lure us into a deeper engagement with the landscape so that over time we may potentially discern reflections of our own humanity in Inness' visionary spaces."[17]

Inness's *Sunrise* (1887) represents the later phase in his use of the pictorial device of the anonymous figure. In his earlier renditions of the anonymous figure in 1860–1873, including *Sunset* (c. 1860–1865), *Christmas Eve* (1866), *Lake Nemi* (1872), and *The Monk* (1873), the anonymous figure—or figures—is centrally located in the scene and is clearly visible. In the two latter paintings, one is wearing black, the other white, and both stand out against the scenic background. As Bell points out, Inness manifests their contemplative identities by means of their religious garb.[18] But in the later phase the anonymous figure is dramatically reduced in size and does not stand out nearly as much against the background scene. This is especially true of *Sunrise* (1883), *Sunset Glow* (1883) and *Hazy Morning, Montclair* (1893).

On the other hand, the human figure in *Sunrise* is centrally located in the painting and is quite visible due to his black garb. Also, like the religious contemplatives in *Lake Nemi* and *The Monk,* he appears to have been walking along a path, and, like the monk, he seems to have paused to gaze at something—wildflowers perhaps—alongside the path.

However, because the anonymous figure is *not* identified by religious garb, the viewer is able to identify with him. He is alone and not, as in *Sunset,* accompanied by another person, but there is a tree a few feet away with limbs that almost resemble human arms raised upward. The sun, however, is the real subject of the painting as its light creates a sense of wholeness, one in which the anonymous figure is integral to everything that surrounds him. The light itself is subdued and nonglaring. The scene is one of quiet, calm, lack of strain, and economy of effort. And most important, the viewer is *in* the scene, not *outside* it. Through the simple device of an anonymous figure—a figure that is not identifiable by what he does but solely by who he is—Inness enables us to find ourselves back home in the world.

17. Ibid., 66.
18. Ibid., 58.

George Inness, *Sunrise*, The Metropolitan Museum of Art. Photo credit: Art Resource, New York.

WILLIAM JAMES AND THE MELANCHOLY SELF

Angela Miller's interpretation of Sanford Gifford's *Kauterskill Clove* as maternal space and Adrienne Baxter Bell's discussion of George Inness's paintings as reflecting William James's views on the visionary experience, as presented in *The Varieties of Religious Experience*, invite us to take a closer look at James's writings, especially those that have relevance to the concern of this book with the *melancholy self*.

It is important that we keep in mind that although James began publishing articles in 1878, his first major work *The Principles of Psychology* was published in 1890 when Inness's "visionary landscapes" were already well known; and *The Varieties of Religious Experience* was not published until 1902, eight years after Inness's death. Thus, Inness's paintings predated the major portion of James's writings. So if one is concerned with the question of influence, one could make the case that Inness's paintings had greater influence on James than James's writings had on Inness's art. The very fact that James, as a young man, had aspired to become an artist but decided, under considerable paternal pressure, to turn his attention to science, would support this argument, and Freud's concept of displacement would provide a psychodynamic explanation for how he kept his artist self alive through his scientific and philosophical writings.

In fact, Inness's "anonymous figure" provides a case in point, and one that has direct bearing on our theme of the *melancholy self*. It is a well-established fact that James's case of "the worst kind of melancholy" (i.e., one that takes the form of panic fear) in his "The Sick Soul" lecture in *The Varieties of Religious Experience* is an account of his own experience disguised as that of a French correspondent.[19] This account describes an experience when he was in his mid- to late-twenties and in a "state of philosophic pessimism and general depression of spirits about my prospects," in which

> there arose in my mind the image of an epileptic patient whom I had seen in the asylum, a black-haired youth with greenish skin, entirely idiotic, who used to sit all day on one of the benches, or rather shelves against the wall, with his knees drawn up against his chin, and the coarse gray undershirt, which was his only garment, drawn over them inclosing his entire figure. He sat there like a sort of sculptured Egyptian cat or Peruvian mummy, moving nothing but his black eyes and looking absolutely non-human. This image and my fear entered into a species of combination with each other. *That shape am I*, I felt, potentially.[20]

He added that there was nothing he possessed that could defend him against that fate "if the hour should strike for me as it struck for him." There was "such a horror of him, and such a perception of my own merely momentary discrepancy from him, that it was as if something hitherto solid within my breast gave way entirely, and I became a mass of quivering fear." The experience "was like a revelation," and although it "gradually faded," he was unable for months "to go out into the dark alone."[21]

In short, among the two hundred or so cases that James presents in *The Varieties of Religious Experience*, he is among them, but he is there by means of the simple device of "the anonymous figure."[22] Of course, the fact that both Inness and James employ the device of "the anonymous figure"

19. James, *The Varieties of Religious Experience*, 149–51.

20. Ibid., 149–50 (italics original).

21. Ibid., 150.

22. As indicated, James's case of the "French Sufferer" is widely known to have been his own. In his editorial notes in *William James: Writings 1902–1910*, Bruce Kuklick writes, "James later wrote to Swiss philosopher Frank Abauzit, who was translating *The Varieties* into French, that this account 'is my own case—acute neurasthenic attack with phobia. I naturally disguised the *provenance*! So you may translate freely'" (1362).

may be a mere coincidence. Nonetheless, it invites us to explore Bell's identification of associations between Inness's landscapes and James's view of the world by discussing certain of James's writings in greater detail. As Bell notes, the relevance of William James's psychological views to Inness's artistic understanding is that Inness was especially concerned that his art would not merely reflect his theological/mystical passions but that it would also be grounded in scientific or empirical truth. She points out that "critics, friends, and family members described Inness as 'devoted to mystical speculations' and engaged in 'metaphysical labors'" and that toward the end of his life he "acknowledged this passion when he described his investigations of art and theology as kindred pursuits."[23] When asked what he did when he grew weary of painting he replied that he then takes to theology, which is "the only thing except art which interests me," but then he added, "In my theory, they are very closely connected. That is, you may say it is theology, but it has resolved itself gradually into a scientific form and that is the development which has become so very interesting to me."[24]

Bell points out that this resolution of theology into "a scientific form" is what made Inness's art and James's writings so compatible. For example, Inness' anonymous figures "find their philosophical counterpart not in the idealism of Transcendentalism but in William James' pragmatic research into psychical states of consciousness."[25] The same is true of Sanford Gifford's work, as it finds its "philosophical counterpart" in William James's argument in *A Pluralistic Universe* for a pluralistic empiricism that avoids, on the one hand, materialists' tendency to treat the natural world as mere matter and, on the other, idealists' tendency to argue for a supernatural reality that exists over and above the natural world.[26]

In exploring James's writings in greater detail, I will focus on two issues: his reflections on the reality of the unseen world in *The Varieties of Religious Experience* and his conception of the world as inherently sympathetic in *A Pluralistic Universe*. The former, presented as the Gifford Lectures in 1901–1902, was published in 1902. The latter, presented as the Hibbert Lectures in 1909, was published the same year. James died a year later at the age of 68.

23. Bell, *George Inness and the Visionary Landscape*, 18.
24. Ibid.
25. Ibid., 60.
26. James, *A Pluralistic Universe*, lecture 1.

The Reality of the Unseen World

Angela Miller's interpretation of American landscape art in *The Empire of the Eye* and James's effort in *The Varieties of Religious Experience* to relate the psychology of melancholia to the religion of animism have a great deal in common. In his discussion of melancholia in his lectures on the sick soul, James points out that the external world appears dead and lifeless to the person suffering from extreme forms of melancholia. In the experience of conversion or religious regeneration, "a not infrequent consequence of the change operated in the subject is a transfiguration of the face of nature in his eyes," and "a new heaven seems to shine upon a new earth."[27]

In melancholia there is a similar change, only it occurs in the reverse direction: "The world now looks remote, strange, sinister, uncanny. Its color is gone, its breath is cold, there is no speculation in the eyes it glares with." One asylum patient says that he see "everything through a cloud." Another observes, "I touch, but the things do not come near me, a thick veil alters the hue and look of everything." Still another notes, "Everything floats before my eyes, but leaves no impression." What most distresses the melancholy soul is that "the natural world is so double-faced, and unhomelike," raising the question of "what world, what thing is real?"[28] James's use of the words "uncanny" and "unhomelike" recalls Freud's discussion in "The 'Uncanny'" of the "homesickness" of some of his male patients.[29]

Later, in his chapter "Conclusions," James discusses the threat that modern science poses for natural theology. He acknowledges that "the books of natural theology which satisfied the intellects of our grandfathers seem to us grotesque, representing, as they did, a God who conformed the largest things of nature to the paltriest of our private wants." On the other hand, the scientific temperament of the current era has its own problems. Specifically, it has reduced the natural world to a set of "mathematical and mechanical modes of conception," and of these conceptions, James can hardly conceal his contempt: "Weight, movement, velocity, direction, position, what thin, pallid, uninteresting ideas!"[30] His point is clear: Science and melancholia are not very different, for with both the natural world becomes impersonal, remote, objectified, disinterested.

27. James, *The Varieties of Religious Experience*, 142.
28. Ibid.
29. Freud, "The 'Uncanny,'" 152–53.
30. James, *The Varieties of Religious Experience*, 445–46.

He admits that the animistic religion of our early ancestors does not hold up well in this age of science. Where it continues to exist, it seems a mere "survival" of an earlier, more primitive era, when the one great object in human dealings with the natural world was to coerce the spiritual powers. On the other hand, animistic religion possesses an aesthetic imagination which is not as primitive or simpleminded as it seems. He asks:

> How could the richer, animistic aspects of Nature, the peculiarities and oddities that make phenomena picturesquely striking or expressive, fail to have been first singled out and followed by philosophy as the more promising avenue to the knowledge of Nature's life? Well, it is still in these richer animistic and dramatic aspects that religion delights to dwell. It is the terror and beauty of phenomena, the "promise" of the dawn and of the rainbow, the "voice" of the thunder, the "gentleness" of the summer rain, the "sublimity" of the stars, and not the laws which these things follow, by which the religious mind continues to be impressed.[31]

To this animistic view of nature, the survival theory is patronizing at best: "Pure anachronism! says the survival theory;—anachronism for which the deanthropomorphization of the imagination is the remedy required." So "the less we mix the private with the cosmic, the more we dwell in universal and impersonal terms, the truer heirs of Science we become."[32]

But James dissents: "In spite of the appeal which this impersonality of the scientific attitude makes to a certain magnanimity of temper, I believe it to be shallow." Why? Because it fails to take account of the fact that the world of our experience "consists at all times of two parts, an objective and a subjective part, of which the former may be incalculably more extensive than the latter, and yet the latter can never be omitted or suppressed."[33] Thus, the "reality" of the external world is confirmed when it becomes the object of our own experience, when we *feel* it, when we have an *attitude* toward it. He will not, therefore, disparage the view of the animists that the world of nature, especially its more picturesquely striking or expressive features, is alive and has feelings, as it were, that are similar to our own feelings toward it.

This, however, raises the question whether the view of nature conveyed by the second generation of American landscape painters as uniquely feminine, even maternal, is one that James would have shared? An affirmative

31. Ibid., 446.
32. Ibid.
33. Ibid.

answer is supported by his discussion of contemporary interpretations of Greek mythology in his lectures on "The Reality of the Unseen." He notes here that contemporary scholars are now asserting that "in their origins the Greek gods were only half-metaphoric personifications of those great spheres of abstract law and order into which the natural world falls apart— the sky-sphere, the ocean-sphere, the earth-sphere, and the like: just as even now we may speak of the smile of the morning, the kiss of the breeze, or the bite of the cold, without really meaning that these phenomena of nature actually wear a human face."[34]

In a footnote to this passage, James cites an example of such "half-metaphoric personifications" from the writings of B. de St. Pierre who writes: "Nature is always so interesting, under whatever aspect she shows herself, that when it rains, I seem to see a beautiful woman weeping. She appears the more beautiful, the more afflicted she is."[35] This example suggests that James views the natural world, at least when it assumes a "face," as feminine.

This suggestion is supported, in turn, by his observation that whatever may have been the *origin* of the Greek gods, we may safely conclude that there is in human consciousness "a feeling of objective presence, a perception of what we may call 'something there,' more deep and more general than any of the special and particular 'senses' by which the current psychology supposes existent realities to be originally revealed."[36] This "sense of presence" is precisely what the second generation of American landscape artists sought to represent by means of atmospherics, especially light and air. Thus, the feminine is experienced precisely as "the reality of the *unseen*." As a reviewer of one of Gifford's paintings expressed it: "Here is a canvas from which light and warmth seem to radiate through air that floatingly fills all space."[37] Air is especially significant because it is *unseen* yet its *reality* cannot be disputed.

There is also a maternal touch to James's reflections in his "Conclusions" on the role that the subconscious plays in religious experience. Discussing the religious "over-beliefs" that allow us to be open to influences from without, he writes: "Although the religious question is primarily a question of life, of living or not living in the higher union which opens itself to us as a gift, yet the spiritual excitement in which the gift appears

34. Ibid., 59.
35. Ibid.
36. Ibid.
37. Miller, *The Empire of the Eye*, 281.

a real one will often fail to be aroused in an individual until certain particular intellectual beliefs or ideas which, as we say, *come home to him*, are touched."[38] James speaks here of *yielding* to the subconscious mind.

Thus, if the "saving experience" for which he is longing is the domestication of the world into which one has been exiled, his yielding to the subconscious mind enables him to attend to those features of the natural world which are quietly atmospheric, redolent of life-giving energies and invisible powers. For James, as for the landscape artists presented here, the issue was the reality of the unseen. Separated from their mothers, and feeling this separation very keenly, men turned to the natural world where they could "sense" that the maternal was still there for them. The very fact that the feminine was "veiled" made its presence more palpably real, for, as James points out, when one experiences the reality of the unseen world, one is impressed by the fact that the "unseen" in such saving experiences seems even more real than the persons with whom we relate in our ordinary social worlds.[39]

A Sympathetic World

In the opening lecture of *A Pluralistic Universe* James presents "two types of thinking": "absolute idealism" and "radical pluralism." The purpose of his lectures is to show that radical pluralism, as he understands it, is better positioned than absolute idealism to address the problem of the perception that we are individually and collectively at odds with the universe, alien to its interests and tendencies, and of how this perception may be met and overcome. Thus, his central concern is with the issue of our relatedness to the universe, the question of how we may feel "at home" within it and feel ourselves to be making some contribution, however intangible, to its maintenance. In this introductory lecture he (uncharacteristically) quotes the German philosopher Georg Wilhelm Friedrich Hegel approvingly: "'The aim of knowledge,' says Hegel, 'is to divest the objective world of its strangeness, and to make us more at home in it.'" James, however, adds this important caveat, "Different men find their minds more at home in very different fragments of the world."[40]

38. James, *The Varieties of Religious Experience*, 459 (italics added).
39. Ibid., 60.
40. James, *A Pluralistic Universe*, 634.

In light of this question of our "at-homeness" in the world, an especially key lecture in *A Pluralistic Universe* is the one titled "Concerning
Fechner." Based on his reading of the philosophical works of the German
physicist-philosopher Gustav Theodor Fechner (1801–1887), this lecture
is concerned to demonstrate the extremely "thin" account of the world
that absolute idealism offers. While Fechner's own views tend in the end
toward a kind of absolutism, his significance for James is in the fact that
the world he portrays is "thick," vivid and pulsating with life. Noting our
tendency to view anything outside ourselves as "so much slag and ashes"
and to settle for a "bodiless" Divine Spirit and a "soulless" natural world,
Fechner asks what comfort, or peace, can come from such a doctrine? As
James expresses it, "The flowers wither at its breath, the stars turn into
stone; our own body grows unworthy of our spirit and sinks to a tenement
for carnal senses only." In effect, "the book of nature turns into a volume
on mechanics, in which whatever has life is treated as a sort of anomaly."[41]

In James's view, Fechner's "great instrument for vivifying the daylight
view is analogy," not, however, as a rationalist uses it, but as employed by ordinary men and women "in practical life." For example, as "my body moves
by the influence of my feeling and will," so "the sun, moon, sea and wind,
being themselves more powerful, move by the influence of some more
powerful feeling and will."[42] While the number of such analogies Fechner
perceived was "prodigious," he also insisted on the differences. By "making difference and analogy walk abreast, and by his extraordinary power of
noticing both," he "converts what would ordinarily pass for objections to
his conclusions into factors of their support."[43]

James devotes much of his lecture to Fechner's portrayal of the earth.
While he has major reservations concerning Fechner's notion of "the earth-
soul," he is strongly supportive of Fechner's personification of the earth
and more precisely, his representation of earth in female form. In behalf
of a feminized earth, Fechner makes the very affirmations that are typically made of God in dualistic theism, a position that James critiqued in
his introductory lecture in favor of a view of God as a finite being who is a
participant in the world, not above or over-against it. For instance, Fechner
says of the earth that "she is self-sufficing in a million respects in which we
are not so," and "we depend on her for almost everything, she on us for but

41. Ibid., 698.
42. Ibid.
43. Ibid., 699.

a small portion of her history." Moreover, earth's complexity "far exceeds that of any organism, for she includes all our organisms in herself, along with an infinite number of things that our organisms fail to include. Yet how simple and massive are the phases of her own proper life! As the total bearing of any animal is sedate and tranquil compared with the agitation of its blood corpuscles, so is the earth a sedate and tranquil being compared with the animals whom she supports."[44]

Another of her characteristics, one also attributed to God by dualistic theism, is that she develops from within instead of being fashioned from without: "It is like that of a wonderful egg which the sun's heat, like that of a mother-hen, has stimulated to its cycles of evolutionary change." In this, she is like all the organisms that inhabit her, but there is a difference, for

> our animal organization comes from our inferiority. Our need of moving to and fro, of stretching our limbs and bending our bodies, shows only our defect. What are our legs but crutches, by means of which, with restless effects, we go hunting after the things we have not inside of ourselves? But the earth is no such cripple; why should she who already possesses within herself the things we so painfully pursue, have limbs analogous to ours? Shall she mimic a small part of herself? What need has she of arms, with nothing to reach for? of a neck, with no head to carry? of eyes or nose when she finds her way through space without either, and has the millions of eyes of all her animals to guide their movements on her surface, and all their noses to smell the flowers that grow? She is, as it were, eye and ear over her whole extent—all that we see and hear in separation she sees and hears at once.[45]

These are signs of her superiority—if not perfection—deriving from the fact that she is the sum of her various parts.

Moreover, she is the giver of life as she "brings forth living beings of countless kinds upon her surface, and their multitudinous conscious relations with each other she takes into her higher and more general conscious life."[46] Yet, her conscious life is different from our own, for she has no need of heart, or lungs, or even a brain, for if the primary function of our brain is "to correlate our muscular reactions with the external objects on which we depend," the earth does this "in an entirely different way," reacting to the objects external to her—other stars and planets—"by more

44. Ibid., 701.
45. Ibid., 701–2.
46. Ibid., 702.

exquisite alterations" in the "total gait" of her whole mass, "and by still more exquisite vibratory responses in its substance. Her ocean reflects the lights of heaven as in a mighty mirror, her atmosphere refracts them like a monstrous lens, the clouds and snow-fields combine them into white, the woods and flowers disperse them into colors. Polarization, interference, absorption, awaken sensibilities in matter of which our senses are too coarse to take any note."[47] Thus, insisting on the differences as well as the resemblances, Fechner's imagination "tries to make our picture of the whole earth's life more concrete."[48]

As indicated, the reader of James's summary of Fechner's ideas can hardly escape the fact that for Fechner the earth is deeply feminized and disposed to be maternal as, for example, in her capacity as the giver and sustainer of life itself. For Fechner, but less so for James, this justifies viewing her as "the earth-soul." The reader also realizes that James has contributed his own imagination to Fechner's portrayal of the earth, making it difficult to determine where Fechner's analogies end and James's begin. Reminiscent of his lecture on the sick soul in *The Varieties of Religious Experience*, where he points out that the external world appears dead and lifeless to the melancholic patient whereas in the experience of religious regeneration "a not infrequent consequence of the change operated in the subject is a transfiguration of the face of nature in his eyes,"[49] he likens earth's landscape to a human face, one that is "peopled," for humanity's "eyes would appear in it like diamonds among the dewdrops" and "green would be the dominant color, but the blue atmosphere and the clouds would enfold her as a bride is enshrouded in her veil."[50]

We even find James endorsing Fechner's analogy of earth to angels. If the heavens really are the home of angels, the stars and planets being these "very angels, for other creatures *there* are none," then "Yes! The earth is our great common guardian angel, who watches over all our interests combined."[51] And as she watches over us, so we ourselves add to her "perceptive life so long as our own life lasts . . . When one of us dies, it is as if

47. Ibid., 703.
48. Ibid.
49. James, *The Varieties of Religious Experience*, 142.
50. James, *A Pluralistic Universe*, 703–4.
51. Ibid., 704.

an eye of the world were closed, for all *perceptive* contributions from that particular quarter cease."[52]

James follows this acclamation of Fechner's guardian angel analogy for earth with an account of one of Fechner's "moments of direct vision" of the earth's "transfigured" bearing, one in which she turned "her whole living face to Heaven" and carried him "along with her into that Heaven." This experience caused him to wonder how "the opinions of men could ever have so spun themselves away from life so far as to deem the earth only a dry clod, and to seek for angels above it or about it in the emptiness of the sky,—only to find them nowhere."[53]

James concludes this lecture with the observation that Fechner makes the universe "more *thickly* alive than do the other philosophers who, following rationalistic methods solely, gain the same results, but only in the thinnest outlines."[54] Also, because absolute idealism thinks of reality only under intellectual forms, it "knows not what to do with *bodies* of any grade, and can make no use of any psychophysical analogy or correspondence," and the "resulting thinness is startling when compared with the thickness and articulation of such a universe as Fechner paints."[55]

This very allusion to Fechner as a "painter" would be no less applicable to James, whose lecture on Fechner portrays through words what Gifford, Inness, and other landscape painters portrayed on canvas. Both, after all, are representations of the mother we call earth. In effect, they are portraits of her, and this being the case, Richard Brilliant's observation (cited in the introduction) that the "dynamic nature of portraits and the 'occasionality' that anchors their imagery in life seem ultimately to depend on the primary experience of the infant in arms" is relevant to landscape art as well.[56] In effect, landscapes portray the fact that there has been a displacement of feelings toward the original love object onto the mother we call earth. Thus, landscape art reflects and replicates a psychological reality—the birth of the *melancholy self*.

52. Ibid., 707.
53. Ibid., 704.
54. Ibid., 708.
55. Ibid., 709.
56. Brilliant, *Portraiture*, 9.

THE ANONYMOUS FIGURE AS SYMBOL OF HOPE

In her discussion of anonymous figures in Inness's paintings, Adrienne Baxter Bell points out that they "are not intended simply to advance a narrative, and they could not be eliminated or altered without destroying the integrity of the scene." In fact, "They are often our first point of interest in the represented landscape, and in particularly abstract settings, they tend to anchor our cognitive capacities to the realm of the human, the familiar."[57] To be sure, Inness would continue to paint figures in markedly narrative settings. For example, in *Shades of Evening* he portrays a woman in white with her dog waving a handkerchief to three figures in a boat. This painting "is clearly anchored in the realm of narration." But a distinctive feature of anonymous figures is their tendency to disengage the painting in which they appear from the realm of narration: "Often represented in silhouette, or with their backs turned to the viewer, or gazing into the landscape . . . these lone, contemplative beings seem to be thinking about something that we cannot see in the landscape, even something beyond the three-dimensional domain in which physical sight functions. Incarnated in two or three summary dashes of paint . . . their very beings—as ephemeral as any in art—mirror the transience of the activity in which they appear to be deeply engaged."[58]

No longer guided and limited by the "structural imperative" of narration, they embody the disintegration of the narrative and invite the viewer to envision a new and different reality. Through his invention of the anonymous figure Inness, in effect, engages "our own memory in the challenge of identifying the hieroglyphic forms of the 'anonymous figures,' thereby making our own contribution central to the epistemological process of discerning "what we see and what we know."[59]

I suggest, therefore, that the anonymous figure is a symbol of hope, for hope typically depends on the disintegration of the narrative to which our lives have been conformed so that new possibilities may come to life. If the narratives of our lives tell us what we may realistically expect, the very dissolution of these familiar narratives allows us to contemplate the realizable, and the very indeterminateness of the anonymous figure invites not only our identification with this figure but also our engagement in its

57. Bell, *George Inness and the Visionary Landscape*, 118.
58. Ibid.
59. Ibid.

realization.[60] As Bell points out, "these lone, contemplative beings seem to be thinking about something that we cannot see in the landscape, even something beyond the three-dimensional domain in which physical sight functions."[61] In his chapter "Seeing is Hoping," in *Toys and Reasons*, Erik H. Erikson suggests that in the infant's interplay with the mother two forms of vision develop, namely, "the capacity to see what is before us, here and now, and the power to foresee what, if one can only believe it, might yet prove to be true in the future."[62] The anonymous figure in Inness's *Sunrise* seems to embody both forms of vision—seeing and foreseeing—and his contemplative pose manifests the fact that a living hope requires both.

60. Ibid.

61. I discuss the distinction between the realistic and the realizable in Capps, *Agents of Hope*, 71–75. Given the emphasis of the present book on the *melancholy self* that forms in the wake of the loss of infant's original love object, my discussion of the reversibility of loss is particularly relevant (72–73). The fact that Bell emphasizes the solitariness of the anonymous figure suggests that my discussion of hope as a solitary act is also relevant (56–58). Finally, given the focus of the present book on works of art, it is noteworthy that I view hopes as projections (in the photographic sense) and suggest that they are creative illusions (64–67).

62. Erikson, *Toys and Reasons*, 46.

chapter eight

Grandma Moses's *Little Boy Blue*: The Watchful Mother

KARAL ANN MARLING SUGGESTS that for Norman Rockwell there were "two bright spots" in the darkness of the early 1950s: "The first was *Post* cover that modern critics regard as Rockwell's masterpiece: *Shuffleton's Barbershop.*"[1] The second is *Saying Grace*, the 1951 Thanksgiving cover of the *Saturday Evening Post*, "the most popular cover the *Post* ever printed, judging by the volume of requests for copies."[2] Like *Shuffleton's Barbershop* 'it is a study of light and space" but in this case this fact is "disguised as pious anecdote." She adds that the idea for the painting was suggested by a reader's letter to Rockwell, describing something she had witnessed in a Philadelphia branch of a Horn & Hardart cafeteria: "There, she said, she had seen an old Mennonite woman and her grandson saying grace before their humble meal."[3]

Laura Claridge also views *Saying Grace* as a "bright spot" in an otherwise dark period in Rockwell's life. But, for her, the painting is more than a "pious anecdote" for it "celebrates the tolerance at the base of any democracy" and expresses "Rockwell's absolute conviction that self-righteousness is not only unattractive but undermining to a free society."[4] She adds: "Set in a diner outside a railroad yard, the scene centers on two slightly menacing young male types almost bent over a table as they observe the bowed heads of an elderly woman and her charge, a little boy." Thus, Rockwell "reverses

1. Marling, *Norman Rockwell*, 74.
2. Ibid.
3. Ibid.
4. Claridge, *Norman Rockwell*, 383.

the conventions by which such liberal values especially were illustrated, positioning prayer . . . as the anomaly in danger of being treated disrespect-fully." In effect, "the painting narrates the right of deviants to be respected for practices that don't injure others."[5] Moreover, "the implied threat of the young men, the sense that they are potential hoods or testosterone-laden twenty-year-olds looking for a fight, is undercut by their sense of curiosity and engagement, though they don't appear to be converted into potential piety by the sight of the elderly woman praying."[6] This, however, is Rock-well's point: that the young men are drawn to the elderly woman and the boy who are saying grace, finding them irresistible.

Norman Rockwell's *Saying Grace*, Norman Rockwell Family Agency. Photo credit: The Norman Rockwell Museum Collections.

5. Ibid., 383.
6. Ibid.

What especially interests me about the painting is the fact that the occasion that inspired it was an onlooker's witnessing of a grandmother and her grandson saying grace before a humble meal. Was it important to Rockwell that the older woman was the boy's grandmother? Marling does not say, and Claridge makes no reference to the incident that inspired the painting. But it is worth noting that a grandmother is among the neighbors in Rockwell's *Christmas Homecoming*, the *Saturday Evening Post* Christmas cover in 1948, who have gathered together to welcome a young man home from college.

Norman Rockwell's *Christmas Homecoming*: Norman Rockwell Family Agency. Photo credit: The Norman Rockwell Museum Collections.

It was in the fall of 1948 that Mary Rockwell, realizing that her visits to a psychologist in Bennington, Vermont, were not having the desired effect, began treatments at Austen Riggs, and that on several occasions she would return by way of Poughkeepsie to visit her older sons, Jarvis and Thomas. Claridge notes that Rockwell painted *Christmas Homecoming* in the late summer of 1948 just before Jarvis and Thomas returned to Poughkeepsie for the fall semester at Oakwood School. She points out: "The painter's firstborn is the centerpiece, a near prodigal son whose community welcomes him en masse . . . Mary joyously hugs her son [Jarvis], and Peter and Tommy stand at the side, while Rockwell looks the part of the proud father, pipe in hand, sage smile on face. Mary seems slightly frazzled, however, and it turns out that Rockwell was not taking artistic license."[7]

The painting is made the more heartwarming by the fact that the little old woman on the left side of the painting and standing beside Peter is Grandma Moses, the painter who lived in Eagle Bridge, near Hoosick Falls, New York, some twelve miles from Rockwell's home in New Arlington, Vermont. Anna Mary Robertson Moses had begun painting at the age of seventy-eight, and her paintings of the scenes of her childhood and youth became enormously popular in the 1940s. Born in 1860, she would have been eighty-eight years old in 1948. Marling relates that Joyce Hall, the president of the Hallmark Greeting Card Company, producers of greeting cards featuring the works of Moses and Rockwell, had proposed to Rockwell that he arrange to visit Grandma Moses at her home on September 7, her birthday, and bring her a birthday cake, which he had decorated himself. Rockwell agreed. Marling says that Rockwell "was charmed by Moses."[8] She adds that "Mrs. Moses, that day, had no real idea of who Rockwell was but welcomed him anyway as an interested party and a fellow artist."[9] Later, she visited his studio in New Arlington, Vermont, and took particular interest in his brushes, his paints, and how he used photographs in planning his pictures. She noted at the time that she could not do this herself because photography and even live, outdoor scenery "interfered with the flow of memories and imagination from which her works emerged."[10] However, Marling notes that the two artists were very similar in their ability to create art that was commercially successful.

7. Ibid., 351.
8. Marling, *Designs on the Heart*, 189.
9. Ibid., 187.
10. Ibid., 189.

When *Christmas Homecoming* appeared in late December, Norman, Mary, and Peter were in California, and Jarvis had apparently joined them by this time. Thomas was still away at boarding school. Given the events that had preceded this family togetherness—Rockwell leaving for California by himself and placing the condition on Mary's joining him that she had succeeded in controlling her drinking, her episode of apparent inebriation on the train when she and Peter were en route to California—their own Christmas was very different from the one portrayed in *Christmas Homecoming*. But this, after all, is the point. In *Christmas Homecoming* the family is reunited and the community, including members of the Edgerton family who were certainly aware of Mary's drinking problem, look on with pleasure as the mother hugs her returning son.

Christmas Homecoming is ostensibly, then, a heartwarming portrayal of a son's return home for the holidays. In contrast to Rockwell's earlier painting, *Homecoming G.I.*, the *Post* cover for May 26, 1945, it is not a painting of a son, impeccably dressed in a military uniform, returning from his tour of duty at the close of World War II. Rather, in *Christmas Homecoming* the son is wearing an ill-fitting overcoat, and clothing items are protruding indecorously out of the bag he is carrying. On the other hand, there are Christmas gifts in his right hand, suggesting that he too had anticipated his return with the same pleasure and longing as those who were there to welcome him home. And most of those who have gathered to welcome him are smiling. This is a truly beatific scene.

But the frazzled appearance of Mary and the less than impeccably dressed appearance of Jarvis seem to point to something deeper that is also problematic about this scene. Claridge suggests that "Rockwell looks the part of the proud father, pipe in mouth, sage smile on face."[11] On the other hand, there is also a note of bemused observation of a scene in which a mother wraps her arms around her son with greater intensity and desire than she would have felt if it were her husband who had returned for the holidays. We cannot see the look on the son's face, and the father cannot see the look on his wife's face, but the painter, who perhaps knows more than the father is prepared to acknowledge, can witness the joy on the mother's face, and can also witness how she wraps her right arm around her son's neck while her left arm presses his body close to hers.

I am a viewer thinking about these family issues, so my eyes are drawn toward the older woman (Grandma Moses) standing between but slightly

11. Claridge, *Norman Rockwell*, 351.

behind the smiling little girl and the smiling younger brother: she is rather small, has a high forehead, with black and grey hair, and wearing glasses and a black dress with a white lace in the front, and a necklace. She too is smiling, and though she is watching the mother hug her son, her lips are closed. I have the distinct impression that she is a very observant person who sees more than is likely to be apparent to others. In fact, it is as if Rockwell is using her to convey the sense that there is more going on here than meets the eye.

THE GRANDMOTHER'S BLISSFUL SMILE

In this chapter I will explore the relevance of Grandma Moses to the theme of the *melancholy self*. The very fact that she is not only associated with the maternal but was also an artist seems reason enough to engage in this exploration. But more important is the fact that because she was known as Grandma and not Mother she is unlikely to evoke the whole range of ambivalent responses associated with the mother. It is noteworthy in this regard that Freud and his early associates were greatly interested in the psychology of grandparents.[12] They noted, for example, that some individuals, including patients, engage in a "reversal of generations," in which they identify more closely or personally with a grandparent than with a parent. These identifications were not always positive ones. For instance, in his article on the occurrence in dreams of material from fairy-tales Freud notes that one of his patients told him "that her two children could never get to be fond of their grandfather, because in the course of his affectionate romping with them he used to frighten them by saying he would cut open their tummies."[13]

On the other hand, we may also recall that in his study of Leonardo da Vinci, Freud emphasizes that Leonardo presents St. Anne—the grandmother of Jesus—in a very favorable light. Assuming that Leonardo was engaged in painting *Mona Lisa* and *Saint Anne with Virgin and Child* at the same time, Freud suggests that "it was the intensity of Leonardo's preoccupation with the features of Mona Lisa which stimulated him to create the composition of St. Anne out of his fantasy," for if the smile of Mona Lisa

---

12. Rapaport, "The Grandparent Syndrome." See also Capps, "The Reversal of Generations Phenomenon as Illustrated by the Lives of John Henry Newman and Abraham Lincoln"; and Capps, *Men and Their Religion*, 89–96.

13. Freud, "The Occurrence in Dreams of Material from Fairy Tales," 108.

"called up in his mind the memory of his mother, it is easy to understand how it drove him at once to create a glorification of motherhood, and to give back to his mother the smile he had found in the noble lady."[14]

But is Leonardo's St. Anne based only on Leonardo's memory of his mother Caterina? Freud believes not. Rather, the painting "contains the synthesis of Leonardo's childhood," and "its details are to be explained by reference to the most personal impressions in Leonardo's life." That is to say: "In his father's house he found not only his kind stepmother, Donna Albiera, but also his grandmother, his father's mother, Monna Lucia, who—so we will assume—was no less tender to him than grandmothers usually are. These circumstances might well suggest to him a picture representing childhood watched over by mother and grandmother."[15] Freud goes on to note that another striking feature of the picture assumes even greater significance: "St. Anne, Mary's mother and the boy's grandmother, who must have been a matron, is here portrayed as being perhaps a little more mature and serious than the Virgin Mary, but as still being a young woman of unfaded beauty. In point of fact Leonardo has given the boy two mothers, one who stretches her arms out to him, and another in the background; and both are endowed with the blissful smile of the joy of motherhood."[16]

This smile, he notes, is "unmistakably the same as that in the picture of Mona Lisa" but "it has lost its uncanny and mysterious character, what it expresses is inward feeling and quiet blissfulness."[17]

As noted in chapter 1, Freud believes that, in giving the boy Jesus two mothers, Leonardo has represented the very circumstances of his own boyhood, the fact that he "had had two mothers: first, his true mother Caterina, from whom he was torn away when he was between three and five, and then a young and tender stepmother, his father's wife, Donna Albiera."[18] But Freud also implies that these circumstances were insufficient in themselves to account for the fact that Leonardo painted the boy Jesus with two mothers, for it was by "his *combining* this fact about his childhood with the one mentioned above (the presence of his mother and grandmother) and

14. Freud, *Leonardo da Vinci and a Memory of His Childhood*, 61–62.

15. Ibid., 62–63.

16. Ibid., 63.

17. Ibid., 62.

18. Ibid., 63.

by his condensing them into a composite unity" that the design of *St. Anne with Virgin and Child* took shape for him."[19]

Thus, two images—that of his mother and that of his paternal grand-mother—combined to bring about the design of the painting. Freud adds that the very availability of the latter image enabled Leonardo to disavow the problematic features of his image of his mother. He explains: "The maternal figure that is further away from the boy—the grandmother—corresponds to the earlier and true mother, Caterina, in its appearance and in its special relation to the boy. The artist seems to have used the blissful smile of St. Anne to disavow and to cloak the envy which the unfortunate woman felt when she was forced to give up her son to her better-born rival, as she had once given up his father as well."[20] In effect, the image of his tender grandmother enables him to "screen out the unpleasant and disturbing."[21]

In short, Freud's observations here—such as his intuition that St. Anne is based on Leonardo's memory of his paternal grandmother who, we may assume, "was no less tender to him than grandmothers usually are"—suggest that the grandmother evokes none of the negative feelings associated with the mother and that, in fact, she evokes positive feelings that are unique to her.

This overwhelmingly positive portrayal of the grandmother is reinforced by Freud's reflections on the fact that St. Anne is "perhaps a little more mature and serious than the Virgin Mary" but is still "a young woman of unfaded beauty."[22] He rejects Richard Muther's explanation that "Leonardo could not bring himself to paint old age, lines and wrinkles, and for this reason made Anne too into a woman of radiant beauty," but neither is Freud persuaded by the countersuggestion of Woldemar von Seidlitz that there really is a significant difference in age in Leonardo's portrayal of the two women. There can be no doubt that "St. Anne has been made more youthful" than we would have expected, and that, as noted, the similarity of St. Anne and the Virgin Mary in terms of age supports Freud's contention that St. Anne "corresponds to the earlier and true mother, Caterina, in its appearance and in its special relation to the boy."[23]

And yet, as Freud also recognizes, St. Anne is nonetheless "a woman of radiant beauty," and her beauty is the more compelling precisely because

19. Ibid., italics added.
20. Ibid., 63–64.
21. Halpern, *Norman Rockwell*, 25.
22. Freud, *Leonardo da Vinci and a Memory of His Childhood*, 63.
23. Ibid., 63.

she is older than the other maternal figure—the Virgin Mary—in the painting. In other words, the fact that the Virgin Mary is a young, beautiful woman is neither surprising nor exceptional. What *is* exceptional—and thus invites scholarly debate—is the fact that the grandmother is also young and beautiful; and the fact that she corresponds to the painter's mother is only a partial explanation for why this is so. As far as her radiant beauty is concerned, what is more significant for Freud is the assumption that the painter has memories of a grandmother who was tender to him, and that this memory accounts for the fact that St. Anne is also "endowed with the blissful smile of the joy of motherhood," and the boy in the painting is the object and beneficiary of her joy. She exudes this joy because, as far as the painter is concerned, there is nothing about her that needs to be disavowed. The boy, whom Freud suggests may well be treating the lamb "a little unkindly," is looking at his mother. But it is the grandmother who "gazes down on the pair with a blissful smile" and, in doing so, is largely responsible for the sense that the boy is secure (despite the symbolic meaning of the lamb and what it portends) because he is the object of the older woman's gaze.

As we now turn to the life and artist of Grandma Moses, it seems appropriate that her first name—Anna—is a derivative of the name of Jesus's grandmother.

GRANDMA MOSES (1860–1961)

Anna Mary Robertson was born in Greenwich, New York, on September 7, 1860.[24] She was the third of ten children of Mary Shannahan and Russell King Robertson, a farmer who had some artistic talent and encouraged his children to paint. When she was twelve, she left home to work as a "hired girl" on a neighboring farm and spent the next fifteen years of her life in this manner, learning to sew, cook, keep house, and tend the family's children. She would occasionally make some visits home. In the 1870s she experienced a few years of schooling with the children of the family for which she worked. In the fall of 1886 she went to work for a family whose hired man was Thomas Salmon Moses. They were married in the minister's parlor in Hoosick Falls, a town not far from where she was born.

24. In addition to Jane Kallir's *Grandma Moses: The Artist behind the Myth*, I have drawn on these sources for the following sketch of Grandma Moses's life: William C. Ketchum Jr.'s *Grandma Moses: An American Original*; Karal Ann Marling's *Designs on the Heart: The Homemade Art of Grandma Moses*; Zibby Oneal's *Grandma Moses: Painter of Rural America*; and Adam Schaefer's *The Life and Work of Grandma Moses*.

Anna and Thomas had said goodbye to her family several days earlier, and following the ceremony, they boarded a train headed for New York City. Four days later they arrived in Staunton, Virginia. They had planned to go to North Carolina, but there was a farm for rent in Staunton, and they decided to settle there. Over the next several years, Anna contributed to the family income by producing butter and potato chips. They had ten children, five of whom died in infancy. In 1905 they returned to New York State because Thomas was homesick for the North. They purchased a farm in Eagle Bridge, not far from where she was born, and their children went to the same one-room schoolhouse their mother had attended. They named the farm Mount Nebo after the mountain from which the biblical Moses (their namesake) viewed the promised land (Deuteronomy 34:1–6). As her children grew up and began to leave home, Anna began dabbling in artistic projects.

The initial inspiration to paint derived from a few accidental circumstances—such as running out of wallpaper, which led to the decision to decorate a fireboard with a landscape. But the real impetus came when her daughter Anna, who had seen an embroidered picture somewhere, asked her mother for one like it. This worsted yarn piece was a great success, and she received requests for more. However, in time, she worried about the impermanence of yarn pieces, which were vulnerable to moths and faded after prolonged exposure to sunlight. Moreover, arthritis made it increasingly difficult for her to use a needle. So she readily adopted her sister Celestia's suggestion that it might be less painful to paint.

After her husband, Thomas, died in 1927, Anna continued to make pictures for family and friends but did not consider the possibility that painting might become a full-time occupation. However, she continued to paint, and when she had quite a few paintings on hand, someone suggested that she take some of them down to the old Thomas drugstore in Hoosick Falls. Mrs. Thomas, the owner, wanted to establish a sort of women's exchange, an outlet where local residents could sell their goods, so she was more than happy to display Anna's paintings.

In 1938 Louis J. Caldor, a civil engineer who lived in New York City and was on vacation with his wife and daughter, happened to notice the paintings—there were four of them—in the drugstore window. An amateur art collector, he asked the store manager if there were any more. There were a dozen paintings in all, the others having been stored in the back room, and none had sold in the year that they had been on consignment. The price was so low that Caldor bought all of them. He began to promote Moses's work in New York City but with little success. Then, however, in the summer of 1939, he made contact with Otto Kallir, a dealer in modern art who had fled to the United States after the Nazi takeover of his native Austria. Kallir was interested in the work of "primitive" or "naïve" artists. He liked what Caldor showed him and arranged for a one-woman exhibition in the fall. It was titled "What a Farm Wife Painted."

Although only three of the thirty-four paintings sold, Gimbels Department Store reassembled the exhibition on its premises for a Thanksgiving festival and invited Anna to come to New York for the event. Gimbels's publicity department prepared advertisements calling Grandma Moses "the white-haired girl of the U.S.A.," but what charmed the New York City press was the presence of Grandma Moses herself. One headline asserted that "Grandma Moses Just Paints and Makes No Fuss about It." Her work began to catch on, and the printing of a line of greeting cards, together with the publication of a book titled *Grandma Moses, American Primitive* (both occurring in 1946) catapulted her from local to national stature. As Jane Kallir points out, "The name 'Grandma Moses,' which was entering the vernacular, was becoming a generic term connoting old age, unexpected talent, or potential realized. She had come to symbolize all amateur artists and was credited with initiating a boom in amateur art."[25]

As time went on, her art was exploited by proponents of realism against abstract expressionism. As Kallir notes, abstract expressionism was in part a direct response to the existential uncertainty—the possibility of atomic holocaust, the cold war—that pervaded the United States following World War II. Thus, "its mythos was a tragic one, fueled by the brutal circumstances under which several of its heroes perished," for "young and vital artists like Gorky, Rothko, and Pollock died tragically." In contrast, "Moses lived to be 101. She countered their pessimism with her optimism. She was the other side of the coin, the silver lining in the gray cloud. There was something almost miraculous, in these nervous times, about an old woman who could go on national television and say, in effect, 'I am not afraid to die.'"[26]

Kallir also notes that easy explanations have been offered for why "the Moses phenomenon" lasted far longer than anyone might have predicted. The reasons for the enduring popularity of her art include her personality, her age, escapism, and nostalgia. The first two, however, would have been insufficient to maintain her enterprise, while the second two were

25. Kallir, *Grandma Moses*, 19.
26. Ibid., 23.

irrelevant. Moses's personality was important, but what mattered more was the fact that her art and personality were complementary, for she was "as unaffected as her paintings."[27] As for the escapism and nostalgia explanations, her art involved neither:

> Moses was not preaching a return to the past, though she did paint partly from memories of a life that extended back into the previous century. The "old-fashioned" details in her pictures were, because of their stylistic simplicity, incapable of evoking the past in any but a symbolic sense. Her landscapes, on the other hand, were portrayed with an accuracy that was very much of the present. Ultimately, in both art and life, the forms of nature are the most enduring; they are eternal. There was a link between the present and the past in Moses' work that seemed to secure the future. The message was that some things—the scent of summer on the winds of spring, the bite of the first snow in November—do not change. She inspired not longing, but hope.[28]

In effect, she was the very personification of Sanford Gifford's project —the domestication of the sublime—and the fact that she lived to 101 was itself symbolic of the endurance of the forms of nature. Also, the fact that she lived on a farm christened Mount Nebo—where Moses stood to view the promised land before he died (Deuteronomy 32:48–52)—supports her association with hope, the promise of good things to come.

GRANDMA MOSES'S LITTLE BOY BLUE

Grandma Moses painted *Little Boy Blue*, *Tom Tom the Piper's Son*, and *Mary and Little Lamb* in 1947. All three were inspired by well-known nursery rhymes. The various versions of "Little Boy Blue" have small differences in wording, but this one is representative:

> Little boy blue come blow your horn,
> The sheep's in the meadow the cow's in the corn;
> But where's the boy who looks after the sheep?
> He's under a haystack fast asleep.
> Will you wake him? No, not I.
> For if I do, he's sure to cry.[29]

27. Ibid., 29.
28. Ibid.
29. "Little Boy Blue Rhyme." Online: http://www.rhymes.org.uk/little_boy_blue.htm/.

Grandma Moses's *Little Boy Blue*, Grandma Moses Properties Co., New York.
Photo credit: Grandma Moses Properties Co.

In each of her paintings of nursery rhyme scenes, Grandma Moses transposed the rhyme from its original English context to her familiar Hoosick Valley. Thus, as William C. Ketchum Jr. points out, "In *Little Boy Blue* the forgetful protagonist snoozes peacefully within feet of a center-hall colonial farmhouse (a prototypical American form), while the 'cows in the corn' and the 'sheep in the meadow' are set against the same rolling Washington County hills seen in countless other of her works."[30]

That Moses transposed the scene to her own familiar surroundings was not at all surprising or even especially noteworthy. As Marling points out, Mother Goose rhymes were first published in America in 1787, and were "printed so frequently thereafter as suitable moral fare for children that their European origin was eventually forgotten."[31] In fact, in 1860,

---

30. Ketchum, *Grandma Moses*, 68–69.
31. Marling, *Designs on the Heart*, 53.

the year that Anna Mary Robertson was born, New Englanders made the unsubstantiated claim that Mother Goose was actually Elizabeth Goose of Boston, great-grandmother of the wife of publisher Isaiah Thomas. This claim led many tourists to make the pilgrimage to the Old Granary Burial Ground in Boston to pay homage to her. In subsequent decades, picture books, dime-store ceramics, printed embroidery patterns, and valentines featured Jack and Jill; Tom, the piper's son; and the other dramatis personae of the Goose anthology.

Marling notes that several illustrators created fresh interpretations of "Little Boy Blue" for reprintings of the Mother Goose rhymes, but an especially appealing rendition was Maud Humphrey's "chubby, rosy-lipped, curly-headed boy in blue slumbering on a bed of hay, an image awash in the Victorian child-worship and mother-love of her day."[32] She adds, "It would have been an act of unspeakable cruelty to wake Maud Humphrey's dimpled darling, and so he dreamt on as a million doting Mamas of the Gilded Age watched and sighed in pleasure."[33]

Noting that "Mother Goose, it seems, was everywhere," Marling suggests that

> she also hovers over Grandma Moses' *Little Boy Blue* (1947), an intriguing composition in which no fewer than eight brown cows wreak havoc in the corn. The sleeping boy in blue, splayed out like a Hellenistic faun on a mound of new-mown green hay, with a round brown object (Humphrey's straw hat?) abandoned by his side, seems almost incidental to the action, however. Haymakers toil. A carefree boy and girl romp through the hayfield. A hired hand gets after the errant cows. A farmer plows behind a team. Another man in a straw hat chases a dog.[34]

Off to the right, "at the very edge of the picture, stands an old well house of Disneyesque design, from which a wispy old lady in a lavender dress has drawn a bucket—an *Old Oaken Bucket*—of water." Is she Mother Goose herself? Or is she Grandma Moses, "watching out for the little fellow dreaming away, safe and sound, as the life of the farm bustles around him?"[35]

As Marling also suggests that the father, mother, and little girl in *The Old Oaken Bucket* (painted the same year) are "watched over by a wraith

32. Ibid., 55–56.
33. Ibid., 56.
34. Ibid., 56–57.
35. Ibid., 57.

of an old lavender-lady in the doorway, who may be Mrs. Moses herself,"[36] we seem here to be witnessing in *Little Boy Blue* Grandma Moses's own version of George Inness's pictorial device of the anonymous figure. Here the painter has inserted herself into the picture. If so, it is significant that she has transformed the viewer or observer who is within the scene into a more intentional watching over of others who are also in the scene.

Like St. Anne in Leonardo's *St. Anne with Virgin and Child*, she is the one whose role is to "watch over" while others are engaged in various activities. No doubt there is a contemplative quality to her role, but it is less the contemplation of the world around her and more the contemplation of what is—or will—become of the ones who are the object of her gaze. As a mother who lost five of her ten children in infancy, Grandma Moses had considerable experience of the agony of a mother watching her child pass away. Now she was a grandmother, and her maternal role was less immediate, less charged with overwhelming emotions, and more transcendent, similar to that of St. Anne watching over her daughter and grandson with a blissful smile on her radiant face.[37] In *Little Boy Blue*, she watches from a distance, with the man chasing the dog midway between her and the sleeping boy.

THE RUDE AWAKENING

Following her observation that doting mothers of the Gilded Age would not have awakened Maud Humphrey's "Little Boy Blue" but would instead have

36. Ibid., 48.

37. St. Anne's contemplation of what will become of her grandson is expressed in a letter written on April 3, 1501 by the Carmelite monk Fra Pietro da Nopvellara in which he mentions Leonardo: "Leonardo's lifestyle is erratic and very fickle, and it would appear that he just lives from one day to the next. Since he has been in Florence he has only made one cartoon, with the Holy Child at about the age of one, almost escaping from His mother's arms. He is turned towards a lamb and seems to be embracing it. His mother, almost getting up from the lap of St. Anne, is clinging on to the Child, trying to pull Him away from the lamb (a sacrificial animal that stands for Christ's Passion). St. Anne, slightly rising up, seems to want to hold her daughter back so that the latter cannot separate the Child from the lamb. Perhaps Anne represents the Church which does not want anything to stand in the way of Christ's Passion" (Zöllner, *Leonardo 1452–1519*, 65). Whether or not Leonardo had this representation in mind, it is noteworthy that the monk attributes the separation of mother and child to the child's own maturation, not to the mother's own initiative, which is directed towards pulling him back to her. It is significant in this regard that Erik H. Erikson, in his discussion of melancholia in *Young Man Luther*, attributes the infant's separation from the mother to his gradually maturing organs and the accompanying development of a will of his own (120–21).

"watched and sighed in pleasure" as he dreamt on, Marling suggests that a "similar case of motherly nostalgia flavored Eugene Field's poetic recasting of the story of 'Little Boy Blue' in his beloved *Poems of Childhood*." She writes: "This time, the little boy has vanished from his nursery. The speaker fondly, sadly, takes stock of a dusty toy dog, a tin soldier, a trundle bed, and remembers the night when the child lay dreaming and 'an angel song awakened our Little Boy Blue' to a new life in heaven above."[38] If "motherly nostalgia" flavored this poetic recasting of the story of "Little Boy Blue," the pervasive mood of the poem is that of the *melancholy self*. The poet is undoubtedly reflecting on his own experience as a little boy. Field was born in St. Louis in 1850. After his mother died six years later, he was raised by a cousin in Amherst, Massachusetts. He began publishing his poetry in 1879, and his first book of poetry was published in 1889.[39] *Poems of Childhood* was published posthumously in 1904, nine years after his death in 1895. Here is the poem:

LITTLE BOY BLUE

The little toy dog is covered with dust
But sturdy and staunch he stands;
And the little red soldier is red with rust,
And his musket moulds in his hands.
Time was when the little toy dog was new,
And the soldier was passing fair;
And that was the time when our Little Boy Blue
Kissed them and put them there.

"Now, don't you go till I come," he said,
"And don't you make any noise!"
So, toddling off to his trundle-bed,
He dreamt of the pretty toys;
And, as he was dreaming, an angel song
Awakened our Little Boy Blue—
Oh! The years are many, the years are long,
But the little toy friends are true!

Ay, faithful to Little Boy Blue they stand,
Each in the same old place—
Awaiting the touch of a little hand,
The smile of a little face;
And they wonder, as waiting the long years through

38. Marling, *Designs on the Heart*, 56.
39. "Eugene Field." Online: http://en.wikipedia.org/wiki/Eugene_Field/.

> In the dust of that little chair,
> What has become of our Little Boy Blue,
> Since he kissed them and put them there.[40]

The *Wikipedia* article on the poem begins with the assertion that in this "melancholy" poem "the boy dies in his sleep, thus leaving the toys there forever." Then it later suggests that the "angel song" that Field writes about "could be one of two things":

> It could either be an Angel of God, or it could be a beautiful woman, possibly his mother, to tell him *they* were leaving. Most people believe that in the end, Little Boy Blue is dead. Or could it just be simply a bittersweet story of growing up that captures the exact moment in time that the little boy was awakened by an Angel's song to wake up as a boy who is old enough not to "toddle" off to his pretty toys? A young man who forgot all about the old toys or at least the last words of promise that he'd made to them.[41]

In light of Field's loss of his mother at the age of six and the fact that he then went to live with his cousin, another possibility is that the Angel is, indeed, the boy's mother, who has awakened him with the news that *she* is leaving and will no longer be with him in the flesh. In this sense, Marling's suggestion that "it would be an act of unspeakable cruelty" to awaken the boy would be deeply and tragically true, and the concluding lines of the nursery rhyme ("Will you wake him? No, not I. / For if I do, he's sure to cry") would have less to do with the fact that the little boy dislikes being aroused from his peaceful slumbers and more to do with the reason why he has been awakened from them.

However, in the end, the poem draws our attention to the fact that the death is that of the boy himself. That two interpretations of the poem are possible means perhaps that, either way, the boy has passed from the scene. He may, as Marling suggests, have been awakened by the angel song to a new life in heaven above. Or he may, as the *Wikipedia* article suggests, have been awakened by the angel's song to "wake up as a boy who is old enough not to 'toddle' off to his pretty toys." The toys are living witnesses to the fact that the boy is no longer with them, and the poet, now adult, views the scene as an outsider: he sees the toys standing there, each where the little boy placed it, and he notices that they are still awaiting "the touch

40. Field, *The Poems of Eugene Field*, 248–49.

41. "Little Boy Blue." Online: http://en.wikipedia.org/wiki/Little_Boy_Blue/ (italics added).

of a little hand, the smile of a little face." But perhaps in this daydream of his own,[42] the poet—the viewer—feels the touch of that little hand and sees the smile on that little face, then reassures the toy dog and toy soldier that the little boy is alive and well, for somewhere in that little room is someone who watches over him—like a tender grandmother watching over the boy reaching out to play with a young lamb, in anticipation of the day when he will look after the sheep and just as surely cry.

On the other hand, there was also a grandmother, less tender, perhaps, yet even more reassuring, who was content to paint the nursery-rhyme version and to envision Little Boy Blue asleep on the hay. Watching him from the old well where she has just drawn a bucket of water, she may have considered walking over to where he lies to awaken him and remind him that he has work to do. Had this grandmother, Grandma Moses, been her neighbor, Norman Rockwell, she may have thought that the perfect way to awaken a sleeping boy would be to throw a bucket of water on his head. But no, she stands there, simply watching, and this is all he needs to know.

42. Freud, "The Relation of the Poet to Day-dreaming."

chapter nine

Irving's "Rip Van Winkle": Imitating Nature's Repose

As WE HAVE SEEN, Grandma Moses's *Little Boy Blue* illustrates the fact that the desire to be at home in the world has roots in early childhood. The boy asleep in the hay thus symbolizes the desire of every male, whatever his chronological age may be, to experience a sense of being at home in the world, to recover what he associates with the maternal environment of early infancy. Because *Little Boy Blue* is a work of art, it does not presume to tell us whether the sense of having once been at home in the world was an objective reality. Nor have I discussed this question in any systematic way throughout this study. In focusing on Freud's essays on "Mourning and Melancholia" and "The 'Uncanny,'" I have been concerned with the boy's sense of loss and have viewed this sense of loss as a subjective reality, whatever its objective reality may have been. A similar point could, of course, be made with the story of Adam and Eve in the garden of Eden. In this view, the human couple was at home in their original world, and were then cast out of this home into a world alien and foreign to them.

By concluding this study with Grandma Moses's *Little Boy Blue* I am also suggesting that every male, whatever his chronological age may be, may identify with this little boy and thus with the implied message that there is a place where he can experience himself to be at home in the world. It is not, of course, for me to presume to specify where this place may be; for this depends on the individual. For some, it is an actual physical place in the world. For others, it is an imaginary place—a mental construction—but no less real than a physical place or location would be.

However, to make this connection between the little boy and the adult man more explicit, I would like to close this study with a brief allusion to a grown man who exemplifies the sense of being at home in the world, and who does so in very much the same way that Little Boy Blue does: by sleeping while others engage in the business of life around him. And perhaps both are modeled after the infant who sleeps soundly in his mother's arms as if he hasn't a care in the world. In any event, the grown man to whom I have reference is Rip Van Winkle, the creation of Washington Irving.[1]

This story, part of a collection titled *The Sketch Book of Geoffrey Crayon*, is set in the years before and after the Revolutionary War. Rip lives in a pleasant village at the foot of the Catskill Mountains. He is an amiable man who is loved by all in town, especially the children, to whom he gives toys and tells stories. Due to his tendency to avoid all gainful labor, his home and farm fall into disarray; this situation evokes his wife's chastisement.

To escape her chastisements he wanders up into the mountains with Wolf, his dog, and meets up with a man who requests his help in carrying a keg up the mountain. They hike together up to a hollow where a group of ornately dressed, silent bearded men are playing ninepins. Rip surreptitiously drinks some of their liquor and soon falls asleep. When he awakens, twenty years have passed and Wolf is nowhere to be found. When he returns to the village, he learns that his wife has since died, and his now-adult daughter takes him in. He resumes his idle ways, and when other husbands hear his story, they wish that they could share in his good fortune of being cared for by a loving daughter and of having had the luxury of sleeping through the hardships of war.[2] In effect, Rip is the object of jealousy precisely because he fulfilled the desire to be at home in the world. The fact that for twenty years he was totally unaware of the fact that he *was* at home in the world does not diminish the power of the scene itself.

We can well imagine that in Rip's life situation before his twenty-year sleep, the experiences that originally formed the *melancholy self* are all too present. We cannot blame his wife for chastising him. After all, their home and farm are a reflection of his indolence. Nonetheless, it is evident that he does not feel at home when he is at home. If he is ever to feel at home, he will need to discover a sense of home in the world outside the maternal environment. So he decides to wander up the mountain accompanied by his dog, and encounters a scene not unlike that to which the viewer of

1. Irving, *The Complete Tales of Washington Irving*, 21–31.
2. "Rip Van Winkle" Online: http://en.wikipedia.org/wiki/Rip_Van_Winkle/.

Rockwell's *Shuffleton's Barbershop* is witness: a group of men playing a game together. Conceivably, Rip Van Winkle would have experienced a sense of being at home if he had simply joined them in their game, but it seems rather clear that he is not one of them: their ornate costumes set them off from him, and, in any event, they do not invite him to join in their game. His experience of being at home in the world will reflect, instead, his rather solitary nature, but he will not be alone, for during his twenty-year sleep he will be visited by the living creatures of the area and will be the object of the attentive gaze of Mother Nature herself. Billy Collins's poetic tribute to Rip Van Winkle is noteworthy in this regard.

RIP VAN WINKLE

The illustrations always portray him outdoors,
sleeping at the base of a generous oak,
acorns bouncing off his elfin cap,
the beard grown over him like a blanket.

Here reclines the patron of sleep,
He has sawed enough logs to heat the Land of Nod.
His dreams are longer than all of Homer.
And the Z above his head looks anchored in the air.

You would think a forest animal would trouble
his slumber, the paw of a bear on his paunch,
but squirrels hop over his benign figure
and by now the birds are unafraid of his rhythmic snoring.

In the next valley the world probably goes on,
hammering and yelling and staying up late at night
while around his head flowers open and close
and leaves or snow fall as he sleeps through the seasons.

Some mornings, awakened by the opera of dawn,
I think of his recumbrance, his serene repose
as I open my eyes after a paltry eight hours,
pointlessly alert, gaudy with consciousness.[3]

---

3. Collins, "Rip Van Winkle." His reference to illustrations in the first line suggests that this poem is an example of *ekphrasis*, the literary representation of visual art. See Heffernan, *The Museum of Words*, 1. In light of our earlier discussion of Leonardo da Vinci's *Mona Lisa*, Collins's use of *ekphrasis* in his poem "Sweet Talk" is also significant. In it he tells his beloved that she is "not the Mona Lisa / with that relentless look" but is "more like the sunlight / of Edward Hopper, / especially when it slants / against the eastern side / of a white clapboard house / in the early hours of the morning" (*The Art of Drowning*, 66).

Note Collins's observation that Rip sleeps at the base of "a generous oak," that he is not troubled by forest animals, and that his snoring no longer causes fear among the birds. While hammering and yelling take place in the next valley, he lies in "serene repose." These observations recall my earlier reference (in chapter 6, footnote 31) to Annie Payson Call's *Power through Repose*, in which she advises her readers to imitate "the work and quiet economy, the lack of strain and false purpose, in fine old Nature herself," thus advocating the imitation of "Nature's repose," of "her permanent moods rather than . . . her fitful phenomenal display."[4] It is no accident that Rip Van Winkle fulfills the desire to be at home in the world in the act of imitating Nature's own repose. He is able to sleep in "serene repose" because he is the object of Mother Nature's watchful gaze. His body is relaxed, his mind is free, and his emotional state is one of infinite calm.[5] Moreover, we should not overlook the fact that the target of the poet's ironic sensibility is not Rip Van Winkle but himself, for unlike Rip, he awakens after a "paltry eight hours, pointlessly alert, gaudy with consciousness."

It is probably no accident that the initials of Rip Van Winkle's given name invoke the familiar "Rest in Peace" carved in many of the gravestones in the cemetery of Sleepy Hollow. But as Jesus said of the daughter of Jairus, "The child is not dead but sleeping" (Mark 5:39). There are other ways besides sleeping to be at home in the world, but the infant who continues to live inside us has much to teach us in this regard, for to be at home in the world is often to be oblivious to the hammering and yelling in the next valley.

4. Call, *Power through Repose*, 165; Miller, *The Empire of the Eye*, 251.
5. Capps, "Relaxed Bodies, Emancipated Minds, and Dominant Calm."

Bibliography

Agnes, Michael, editor. *Webster's New World College Dictionary.* Foster City, CA: IDG Books Worldwide, 2001.

Allport, Gordon W. *The Individual and His Religion.* New York: Macmillan, 1950.

Anderson, Ronald and Anne Koval, *James McNeill Whistler: Beyond the Myth.* New York: Carroll & Graf, 1994.

Artchive. "George Inness (1826-94)" Online: http://archive.com/artchive/I/nness.html/.

Austen, Ian. "New Look at 'Mona Lisa' Yields Some New Secrets." *The New York Times,* September 27, 2006.

Avery, Kevin J., and Franklin Kelly, editors. *Hudson River School Visions: The Landscapes of Sanford R. Gifford.* New Haven: Yale University Press, 2003.

Baden-Powell, Robert. *Scouting for Boys: Handbook for Instruction in Good Citizenship,* edited by Elleke Boehmer. Oxford: Oxford University Press, 2004.

Bates, Theunis B. (2010). "Did High Cholesterol Dim Mona Lisa's Smile?" Online: http://www.aolnews.com/2010/01/06/did-high-cholesterol-dim-mona-lisas-smile/.

Bell, Adrienne Baxter. *George Inness and the Visionary Landscape.* New York: Braziller, 2003.

Berman, Avis. *First Impressions: James McNeill Whistler.* New York: Abrams, 1993.

Bogart, Michelle. *Artists, Advertising, and the Borders of Art.* Chicago: University of Chicago Press, 1995.

Bowlby, John. *Maternal Care and Mental Health.* Geneva: World Health Organization, 1964.

Brilliant, Richard. *Portraiture.* Cambridge: Harvard University Press, 1991.

Bryson, Norman. *Looking at the Overlooked: Four Essays on Still Life Painting.* Cambridge: Harvard University Press, 1990.

Call, Annie Payson. *Power through Repose.* Boston: Roberts Brothers, 1891.

Capps, Donald. *Agents of Hope: A Pastoral Psychology.* Eugene, OR: Wipf & Stock, 2001.

————. "Erik H. Erikson, Norman Rockwell, and the Therapeutic Functions of a Questionable Painting." *American Imago* 65 (2008) 191–228.

————. "Erikson's Schedule of Human Strengths and the Childhood Origins of the Resourceful Self." *Pastoral Psychology* 61 (2011) 269–83.

————. *Men and Their Religion: Honor, Hope, and Humor.* Harrisburg, PA: Trinity, 2002.

————. *Men, Religion, and Melancholia: William James, Rudolf Otto, C. G. Jung, and Erik H. Erikson.* New Haven: Yale University Press, 1997.

————. "Relaxed Bodies, Emancipated Minds, and Dominant Calm." *Journal of Religion and Health,* 48 (2009) 368–80.

————. *Striking Out: The Religious Journey of Teenage Boys.* Eugene, OR: Cascade Books, 2011.

————. "The Reversal of Generations Phenomenon as Illustrated by the Lives of John Henry Newman and Abraham Lincoln." *Pastoral Psychology* 55 (2006) 3–25.

Carroll, Michael P. *Madonnas That Maim: Popular Catholicism in Italy since the Fifteenth Century.* Baltimore: Johns Hopkins University Press, 1992.

Claridge, Laura. *Norman Rockwell: A Life.* New York: Modern Library, 2003.

Cochran, Sam V., and Fredric E. Rabinowitz. *Men and Depression: Clinical and Empirical Perspectives.* Practical Resources for the Mental Health Professions. San Diego: Academic Press, 2000.

Collins, Billy. *The Art of Drowning.* Pittsburgh: University of Pittsburgh Press, 1995.

———. "Rip Van Winkle." In *Questions about Angels: Poems.* Pittsburgh: University of Pittsburgh Press, 1999.

Collins, Bradley I. *Leonardo, Psychoanalysis, & Art History: A Critical Study of Psychobiographical Approaches to Leonardo da Vinci.* Psychosocial Issues. Evanston: Northwestern University Press, 1997.

Dali, Salvador. "Why They Attack the 'Mona Lisa.'" *ArtNews* 91/9 (1992) n.p.

Davies, Christie. *Jokes and Their Relation to Society.* Humor Research 4. Berlin: Mouton de Gruyter, 1998.

Dawson, Jim. *Who Cut the Cheese?: A Cultural History of the Fart.* Berkeley: Ten Speed, 1999.

Eissler, Kurt R. *Leonardo da Vinci: Psychoanalytic Notes on the Enigma.* New York: International Universities Press, 1961.

Epstein, Daniel Mark. *Nat King Cole.* New York: Farrar, Straus & Giroux, 1999.

Erikson, Erik H. *Childhood and Society.* New York: Norton, 1950.

———. *Identity: Youth and Crisis.* New York: Norton, 1968.

———. *Insight and Responsibility: Lectures on the Ethical Implications of Psychoanalytic Insight.* New York: Norton, 1964.

———. *Toys and Reasons: Stages in the Ritualization of Experience.* New York: Norton, 1977.

———. *Young Man Luther: A Study in Psychoanalysis and History.* New York: Norton, 1958.

Field, Eugene. *The Poems of Eugene Field.* New York: Scribner, 1917.

Freud, Sigmund. "Humor." In *Character and Culture,* edited by Philip Rieff, 263–69. New York: Collier, 1963.

———. *Jokes and Their Relation to the Unconscious.* New York: Norton, 1960.

———. *Leonardo da Vinci and a Memory of His Childhood.* New York: Norton, 1964.

———. "Medusa's Head." In Sigmund Freud, *Writings on Art and Literature,* edited by Werner Hamacher and David E. Wellbery, 264–65. 1940. Reprinted, Stanford: Stanford University Press, 1997.

———. "Mourning and Melancholia." In *General Psychological Theory,* edited by Philip Rieff, 164–79. New York: Collier, 1963.

———. "Psychoanalytic Notes Upon an Autobiographical Account of a Case of Paranoia (Dementia Paranoides)." In *Three Case Histories,* edited by Philip Rieff, 83–160. New York: Simon & Schuster, 1963.

———. *The Future of an Illusion.* New York: Anchor, 1964.

———. *The Interpretation of Dreams.* New York: Avon, 1965. Original published in 1900.

———. "The 'Uncanny.'" In *On Creativity and the Unconscious,* edited by Benjamin Nelson, 122–61. New York: Harper & Row, 1958.

———. "Thoughts for the Times on War and Death." In *On Creativity and the Unconscious,* edited by Benjamin Nelson, 206–35. New York: Harper & Row.

Halpern, Richard. *Norman Rockwell: The Underside of Innocence.* Chicago: University of Chicago Press, 2006.

Heffernan, James A. W. *Museum of Words: The Poetics of Ekphrasis from Homer to Ashbery.* Chicago: University of Chicago Press.

Irving, Washington. "Rip Van Winkle." In Washington Irving, *The Complete Tales of Washington Irving,* edited by Charles Neider, 21–31. New York: Da Capo.

James, William. *A Pluralistic Universe.* In *William James: Writings 1902–1910,* edited by Bruce Kuklick, 625–819. New York: The Library of America, 1987.

———. "The Gospel of Relaxation." In *William James: Writings 1902–1910,* edited by Gerald E. Myers, 825–40. New York: The Library of America, 1992.

———. *The Principles of Psychology,* 2 vols. New York: Dover, 1950.

———. *The Varieties of Religious Experience.* In *William James: Writings 1902–1910,* edited by Bruce Kuklick, 1–477. New York: The Library of America, 1987..

Johns, Elizabeth. *Thomas Eakins: The Heroism of Modern Life.* Princeton: Princeton University Press, 1983.

Kallir, Jane. *Grandma Moses: The Artist behind the Myth.* New York: Potter, 1982.

Keele, Kenneth D. "The Genesis of Mona Lisa." *Journal of the History of Medicine and Allied Sciences* 14 (1959) 136–59.

Ketchum, William C. Jr. *Grandma Moses: An American Original.* Singapore: New Line, 2006.

Kristeva, Julia. *Black Sun: Depression and Melancholia.* European Perspectives. Translated by Leon S. Roudiez. New York: Columbia University Press, 1989.

Leader, Darian. *Stealing the Mona Lisa: What Art Stops Us from Seeing.* New York: Counterpoint, 2002.

Levin, Gail. *The Poetry of Solitude: A Tribute to Edward Hopper.* New York: Universe, 1995.

MacDonald, Margaret F. "The Painting of Whistler's *Mother.*" In *Whistler's Mother: An American Icon,* edited by Margaret F. MacDonald, 29–63. Aldershot, UK: Lund Humphries, 2003.

Marling, Karal Ann. *Designs on the Heart: The Homemade Art of Grandma Moses.* Cambridge: Harvard University Press, 2006.

———. *Norman Rockwell 1894–1978: America's Most Beloved Painter.* Los Angeles: Taschen, 2005.

Miller, Angela. *The Empire of the Eye: Landscape Representation and American Cultural Politics, 1825–1875.* Ithaca, NY: Cornell University Press, 1993.

Nuland, Sherwin B. *Leonardo da Vinci.* New York: Penguin, 2000.

Nursery Rhymes Lyrics and Origins. "Little Boy Blue Rhyme." Online: http://www.rhymes.org.uk/little_boy_blue.htm/.

Oneal, Zibby. *Grandma Moses: Painter of Rural America.* New York: Puffin, 1986.

Pater, Walter. "The Child in the House." In *Selected Writings of Walter Pater,* edited by Harold Bloom, 1–16. A Signet Classic. New York: Columbia University Press, 1974.

———. *The Renaissance: Studies in Art and Poetry: The 1893 Text,* edited by Donald L. Hill. Studies in the History of the Renaissance. Berkeley: University of California Press, 1980.

Pruyser, Paul W. *The Play of the Imagination: Toward a Psychoanalysis of Culture.* New York: International Universities Press, 1983.

Questroyal. "Sanford Robinson Gifford (1823–1880)." Online: http://www.questroyal fineart.com/artist/sanford-robinson-gifford/.

Radden, Jennifer. "Love and Loss in Freud's *Mourning and Melancholia.*" In *The Analytic Freud: Philosophy and Psychoanalysis,* edited by Michael P. Levine, 211–30. London: Routledge, 2000.

————, editor. *The Nature of Melancholy: From Aristotle to Kristeva*. Oxford: Oxford University Press, 2000.

Rapaport, Ernest A. "The Grandparent Syndrome." *Psychoanalytic Quarterly* 27 (1958) 518–38.

Richardson, Robert D. *William James: In the Maelstrom of American Modernism—A Biography*. Boston: Houghton Mifflin, 2006.

Rockwell, Norman. *My Adventures as an Illustrator*. Garden City, NY: Doubleday, 1960.

Rosenthal, Angela. "She's Got the Look! Eighteenth-Century Female Portrait Painters and the Psychology of a Potentially 'Dangerous Employment.'" In *Portraiture: Facing the Subject*, edited by Joanna Woodall, 147–66. Critical Introductions to Art. Manchester: Manchester University Press, 1997.

Sassoon, Donald. *Becoming Mona Lisa: The Making of a Global Icon*. New York: Harcourt, 2001.

Schaefer, Adam. *Grandma Moses*. The Life and Work Of. Chicago: Heinemann Library, 2003.

Sharp, Kevin. "Pleasant Dreams: Whistler's *Mother* on Tour in America, 1932–4." In *Whistler's Mother: An American Icon*, edited by Margaret F. MacDonald, 81–99. Aldershot, UK: Lund Humphries, 2003.

Shorter, Edward. *From Paralysis to Fatigue: A History of Psychosomatic Illness in the Modern Era*. New York: Free Press, 1992.

Snow, Edward. *A Study of Vermeer*. Berkeley: University of California Press, 1994.

Spalding, Frances. *Whistler*. London: Phaidon, 1979.

Taylor, Robert. "Norman Rockwell and the Spirit of '76." *Boston Sunday Globe*, January 3, 1971.

Tedeschi, Martha. "The Face that Launched a Thousand Images: Whistler's *Mother* and Popular Culture." In *Whistler's Mother: An American Icon*, edited by Margaret F. MacDonald, 121–41. Aldershot, UK: Lund Humphries, 2003.

The New York Times. "James M'N. Whistler Dies in London: Celebrated American Artist Unexpectedly Passes Away." Obituary July 18, 1903. Online: http://www.nytimes.com/learning/general/onthisday/bday/0714.htm/.

Vidler, Anthony. *The Architectural Uncanny: Essays in the Modern Unhomely*. Cambridge: MIT Press, 1992.

Walden, Sarah. *Whistler and His Mother: An Unexpected Relationship*. London: Gibson Square, 2003.

Weintraub, Stanley. *Whistler: A Biography*. New York: Da Capo, 1974.

Wheelis, Allen. *The Quest for Identity*. New York: Norton, 1958.

Whistler, James Abbott McNeill. *The Gentle Art of Making Enemies*. New York: Dover, 1967.

Wikipedia. "Eugene Field." Online: http://en.wikipedia.org/wiki/Eugene_Field/.

————. "George Inness." Online: http://en.wikipedia,org/wiki/George_Inness/.

————. "Little Boy Blue." Online: http://en.wikipedia.org/wiki/Little_Boy_Blue/.

————. "Rip Van Winkle." Online: http://en.wikipedia.org/wiki/Rip_Van_Winkle/.

————. "Sanford Robinson Gifford." Online: http://en.wikipedia.org/wiki/Sanford.Robinson.Gifford/.

Zöllner, Frank. *Leonardo da Vinci, 1452–1519*. Köln: Taschen, 2000.

Index